Uncle Joe's

W9-BRY-668

Also by Richard White

The Organic Machine

The Middle Ground

"It's Your Misfortune and None of My Own"

The Roots of Dependency

Land Use, Environment, and Social Change

The Frontier in America
(with Patricia Nelson Limerick and James Grossman)

REMEMBERING
AHANAGRAN

REMEMBERING AHANAGRAN

Storytelling in a Family's Past

RICHARD WHITE

ⓌHill and Wang

A division of Farrar, Straus and Giroux

New York

Hill and Wang
A division of Farrar, Straus and Giroux
19 Union Square West, New York 10003

Copyright © 1998 by Richard White
Distributed in Canada by Douglas & McIntyre Ltd.
Printed in the United States of America
Designed by Jonathan D. Lippincott
First edition, 1998

Library of Congress Cataloging-in-Publication Data
White, Richard, 1947-
    Remembering Ahanagran : storytelling in a family's past / Richard
White. — 1st ed.
        p. cm.
    ISBN 0-8090-8071-0 (alk. paper)
    1. White, Sara, 1919-   , 2. Irish Americans—Biography.
3. Ahanagran (Ireland)—Biography.   4. Chicago (Ill.)—Biography.
5. Boston (Mass.)—Biography.   I. Title.
CT275.W55416W48   1998
973'.049162'00922—dc21
[B]

To Sara

Acknowledgments

This is a book about my family and its stories; it largely concerns events and places outside my experience. There is no such thing as blood knowledge. The Ireland of my mother's youth is foreign to me. I need guides through it. The same, to a lesser degree, is true of the Irish American communities of Chicago and the Jewish American communities of Boston. I inherited only piece-meal knowledge of these places.

I am a historian, and I sought out other historians to help me with the materials I found. I would like to thank my colleagues at the University of Washington Robin Stacey and George Behl-mer, who helped me with the Irish language and Irish history. Both kindly read large sections of the Irish chapters. Hillel Kieval, also my colleague at Washington, helped me put my father's studies at the Mishkam Tefila School in Dorchester and at the Hebrew Teachers College in context. Above all, I want to thank Thomas Pressly, now a professor emeritus at the University of Washington. I have benefited from his professional generosity for twenty-five years, and once more he gave me much-needed aid and advice.

Peter Levine and Jim Grossman, good friends and critical readers, brought their knowledge of immigration history and American social history to their readings of the manuscript. Both did more than this. Jim proved invaluable in helping me to find Chicago sources and in getting me to think about the story that I had to tell. Peter helped me to clarify key ideas and concepts.

My wife, Beverly, and my brother Stephen both read the manuscript and tried to keep me focused on telling a story. After all these years, responding to Beverly's criticisms remains the most daunting task I face. My stepdaughter, Teal Purrington, drew the maps and gave form to spaces my mother lived in but Teal had never seen.

I owe, of course, an immense debt to other members of my family: my aunts and uncles, my cousins Maggie and Sal, and my mother's cousin Teresa. All graciously helped me understand things that were, I realize, sometimes painful for them to discuss and recover or that, to my uncle Johnny, hardly seemed worth recovering at all. I appreciate their kindness and indulgence. In Ireland, Vincent Carmody, with his intimate knowledge of North Kerry and its families, was extraordinarily kind and helpful. Maud Murray, my mother's cousin, provided the only living memory of the time when my Irish grandfather and grandmother were young and courting. Maud Murray remained curious, bright, and active until her death in her nineties, just before this book went to press.

The librarians for the manuscript collections at Trinity College, the Folklore Archives at University College, Dublin, and the National Library in Dublin were all helpful, despite the understaffing that makes their jobs seem so arduous to an outsider. I am grateful for permission to quote from their collections. I am particularly grateful to the head of the Department of Irish Folklore, University College, Dublin, for permission to quote material from the school's manuscript boxes S 402 and S 403 and the Folklore Archives, which provided the bulk of the material in chapter 6. In Chicago the librarians at the Newberry Library, who have helped me with far different projects over the years, once more proved their resourcefulness and got me started with sources where initially I hardly knew my way. Harvard University generously allowed me to see my father's student file. Willy Dobak of the National Archives helped me track down my grandfather's pardon files and to scout what ended up as the dead-end trail of his prison records.

Mort Trachtenberg was gracious, funny, and helpful when I called him out of the blue. He provided me with important details on my father's life in Boston.

I need to thank my agent, Georges Borchardt, who took me on and sold this book, and my editor, Arthur Wang, whose judgment I have come to trust and value greatly. I cannot imagine a closer or more discerning reader of a writer's work.

My research for this book, and the ultimate form the book took, would have been far different without the aid of the Mac-Arthur Foundation. No one deserves a MacArthur fellowship (particularly me), but undeserved generosity makes recipients all the more grateful. It was the foundation's aid which allowed me to do research in Ireland with my mother.

Finally, of course, I need to thank my mother, Sara. Just as her memories have provided the thread along which I have beaded her family's past, so her day-to-day life of letters, phone calls, mediations, admonishments, and advice forms the thread that seems to hold her diverse family together. She was an active participant in the creation of this book. I have written about things she would have preferred to leave untouched, but her stories are the seeds from which everything in this book grew. In the end, I learned far more from my mother and her stories than I can ever thank her for.

Family Tree

William Walsh
m. Ellen Carr

- Mary b. 1870
  m. Connors 1872

- Bridget (Bea) b. 1871
  m. Ed Mulvihill
  - William
  - Jerry

- Catherine (Kitty) b. 1873
  m. Thomas O'Brien
  - Timothy b. 1897

- Edmund b. 1875

- Honora (Nora) b. 1876
  m. Will Lynch

- Margaret b. 1878
  m. Pierce

- John (Jack) b. 1880
  m. Margaret Hegarty
  b. 1883
  - Mary b. 1914
    m. John Bambury
  - Nell b. 1914
    m. Pat O'Hara
  - Gerard b. 1917
    m. Josie Collins
  - Sarah (Sara) b. 1919
    m. Harry E. White
  - William b. 1921
    m. Margaret Doyle
  - Johnny b. 1924
    m. Sheila Dooling
    - William (Billy)
    - John (Jackie)

- Helen (Ellie) b. 1881
  m. William Butler

- Eliza (Liz) b. 1883
  m. Ahern

- Hannah (Han) b. 1885
  m. Patrick Holly

- Sarah b. 1889
  m. Ed Leahy

- Wilhelmina b. 1894

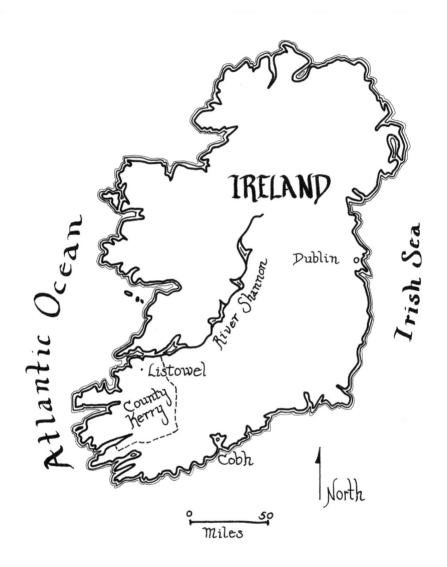

IRELAND

Atlantic Ocean

Irish Sea

River Shannon

Dublin o

· Listowel

County
Kerry

Cobh

North

0   50
Miles

River Shannon

Carrig Island

Ballylongford Bay

TO TARBERT

Carrigafoyle Castle

Slough

Lislaughtin Abbey

Gurtard

Doctor's Cross

National School

TO BALLYBUNNION

Hollys Farm

Johnny's Farm

Creamery

ASTEE

Walshs Farm

BALLYLONGFORD

Ahanagran

Guhard

Heagartys Farm

Ballyline

Ballyline Road

Shronowen Bog

North

Pollagh

0   Miles   1

TO LISTOWEL

REMEMBERING
AHANAGRAN

Introduction

Sara Walsh, who married and became Sara White, is my mother, and she has told me stories about her life since I was a child. She sets these stories in County Kerry, Ireland, where she was a girl. She sets them on South Mozart Street in Chicago, where she was a young woman. She sets them in New Orleans, where she met my father. She sets them in and around Boston, where she visited briefly when my father returned from overseas after World War II.

In my mother's stories the world constantly takes her by surprise. The stories say that although she was born into a complicated world she was raised to lead a simple life. She casts her life almost as a work of fiction so that in a sentence she can move into worlds neither previously known nor imagined by her. She moves from rural Ireland to the Southwest Side of Chicago; she passes through Jewish Dorchester on the edge of Boston and then on to New York. Yet only in the brief times of passage is she alone. Once in place she is wrapped up in and ensnared, protected, and neglected by family.

My mother was born and baptized Sarah Walsh; she became Sara Walsh when she dropped the *h* while living in Chicago. The dropped *h* is the mark of her Americanization. A life is more complicated than any narrative of it, and for me that lost *h* has come to symbolize not only her Americanization but my necessary simplification of her life. Except when citing documents that contain the original spelling—Sarah—I will refer to her as Sara. I will tell the story of the lost *h* when I explain the conditions that caused her to drop it.

Most of us live with our family stories, but generally we don't think about them very often. I think about them constantly. Al-

though she never intended this, my mother's stories taught me
the discontinuity and strangeness of the world. Intended to
make sense of her own life, they left me fascinated with difference and unfamiliarity and the surprising turns of life itself.

I once thought of my mother's stories as history. I thought
memory was history. Then I became a historian, and after many
years I have come to realize that only careless historians confuse
memory and history. History is the enemy of memory. The two
stalk each other across the fields of the past, claiming the same
terrain. History forges weapons from what memory has forgotten
or suppressed. Few non-historians realize how many scraps a life
leaves. These scraps do not necessarily form a story in and of
themselves, but they are always calling stories into doubt, always
challenging memories, always trailing off into forgotten places.

But there are regions of the past that only memory knows. If
historians wish to go into this dense and tangled terrain, they
must accept memory as a guide. In this jungle of the past, only
memory knows the trails. But memory, like history, is better
thought of as plural rather than singular. Historians have to follow cautiously. When left alone with memories, historians treat
them as detectives treat their sources: they compare them, interrogate them, and match them one against the other. Memory
can mislead as well as lead.

I have spent much of my adult life writing histories. My
mother was proud of them because I wrote them. She tried to
read them, but I think they seemed strange to her. They were
what professors did. She preferred to display them. Then several
years ago, she told me, half jokingly, but only half, that her life
was more interesting than my latest book. Why didn't I write a
book about her? I told her, not joking at all, that I would.

And so we have gone back to the stories and necessarily to
my mother's memories. And, both together and separately, we
have traveled to Chicago, to Dublin and County Kerry, and to
Boston. I have talked to others who remembered what my
mother remembered. But this time I was not just a child listening. I was an adult and a historian, and I could not take even
my own mother at her word.

There is nothing my mother has told me that is without some basis in the past. But neither, at least in those cases where I can recover the historical scraps, is there a story that to a historian sifting through the evidence clearly happened the way she remembers.

This book is a collaboration. It is, for the most part, an easy collaboration between me and my mother and an uneasy collaboration between history and memory. But the two pairs cannot be so readily disentangled. History is not separate from the historian, and in this case the historian is my mother's son. My mother would prefer to let her stories stand and her workings of the past remain definitive. She is more forgiving than I am. She does not always want to know about the lies, cruelties, and injustices that I find and would sometimes prefer they remain forgotten.

These stories and our collaboration have taught me much about the relation of history and memory. They have made me face in at least a small way the cruelty of recovering what memory seeks to bury or disguise. It is no wonder people prefer memory to history.

But I have learned more than that. My mother formulates her life as a set of relationships. Her stories are not an autobiography: not a classic account of self. To center these stories totally on her would be to reinvent my mother and how she understands her life. Sara sees her life as one among many. Her narratives turn away from herself because she considers her life so entwined with others that she could never stand alone. She has lived, and continues to live, in a world dense with people; the people in her past are now mostly dead, but here she calls them back into being.

This book grows out of my mother's stories. Partly it is a memoir of her life. To me it is also an aide-mémoire because details that I recovered or questions that I asked sparked other memories in my mother and uncles and aunts. But partly it is also an anti-memoir, for when her memory is challenged by my rendering of history, the two sometimes clash. My hope is that the conversations of my mother and myself, our mutual questioning, our mutual subversion, can ultimately enrich in a small way both memory and history.

Sometimes in this book I can only follow memory; more rarely there is only history; but the heart of the book are those places where history and memory meet. There I can juxtapose the two, compare them, and sometimes suture them together into a fuller, if never certain, account of the past.

Memory and identity are too powerful to go unquestioned and too important to be discarded as simply inventions and fabrications. They are the stuff from which we fashion our lives and our stories. History can interrogate these stories; it can complicate them, but it cannot kill them. And I have no desire to do so. My questioning is more complicated than that. I respect my mother's stories because I respect the life she has led, and these stories are the sense she makes of her seventy-odd years.

I want to interrogate and understand her stories because I think that, at the close of an American century where cruel and idiot simplicities about memory, identity, and history can do so much damage in a country she has come to love, my mother's stories still have work to do in the world. Beneath these personal stories simmers an ongoing contest over what America is and means and who gets to define it.

This is an important contest. It has been central to my mother's life. It is central to American history. Immigration is not always about leaving a past behind, but neither is it simply the transportation of culture or traditions from one place to another. American is not something a person learns to be; it is an identity contested and fought over. Boundaries do not create identities; boundaries are permeable. There is no category other than human that can embrace us all; there is no single category that can embrace even one of us. By the time history is through with us, we are all many people.

My mother's stories have led me to write a book that I never expected to write. Sara has surprised me.

 # PART I

❧ 1 ❧

Ahanagran's gone.   —My mother, Sara, 1995

The winter of 1994–1995 was one of the wettest the west of Ireland had ever seen, and when the ditch that drained the fields along the road overflowed its banks, Gerard and Josie Walsh's house flooded for the first time in memory. The family's memory was a long one. Gerard had received the house in the townland of Ahanagran from his father, Jack, who had, inherited it from his parents. Gerard's grandfather had come to live in the house more than a century earlier when he married Ellen Carr.

Gerard and Josie cleaned the old house when the flood receded. They remained watchful when the storms resumed.

On a January night in 1995, it was not the noise of a storm but the noise of a fire in the wall that woke Josie. She thought she was hearing her daughter Sal returning from visiting Nell, another daughter, married and living down the road toward Ballybunnion. It was near midnight, about the time she expected Sal home. Josie rose from the bed, her body as always heavy with pain. Arthritis had twisted one hand into a half fist. A knee was almost gone, and she was waiting for an artificial replacement. She had an open, ulcerated sore on one leg.

The pain and her seventy-five years show in her movements, but the impression she leaves is never one of pain or age. There is something transcendent about her. She appears to be somehow detached from the very surroundings that in fact define her: kitchen, farm, and family. She is always in the midst of family, but you always remember her as separate and removed.

Josie crossed the room and opened the bedroom door. She expected only to repeat an act performed so many times in that house, to greet a daughter returning home. But instead something happened that had never happened there before. Smoke and the heat from the flames met her. They threw her backward into the bedroom.

After that, everything is an astonishment, for, while everyone knows *what* happened, no one is quite sure *how*. Josie and her husband, Gerard, were two old people trapped in a bedroom where only one small casement window, narrow and at chest height, gave direct access to the outside. Gerard had got up as Josie opened the door, but the smoke almost immediately overcame him, and he passed out. Luckily, he fell forward, shutting the door against the fire. Still Josie could not rouse him, and she was too old and crippled to climb up and through that narrow window.

That should have been the end of this tragedy. On an ordinary night, with, perhaps, another person and in a different house with a different history, that might have been true. But the particular death that she and Gerard faced did more than frighten Josie. It angered her.

There was a history to this place now in flames on a January night in 1995; the flames were eating a lifetime of hard and vividly remembered labor. Josie told her daughters later what she thought of amid the smoke and noise. What she thought with her husband collapsed on the floor was that Gerard had put too much work into this farm to die in its destruction. He deserved better. This death, she decided, would not happen, not this way. Gerard would, she said, die of natural causes. She was determined to see to that. But how Josie got her crippled body and ulcerated leg out of that high, narrow window, no one, not even Josie, can understand. And how she made her way barefoot in the pitch dark on the pitted ground to her son John Joe's, none of her sons and daughters can understand. And how John Joe got his six-foot two-inch, 220-pound body back in that slit of a window, no one can understand. Avoiding death meant passing through a needle's eye that night, and somehow they did it.

In the smoke and the heat, John Joe luckily stumbled on his father passed out on the floor. In an instant, things you never imagine happen. The house in flames, you step on your father and save his life.

Gerard and Josie were saved, but initially what was lost was what mattered. The house had burned. It burned so hot that the slates on the roof exploded, making a tremendous noise and attracting people from Ballylongford, the village more than a mile away. When the firefighters arrived from Listowel, they were far too late to save the house. People were already mourning it.

Gerard's brother Johnny came across the fields from Guhard and stood in the road crying and wailing, "Our home is gone, our home is gone." A man in his seventies watched his childhood home in flames. And although his own house stood safe not a mile away, it was still "our" home that was gone. He could not be comforted. In Chicago, his brother Bill, nearly fifty years gone from Ireland, wailed nearly the same words.

In California, seven thousand miles from Ahanagran, my mother, Sara, cried over the phone to me as I sat in my kitchen in Seattle. "Ahanagran's gone," she said, collapsing the whole Irish townland into that house. She had left that home nearly sixty years before. This was the house in which she was born.

In this house people had told stories and listened to stories; it was the site and source of stories; and after it burned, it became only a story. The opening heroics of the night faded with the flames into sickness, disorientation, and loss. Josie wandered dazed into the road, thinking her daughter Sal, whom she had risen to greet, lay dead in the flames. Sal's car was still parked in front of the house. P. J. Cavanaugh, whom people call the Bull because he is larger even than John Joe, found Josie there in the road. He talked to her. She did not respond. He saw her bleeding feet, threw her over his shoulder, and carried her to John Joe's.

He carried Josie in her silent anguish over the loss of a child, but Sal was safe. She had got a ride to Nell's with another sister, Ann. It later amused Sal that her mother could have thought she was making the noise that roused her from sleep. She would have to be "ossified drunk" to make so much noise, she said. When Josie saw Sal, though her home was in embers, she said everything would be all right now.

They took Josie and Gerard to the hospital in Tralee. The medics initially thought they had lost Gerard, but they revived him. He was conscious the next morning, but when the doctor asked him if he knew where he was, he said, of course, he was at Jerry Dee's playing cards. Jerry Dee had lived down the road. Gerard was more confused than the doctor knew, for Jerry Dee was dead twenty years. And even when Gerard became more lucid, his daughters could not convince him of the destruction of the house in which he had spent his entire life. They could not convince him it was gone. It was a shock to him when he returned and saw the ruins. And when his son Jimmy, intending to comfort him, told him that it was the kindness of God that he and Josie had escaped that inferno, Gerard said only that if God were kind he, Gerard, would be lying in the abbey beside his father and mother.

These people are my relatives—my mother, uncles, aunt, and cousins—but in the light of that burning house, they all became strangers to me. Confronting the depth of their pain and loss, I realized that I have no equivalent for what that home was for them, what Ahanagran was. I know no equivalent for the deep emotional ties whose rupture left them so distraught. It was as if in the loss of that house a person had died; no, something longer-lived than a person, more nurturing, domineering, and tenacious of life.

The house is now a pile of rubble behind the new house that Gerard and Josie have built on the same site. The old house was built of stacked stone—flat stones and round ones—mortared together and eventually plastered over. Gerard and Josie lived in the earth of the place itself in the same way that when they burned turf they burned the earth itself and that in Gerard's and my mother's childhood they had eaten only the products of this earth. They quite literally were part of this place in ways I can only imagine.

Since I was a child, my mother has told me stories of Ireland and her migration and her life in America. I realize now that I understood none of them. This is an embarrassing admission, for, as a historian, I claim to understand stories about the past. I claim the ability to tell such stories myself. I think they are important.

I realize now that only in the light of that burning house can I hope to understand my mother's story, for the burning house suggested to me the strangeness of her past. Any good history begins in strangeness. The past should not be comfortable. The past should not be a familiar echo of the present, for if it is familiar why revisit it? The past should be so strange that you wonder how you and people you know and love could come from such a time. When you have traced that trajectory, you have learned something.

The key to the past that my mother tried to tell me about in her stories lies in that house in Ahanagran. My mother was born there in 1919; her father was born there before her, and it sheltered his parents before him and his grandparents before them. The house had been there long before any Walsh knew it. It seems to have been there in 1841–1842 when the English conducted their famous Ordnance Survey that mapped all of Ireland. It seemed, my mother says, that the house would be there forever.

The power of that house, visible to me only after it burned, had been always visible to Sara Walsh. It marked the distance she had traveled in the world, and it was the cause of her travels. Acquiring that farm and keeping it were the great collective work of my mother's family. That land was their home in a way

I can never fathom; that land was a monster in a way I can understand all too well, for behind everything that happened—my grandmother's suffering, my grandfather's departure for Chicago, my mother's coming to America—was the power of that land. It drove the family it was meant to support. My mother's entire life has been lived in the shadow of that house and farm she left so long ago. It had to burn for me to comprehend that.

2

I was born in the bog lands of Co. Kerry in Ireland in 1919, just a few fields away from the sea. It was a cold wet climate in the North Atlantic but very beautiful. I was the 5th of seven children, one dead as a baby. We were very poor; our diet consisted of bread, tea, potatoes, cabbage, once in a while some salt pork from a pig we killed once a year. My parents worked very hard on the farm. We had 6 or 8 milking cows and sold the milk at the creamery in the little village of Bally-longford. My mom had chickens and the eggs were also sold. The only thing that wasn't sold was enough milk for our tea.

The kitchen had a half door, the top was always open, probably to let the fumes of the burning turf escape. When the animals were in the kitchen, it helped clear the air. There was one small window in the kitchen; the window did not open. A kerosene lamp hung by the window. This was our only light. We had a wooden table between the door and the window; we had chairs woven from straw which Tim kept in shape. We had a cabinet which kept dishes and a few other items. Next to the turf fire was a press where the clothes were put to keep out the dampness. This was all the furniture. Every house had a picture of the Sacred Heart of Jesus with a votive candle always burning and inside every door is a holy water font to make the sign of the cross as you leave the house. We had two bedrooms, one behind the fire had two beds, two very tiny windows which did not open. The beds were the only furniture in the room. —Sara's memories of Ahanagran in the 1920s

My mother, Sara, is a creator, maintainer, and repairer of relationships. She presents herself as the sum of her relations. It would be false to her to present her in any other way. She is Gerard's sister. She is Josie's sister-in-law. She is Margaret's daughter. She is my mother. She understands herself in relation to others. It is what she does. She does it patiently and relentlessly, even when the relationships have become but raw nerves that should, I think, be cut and cauterized.

Her stories are about people she knew, about places she has lived, about the relations she established with the world. There is a core to her that is stubborn and indomitable, but that is only a place she retreats to. Her life is lived farther out, on her margins, where she connects with others. She does not understand herself as people who write autobiographies usually understand themselves. She does not see herself as a distinctive self developing as she journeys through the world. She speaks more easily about others than about herself. It is the relations with others that matter; it is these relations that have defined the world she has known and made.

After the house burned, three-quarters of a century after her own birth, Sara returned to Ahanagran. I went with her. She sat in Josie's new kitchen and talked with Josie and Gerard. Later, outside and alone, she tenderly examined the rubble of the old house as if preparing a body for burial. I watched. She gathered a few small stones and carried them with her when she returned to California. I could only wonder how so much stone could have burned so hot.

This stone was the house she was born in. This stone was the house in which her mother, Margaret, lived. Jack Walsh fathered them all in this house, and Margaret Walsh bore them there. This stone marked the space where she and her brothers and sisters had once been together. The house received them as it had received Jack Walsh and his brothers and sisters before them and Jack Walsh's own mother before that.

This is the order in which Margaret Walsh bore them in the thatched cottage in Ahanagran. The twins, Nell and Mary, as different as any two people in the family, came first. Next, the

child that died and always goes unnamed passed briefly through
the house. Gerard, who so nearly died in this same house, followed. Sara Walsh was born on St. Stephen's Day, December
26, 1919. In Ireland at that time, gangs of boys would kill a wren
on St. Stephen's Day and tie it to a piece of holly bush. These
wren boys went from house to house, and at each house they
sang and danced and were awarded with a few pence to bury
the wren. On St. Stephen's Day the wrens died and my mother
was born, just as her twin sisters, Nell and Mary, had been born
on St. Stephen's Day before her. After her came her brother Bill,
and, finally, the youngest, Johnny, arrived.

They grew up together in that small house. They took measure of one another, and sometimes it now seems to me that
there must not have been space enough for two to share the
same traits. If Mary grew to be in perpetual complaint against
the world, then Nell eventually resigned herself to bearing much
quietly. And if Gerard demanded activity, if he could only know
the world through his work, then Johnny, as Johnny himself says,
was retired since he was born and "maybe a little before that."

To see them separately, you would not guess they had been
raised together, that they were brothers and sisters. To see them
together, you would never doubt it. Sara, when she visits, becomes one with them once more, as she does with her even more
numerous cousins, the Hollys. Her upbringing makes it impossible for her to imagine moving through the world alone, and
she never has. She directs and watches and plans, but she is far
too wise to think that anyone, particularly a woman of her time
and place, can do without others.

When she writes of her own birth, she is careful to place
everything in relation to something else and to put herself in
relation to all. When she tells where she was born, she places
her birth in a particular world. She places herself in relation to
her family. She has always lived in engagement with the world,
sometimes passionate, sometimes wary. She comes from a place
where there is much madness and suicide; she knows madness
and death come when you retreat from the world.

She knows both that the world is beautiful and that there are good reasons to retreat from it. Things have not gone as well as they might have in the corner of the world the Walshes come from. The townlands near the mouth of the Shannon River remain undeniably beautiful, but the body of the land bears the scars of a losing duel with history. Its forests are gone. Ruins are everywhere. The Shannon has provided an avenue for invaders. It has brought trouble: in and around Ahanagran lie burned abbeys and the blasted castle of Carrigafoyle. The land itself testifies to violence and conquest: to the troubled times that stretch back for half a millennium and more.

The children of Margaret and Jack Walsh have scattered. Some still live in Kerry. Mary is in County Meath. Bill is in Chicago and Sara in California. But once the house in Ahanagran held them all, and, even as all their lives but Gerard's took them away from the house, they remained tethered to it. It is the site of Sara Walsh's first stories. It is where she still stands to make sense of her life.

She says the house in Ahanagran had adobe walls and an adobe floor, but adobe is a word that comes from her later life in California. The house was stacked stones and mortar, with walls more than a foot thick. The roof was a wood frame covered with woven thatch. The floor was packed earth. There were then three rooms and a loft. The doors, front and back, opened into the kitchen, the biggest room. It had but one small window, and before that window hung their only light, a kerosene lamp. In the kitchen was the hearth with its turf fire and above it a long, black iron bar from which hung a big black pot. That pot and a heavy teakettle were their only cooking utensils. There was a hot press built in by the fire. It held wet clothes that the family placed there to dry. The rest of the furniture was a table and wooden chairs with seats of woven straw.

At the back of the fire was the long room. It held two featherbeds. Her mother and father slept in one; Sara and her two sisters, Nell and Mary, slept in the other.

At the other side of the kitchen was a small room with an unused loft overhead. This small room held two more beds, a barrel full of grain, and the mice attracted by the grain. Sara's brothers, Gerard, Bill, and Johnny, and her cousin Tim, who lived with them, slept there. At night, when she and the family recited the rosary in the kitchen, Sara would watch mice race along the ledge at the foot of the loft.

Ahanagran is a medium-sized townland. Although Sara and her brothers and sisters call Gerard's farm Ahanagran, Gerard's farm is but part of Ahanagran. When they were growing up, the townland held from 120 to 200 people. It had once held far more. On the old maps there are actually three Aghanagrans—upper, middle, and lower. It is spelled with an additional *g* on those old maps, but the changes of a century wore the *g* away. The distinction between the three Ahanagrans survived into my mother's time, but it, too, gradually faded.

A townland is not a village, although part of the village of Ballylongford lies within Ahanagran. Nor is a townland some purely geometrical, endlessly duplicated division of the land like an American township that is designed to make land sales and taxation easier. Once, before the famine, townlands had been nearly independent communities, groups of farming families tied by marriage and the tools and land and animals they shared. But by 1919 that was no longer true, or not completely true, yet townlands remained more than rural neighborhoods. The people who lived in them were still tied by proximity, by some common labor, and by gossip and stories.

Ahanagran was not a prosperous place. The farms were not small by Irish standards—the Walsh farm contained twenty-eight acres when Jack Walsh inherited it—but the land was poor. It was reclaimed bog land whose soil was light and unproductive. In the 1820s only fourteen acres in the townland were classified as first-class land. In the 1880s a land agent for Trinity College in Dublin dismissed the land of the estate of Rusheen, of which Middle Ahanagran was then a part, as "cold and half reclaimed with poor shallow surface." In the 1930s, when twelve-year-olds, at the request of their teacher, gave an account of the townland, their evaluation, learned from their parents, was much the same:

"Some of the land is bad and more of it is faint, but none of it is good enough for growing wheat."

The location of the Walsh farm made it something of a center for the families nearby. The house was on the side of the road between Ballylongford and Ballybunnion, and nearly everything of moment that happened in Ahanagran depended on that road. When people moved cattle from one field to another, when they drove their asses and carts to the creamery, and when they took their ponies and traps to Mass, they passed the Walshes'. And when they died and their bodies went to the church for burial, they passed the house for one last time. Often, on winter nights, neighbors would come to sit in the kitchen by the turf fire, to play cards, and to tell stories: stories of ghosts and stories of hearing banshees howling in the bogs. They told stories of the Time of Troubles, as the Irish call the nearly one thousand years of invasion, conquest, rebellion, and persecution that began with Vikings and stretched through English rule.

The house was a seat of stories. To be in it long enough was to become part of a set of stories. That was the fate of the people Sara Walsh knew there. They became the stories she now tells. I would not know them at all otherwise. But before they became stories, they had entwined her in stories of their own. She came to define herself by the stories they told her.

My mother Sara's story of her birth is a story told to her. What any of us know of our birth, we learn from others. It is a beginning we ourselves cannot recall, so we commit the story to memory. We claim it and incorporate it into our story of ourselves. We thus begin the story of our lives with an intimate event that we can only know secondhand. And so the confusion of history and memory begins.

More than three-quarters of a century after her birth, Sara Walsh remembers and constructs her stories of Ireland from the stories her mother and others told her long ago in Ahanagran and from her own experiences. It is hard to separate these things once you have woven them together in memory. They seem a record of what happened, but memory is the shifting record of the sense we make of things.

We alter stories. We drop some altogether, and we add others. Who is to know? We often do not know ourselves. We change; our stories change.

But our stories make a claim on the past. This is how it happened, they say. It is an unexamined claim; it is a dangerous claim. Our stories are vessels that float on the seas of the past; there are things out there that can sink or redirect them, for the past is full of dead things preserved on paper or in the land itself but unremembered by any living person.

Memory is a living thing vulnerable to this dead past until memory itself dies with its creator. We can record memories, but then they are fixed on the page, pinned like insects in a collection, bodies of what was alive. We can pass memories on, but then they become someone else's memories; they live on like children. They are living descendants of our memories, but no more our memories than children are their parents.

History is a dead thing brought to new life. It is fragments of a past, dead and gone, resurrected by historians. It is in this sense like Frankenstein's monster. It threatens our versions of ourselves.

I live, in a way probably only other historians can fully appreciate, in this junkyard of the past. I haul pieces into the present, and there they confront my mother's memories.

3

Erected to the Memory of The O'Rahilly. Born Here 1875. Killed in Action in Dublin. Easter Rising 1916. . . .
—Plaque put up by the North Kerry Republican Soldiers Memorial Committee, Ballylongford, County Kerry, 1966

The house in Ahanagran where Sara was born produced children more reliably than her father's farm produced crops or cattle. Sara's parents, Jack and Margaret Walsh, lay together, and in ten years Margaret brought forth seven children, six of whom survived.

As a small child, Sara regarded Ahanagran and the surrounding townlands as changeless and complete, but no adult in Ahanagran, no adult in Kerry, could maintain that illusion. The house, women in labor, swarming children, the work of the farm—these seemed constant over three generations, but so much had changed. The very language had shifted from Irish to English. Land reform had come; landlords were vanishing. Now tenants like the Walshes owned the farms they had once rented. Sara was born during a revolution that would free Ireland itself. In many ways the Irish countryside that Sara took as timeless was startlingly new. But one thing had not changed: emigration. Neither Ahanagran nor North Kerry could hold on to its children.

Jack Walsh was one of twelve children, eleven of whom survived. All of them, himself included, eventually migrated, nine for good. He knew how tenuous a hold children born in Ahanagran had on the place. He knew how desperately those who left could long for the townland, and he had only to listen to his children to hear how quickly the townland forgot those who left.

Jack's parents, William Walsh and Ellen Carr, had produced children for America not Ireland. Beginning in 1870, when she gave birth to Mary, Ellen bore children for a quarter of a century. Their births are preserved in the parish records. The priest baptized them in the church in Ballylongford, usually a few days after they were born. These infants came from twelve to twenty months apart until 1878. After that they came slightly less regularly. It was April 1880 when John, whom everyone would call Jack, came to be baptized; a year later Helen arrived, and two years after her, Eliza. Sarah, my mother's aunt, the last child to survive infancy, was born in 1889. Wilhelmina, born in 1894, never made it beyond the house in Ahanagran. She died three days after she was born. They baptized her at home.

Each child received an Irish name at baptism, although none of them would speak the language that created their names. The priest also Gaelicized their parents' names—Hellena Carr and Guilielmo Walsh—as if names alone could conjure up a world that the Irish rather than the English controlled. The irony of this pointed Irishness was that almost all these infants were destined to leave Ireland as adults.

The farm could barely feed them. It never produced enough to provide the girls with fortunes, as dowries were called. It could not be subdivided among the boys; only one son could inherit it. William Walsh paid £27 a year rent for a twenty-eight-acre farm that was largely reclaimed bog. The farm, agents admitted privately, was not worth the rent. William Walsh spent a lifetime of hard labor accumulating his debt and his children. When he died, his rent was £195 in arrears. In 1887 he had seven cows (wet and dry) and ten children. Ten years later his cattle and many of his children were gone. The year before he died his "cow house" had blown down. He was, the estate agent said, in "poor circumstances" and unable to either pay his rent or reduce his arrears. His wife, Ellen, inherited his tenancy: an impoverished farm with seven years back rent due.

Having borne children for twenty-five years, Ellen Carr spent

the rest of her life watching them leave. The first child had
probably emigrated before the last was born. Not counting the
dead infant, Wilhelmina, none of these children would live an
entire life in North Kerry.

When Jack Walsh's daughter Sara was born in 1919, only he
and his sister Hannah, who had already left and come back,
remained in Ahanagran. Hannah had married the widower Patrick Holly, who was in greater need of a wife than a fortune, and
they raised ten children on a farm not half a mile away from the
spot where she was born.

Jack and Hannah could not look around without remembering
all those who were gone, but as a small child Sara thought there
would always be these brothers, sisters, and Holly cousins surrounding her. Sara heard stories of absent aunts and uncles, but
she had no faces, no bodies, had no memories of her own to
attach them to, and so all the stories but one failed to take root.
Except for the story of Aunt Kitty, the stories of all those departures remained alive only among the generation that had
actually known the emigrants. Those stories died as that generation died.

Kitty's story was once one among many. Each new departure
must have yielded stories to occupy the missing person's place,
but now it is hard to discern when the person disappeared and
left only the insubstantiality of stories in his or her wake. When
William Walsh died in 1901, his funeral provided a tally of those
of his children already gone and those remaining. *The Kerry Sen-
tinel* reported that old and respectable men in the village of Ballylongford said they had not seen such a funeral for years. Three
hundred sidecars and fifty horsemen accompanied him to the
cemetery amid "the most heartrending and sorrowful scenes,"
for William Walsh was "the most amiable and benevolent of
men." It had been a year, the paper noted, since William's own
brother, a priest, had died in the States.

Most likely, the account overstated the attendance; certainly,
it exaggerated the number of horses and donkeys carrying and
pulling the mourners. The year before William Walsh died,

Trinity's agent reported, as agents had been reporting for years, that "the tenants on this estate are exceedingly poor." The agent summarized, as he had so many times before, the condition of the farms on the estate: "A considerable number of their holdings consist of partially reclaimed moory land. Many have no effects that could be seized. They meadow the greater part of their holdings, but the produce is so coarse and rushy that very small prices are obtainable. Last year's auctions were a failure; proceeds were not sufficient to pay the very excessive rates levied on this estate." Any donkeys and horses they might have had would presumably have been seized for debt long before.

Alongside William's widow, Ellen, and her son, John (Jack), there stood at the grave four daughters: Ellie (Helen or the Gaelicized Helena), Lizzie (Eliza), Hannie (Hannah), and Sarah. The six children not at the funeral were most likely already in America by 1901. By 1919, when Jack's own daughter Sara was born, only Hannah and Jack Walsh remained. The land, by then, was his. His brother and his other living sisters were gone to Chicago never to return. Chicago held more Walshes than Ahanagran.

It is only because Aunt Kitty left Tim behind that the story of her migration stuck in Sara's memory. Tim, who stayed so close to home that even as an old man he could not see the sense of going so far as Ballybunnion, twenty miles away, became the living memorial of Kitty's departure and the sign of a whole generation's migration. He was the presence that connoted absence. He was the child without a mother. Kitty left for Chicago in scandal, leaving part of herself behind.

Kitty Walsh gave birth to a son in January 1897. She was twenty-four years old. The baby was baptized Timothy a few days later. No father was listed in the record, but everyone knew that the father was Tim Reidy, the creamery manager.

Births with no father listed, or listed with a father but marked illegitimate, were not uncommon in Ballylongford during these years. Tim Reidy seems to have fathered his share, but he also seems to have acknowledged none of them. He "left his rag on every bush," as the saying went around Ballylongford. He would continue like this for more than a dozen years. It was not until 1911 that Maria McElligott got him to marry. They married on May 6 in Ballylongford, not in her own parish, as was customary. She gave birth on May 9.

The year his father married, Timothy Walsh was fourteen years old. He was the only grandchild that William Walsh ever knew, but gaining this grandchild had cost him a daughter. Kitty had little choice but to leave; if she had stayed, the talk would have been vicious. She left her baby with her mother and father, and she went to Chicago. Her brothers and sisters had gone to Chicago before her, other siblings would go after her. Kitty was five years in America when her father died. She was fourteen years in America when Tim Reidy married.

Sara learned this story and told it. A hundred-year-old dalliance still lives in family memory long after Kitty, Tim Reidy, and Tim Walsh are gone. When Tim Reidy seduced Kitty Walsh, he had no idea how long a shadow the seduction would cast over the future.

As Sara grew older, such stories became the stuff to explain the world, why people appeared and disappeared. They were a private accounting that stood alongside a more public memory. The world that private and public rememberings came to recall separately was once a living whole, but it died, and memory and history scavenged it, dividing and carrying off various pieces.

To get a sense of this division, it is only necessary to walk through Ballylongford along the Ballyline Road until you reach the crossroad with what is still the largest building in town. This is the birthplace of The O'Rahilly, Kitty's contemporary, and a plaque commemorates his birth.

The O'Rahilly was born Michael David Rahilly, the son of Richard Rahilly, then "a very respectable and well-to-do man" in Ballylongford. The *O'* was Michael David's affectation. The O'Rahilly might have known Kitty; certainly, in a village that size, he saw her.

The Rahillys and the Walshes were both Catholic, but they were worlds apart. William Walsh was a tenant farmer and a poor one at that. Richard Rahilly knew and consorted with the local landlords, Catholic and Protestant. He shared their ambitions and their fears. In 1887 he was part of a scheme to secure a telegraph connection for Ballylongford. He wanted the assistance of Trinity College, the largest landholder in the area. The telegraph, he informed the college's local agent, would prove a wise investment "should . . . you (anticipate) any troubles with the tenants which would necessitate the services of the constabulary." William Walsh, then withholding his rent and involved with the Land League, was one of the tenants with whom Trinity feared trouble.

The O'Rahilly left Ballylongford for his higher education, but he was back in Kerry in 1896 when Tim Reidy dallied with Kitty Walsh. Maybe he knew Tim Reidy, for being creamery manager was no small position in that time and place. He may have listened to gossip about Tim Reidy. Maybe he laughed about it.

Eventually Kitty and The O'Rahilly left Ballylongford and found their different ways to the United States. Moving across the Atlantic, their trajectories remained as separate as their lives in their native village had been. Kitty was two years in Chicago when The O'Rahilly married Nancy Browne in New York and left on a European honeymoon. She was well established in Chicago when, in 1905, The O'Rahilly began a four-year stay in Philadelphia.

Unlike Kitty, The O'Rahilly would return from America. He came back to Dublin and, in his romantic way, set out to free Ireland from England. Nationalist politics, then a tangle of groups that competed and intermingled, were a village in themselves. The O'Rahilly, for example, was a founder of the Irish Volunteers but no friend of the Irish Republican Brotherhood (IRB). Many members of the IRB were, however, also Irish Volunteers and sought to turn the Volunteers to their own purposes. When in 1916 the IRB maneuvered in secret to have the Irish Volunteers rise against England despite circumstances that made such a rebellion foredoomed, The O'Rahilly made his last journey into the west of Ireland to stay the Volunteers there.

The O'Rahilly stopped the West from rising, but he and his

allies failed to halt the Easter Rising in Dublin. When he learned it was going forward, he got in his car and drove off to join it. He parked his car, by then full of guns and ammunition, and walked into the General Post Office in Dublin. He had not wanted this fight, but, when he came out, he came out fighting, and he died fighting.

The O'Rahilly died in the rising that took place in Dublin on Easter Monday in 1916. His death was a gesture; the Irish Republican Brotherhood intended to conjure up a revolution. They sought a culmination of the Troubles that had racked Ireland for centuries. This demanded blood.

The O'Rahilly distrusted the Irish Republican Brotherhood, but he provided them with blood. He was shot down leading a charge against a military barricade on Moore Street. He dragged himself into a doorway, where he wrote a letter to his family as he was dying. He lived a long time in that doorway with a bullet in his stomach. He cried for water, but no one could bring him water because British soldiers killed anyone who moved in Moore Street. He was the only Volunteer officer to die in the fighting.

The letter was a Kerryman's gesture. Yeats embroidered it. A good enough poet can even gild the lily. In Yeats's poem, The O'Rahilly writes not letters but his own epitaph in the doorway in which he died: "Here lies The O'Rahilly R. I. P." It is written in blood.

The rebels in Ballylongford named their Sinn Fein Club—the largest in North Kerry—after him. Years later Ballylongford marked the building where he was born with a plaque: ERECTED TO THE MEMORY OF THE O'RAHILLY. BORN HERE 1875. KILLED IN ACTION IN DUBLIN. EASTER RISING 1916 . . .

TO THE MEMORY OF . . . , the plaque says, but Kitty Walsh has no memorial. Ballylongford does not wish to remember young women giving birth and fleeing their homeland. They try to remember The O'Rahilly for dying in an attempt to give metaphorical birth to a country. The idea of Ireland often seems to fare better than the Irish themselves. As far as I know, only those who knew her son, Tim, now remember Kitty. It is only my conceit as a historian that now puts her on the page with The O'Rahilly, although once they shared the streets of the village.

The O'Rahilly wanted to free Ireland. Ireland, as far as Kitty Walsh could tell, only wanted to be free of her. To be Catholic and Irish in Ballylongford was not a single identity with a single set of choices. Sara eventually learned that it was a more complicated place than that. The story of Kitty was the first key.

4

I used to hear the stories. I used to tell the stories as a child. I was hiding out on the dike when the Black and Tans came. I was in the fields on the moonlight night. But I wasn't even born.

—Teresa Holly, Sara's cousin

We are a dying race. When we are gone, the bread's gone. The next generation is too lazy to even bake it. The one after that is too lazy to eat it. —Mary Bambury, Sara's sister

Sara Walsh's earliest memories come from before she was old enough to have memories. They are in a real sense four hundred years old. They are memories of the Time of Troubles.

She knows what she remembers, and she remembers that she was very young. She cannot remember the year, but she was very young. The men were shouting at her mother, Margaret Walsh. They were in her mother's kitchen; they were shouting at her mother in her own kitchen. The men were not Irish; they were English, and they had guns. They wanted to know where an Irish Republican Army (IRA) man was, where a rebel was. Her mother would not, or perhaps could not, tell them. In any case, she did not tell them. And then one of the men—a Black and Tan, as she knows now and claims she knew even then—lifted his rifle and drove its butt forward into Margaret Walsh's back. It struck between Margaret's shoulder blades. She staggered. The children screamed and cried. Sara, very young then, cried. She remembers being very young and crying. And then the men were gone. That is her memory.

When Sara talks of the Troubles, her voice gets cold, her diction clipped. She sees the butt of a gun driving into her mother's back. She sees the IRA man, the rebel Eddie Carmody, dead at the Doctor's Cross. That she actually saw the first and not the second does not much matter. They have fused.

When Sara turned these memories into the stories that she told me when I was a child, I fell fully under their sway and made them my own. I knew nothing about Ireland. The IRA just meant the Irish to me, and the Irish meant my mother. The Black and Tans meant the English to me, and I conflated them with Nazis, my prototype for grim indistinguishable European killers of my relatives. I entered into my mother's stories so fully that I am not always sure now whether I remember my mother's stories about a place that I had never seen or my own combinations of the stories. In my memory, which plays without sound, like an old, silent newsreel, the Black and Tans burst into the house. The grandmother I never knew—Margaret Walsh—refuses to reveal the IRA man's hiding place, but the British find him. There is a chase. They kill Eddie Carmody, the IRA man, at the Doctor's Cross. This is the story I recall. It is a story I have created from pieces of my mother's stories.

Possessed by these stories, I imagined that events of such power, so powerfully told, must have been witnessed. I imagined that my mother, not a camera, had seen and recorded these things. But Sara Walsh was not a year old when Eddie Carmody was shot. She was a little more than one when Black and Tans burst into the house in Ahanagran and beat her mother. She claims to remember what she only heard about later. She, too, had made the memory her own. The most powerful stories she told me—the launching point of her life's narrative of struggle—are the most problematic and confusing.

She is not alone in this. Sara's cousin Teresa Holly, who is younger, is amazed at the power of the stories. "I used to hear the stories," Teresa says. "I used to tell the stories as a child." The stories were so compelling that she actually became part of the stories. She was hiding out on the dike when the Black and Tans came. She was in the fields "on the moonlight night." "But," Teresa says now, "I wasn't even born."

These stories matter. They are powerful tools, and the closer you get to County Kerry, the more powerful they become.

How they work is not an easy thing to explain. Eddie Carmody is at the heart of it, for Eddie Carmody is the great symbol of the Time of Troubles in Ballylongford. To claim a part of Eddie Carmody, even a small part, is to have authority in the world. When you speak, others, no matter how grudgingly, have to listen.

In the Walsh family, Sara's older sister Mary tells the most authoritative stories of Eddie Carmody because she is the one living Walsh or Holly who saw his blood. Mary claims that while she was returning from school when she was six years old she saw blood on the road where they had dragged Eddie Carmody. When I was in Ireland in 1981 with my mother, we were in her brother Johnny's house one afternoon. Johnny was not there, but his wife, Sheila, sat in her usual seat by the stove. Sara sat in Johnny's seat. I do not remember where Mary or my cousin Maggie, Sheila's daughter, sat. I do remember the women arguing about the IRA. I was interested. I took notes. I do not have to rely fully on memory.

That year, 1981, was the year of the hunger strikes at the Maze/Long Kesh prison in Belfast. Bobby Sands was dead, and Joe McDonnell died while we were there. Sands and the IRA knew the power of the Troubles. Sands's death purposefully recapitulated Terence MacSwiney's death by starvation in 1920 during the original struggle for independence. Sinn Fein, the political arm of the Irish Republican Army, had condolence books on O'Connell Street in Dublin. Black flags hung on the fences and light posts of Ballylongford. The statues in the squares of Tipperary and Listowel were draped in black. The old struggle was once more everywhere in the air of Ireland. The Troubles seemed to have returned, as the IRA claimed. But had they? Was the death of Bobby Sands the genuine death, the mark of the Troubles?

My mother, her sister Mary, my cousin Maggie, and my then-nine-year-old son Jesse had been in Dublin a few days earlier. Mary had refused to sign the condolence book for the families of the hunger strikers. Mary thought the IRA were idiots (pronounced "idjits" by all my uncles and aunts on my mother's side, whether Irish or American), but she took their paper. She read it at high tea in the Gresham Hotel, where we went because we were tourists. Mary, stooped and in a farm woman's black dress her own mother could have worn, was as out of place there as the IRA paper.

In the kitchen of Johnny's house, Mary and Sheila denounced the recent IRA dead as criminals. They were not the good IRA, and their deaths did not signify the return of the Troubles. In 1981 Sara did not make such clear distinctions between the good IRA of her stories and the present IRA as she does now. She then seemed reluctant to admit that the IRA killed any innocent people. She wanted Bobby Sands and Joe McDonnell united with Eddie Carmody and the martyrs of old in the Troubles.

But Mary held the rhetorical high ground, and she was not about to relinquish it. She dominated the conversation. She was the only witness to the revolution left in the family. She reminded everyone of this. Her everyday walk from school and then her seeing the sign of a singular death meant that she knew firsthand the mark of the Troubles.

In Mary's hands, Eddie Carmody's blood became a dangerous weapon. She wielded it wildly. There was no telling where she would point it or who would be her target. She, in her extravagant way, denounced the IRA and praised Margaret Thatcher. Earlier in the morning, in a different context and in another argument, she had denounced Thatcher and adamantly insisted that British voters were supporting the IRA.

In the end Mary used Eddie Carmody's blood to haul the IRA

into the Court of Mary. That ultimately is the point of all her stories. Mary cultivates a rage against the present and a resentment of the past; her stories are her weapons. Her talk is exhausting because her resentments come out with every word. In every story she establishes the identity of blood relations in fantastic detail. The dead speak in Mary's stories. These are "says he" and "says she" stories. In the Court of Mary everyone is guilty. When Mary denounces the dead, not a piece of gossip, not an offense against God or man, is neglected. But as bad as the dead may be, for Mary the worst is always to come. "We are a dying race," she tells my mother. "When we are gone, the bread's gone. The next generation is too lazy to even bake it. The one after that is too lazy to eat it." Sara loves this. She is exasperated by Mary and repeats everything she says. Only her brothers and sisters can make her laugh so hard.

For Mary the Troubles have become a haven from the everyday life of modern Ireland. There was a bus strike in 1981. It obsessed Mary less as an event in itself than as a symbol of what was wrong with Ireland. Her tirades against the bus strike led to tirades against the Irish in general. "That's the way with us, lazy," she said. "Ireland wants the money, but not the work." I asked her what the strike was about. "Blackguards," she said. "They're too lazy to work. They're too drunk to clean the buses at night. So they fire one, and they all walk out. It's the end of Ireland."

Mary started with the bus strike and produced a vision of an Ireland inert but for starvation and war. Ireland has seen neither starvation nor war since the Troubles, when Eddie Carmody died at the Doctor's Cross. The Troubles had yielded freedom, and to Mary freedom brought decay. Starvation and war are Mary's own form of nostalgia.

Mary baffles me. Her Kerry brogue is so thick that I need my mother to interpret half of what she says. And half of that, when interpreted, seems so wild and extravagant (and vicious and funny) that my first instinct is to discount it all. Why seeing a dead man when she was six should give her authority to interpret Irish politics when she is in her sixties bewilders me.

My confusion showed that I did not understand the Troubles, I didn't understand Kerry, and I didn't understand how time worked in Ballylongford, where Sara forged her first memories and learned her first stories. I have only made things worse by becoming a historian.

When I try to fit these stories into a history, I encounter pasts that do not speak the same language. They do not follow the same rules. In Sara's stories about Ireland when she was very young, time does not always work as I expect it to. I expect people to move through time together; the clock ticks, and they all move forward. I do not expect people to drop out of time. I expect a single category of time with the same uniform minutes, hours, and days.

But in Sara's stories the past is not a single frame. There are different pasts that hang like two pictures on a wall. One frame is the everyday. Within it everyday acts are repeated endlessly. And when acts are repeated, there is no need to specify the time of each act or, indeed, the separateness of each act, or who, exactly, performed it. Who cares who sat in any particular chair that day or the next or the day after that? The point is there was a chair in which he or she sat.

The everyday does not include the extraordinary. To account for the extraordinary, Sara and Kerry have another way of remembering: the Time of Troubles. To historians, extraordinary occurrences seem to erupt out of a daily life where people milk cows, cut turf, and dig potatoes. But Sara and her neighbors in Kerry knew that such events were really visitations. They are things out of ordinary time, and they connect only with other extraordinary events, no matter how far in the past. Heroes and martyrs live with other heroes and martyrs; they are not really of the people who bore them, raised them, and shared their bed and table.

The Time of Troubles is the frame for one set of extraordinary events. It is the frame in which the people of Kerry combine and recombine these images of the past. The Time of Troubles is less a narrative that seeks to chronicle than a matchmaker pairing past and present. I ask my uncles and aunts about the ruins of a medieval tower or a plaque where an IRA man fell, and it is all the same: the Time of Troubles.

The Black and Tans in the kitchen, Eddie Carmody dead in the road—these are part of a near magical combination. Match them up correctly, and the tumblers of some temporal lock click, a door yawns open, and there is a tunnel through time. Through it walks the garrison of Carrigafoyle Castle, put to the sword during the Desmond Rebellion in 1580; through it come the three friars clubbed to death on the high altar at Lislaughtin Abbey that same year; through it come other friars killed by Cromwell's men in the 1640s. And Eddie Carmody merges with them, and the centuries that separate them matter not at all. Many people died in the Troubles, but in Ballylongford Eddie Carmody encapsulates them all; they all, in turn, embrace him.

What history keeps distinct, this common memory of the Troubles joins together. History insists that Eddie Carmody's death was the particular death of an Irish countryman at a particular place and a particular time. The monks died in 1580. Eddie Carmody died in 1920. To a historian these seem separate deaths, centuries apart and for different reasons. But to see all these deaths within the frame of the Troubles is to understand the dying differently. There are not multiple deaths in the Troubles, there is but one death endlessly repeated. It is a heroic death, and it cries for vengeance. In Sara's and Ballylongford's memory, there is only one death at the hands of the English— be they Cromwell's men or the Black and Tans. It is the same death, repeated over and over again. That death is the mark of the Troubles.

The Troubles span centuries, but they are only moments in any individual life. In Sara's life they are the moments when the Black and Tans strike and Eddie Carmody dies. But if the Troubles are to be meaningful, they need their opposite. They need everyday life.

Mary knows this, and she often pairs her stories of Eddie Carmody and the Time of Troubles with her stories of McCabe. In Mary's stories McCabe is the antithesis of Eddie Carmody. He lived among heroes without being heroic. He lived amid tragedy without being tragic. All McCabe wanted to do was avoid trouble, and that was precisely what he could never do in Mary's stories. Eddie Carmody became transcendent; he was a person of the Troubles. But McCabe remained immersed in everyday life.

McCabe was part of the scenery of the revolution and would have been happy to remain that way. Brian O'Grady, an IRA man, remembered that he was standing near McCabe's store when the drunken Black and Tans began shooting the night Eddie Carmody died.

The day the Black and Tans burned McCabe's store is one of Mary's favorite stories. One morning in February 1921, McCabe opened his door to find a group of Black and Tans outside. They were not people he wanted to see. McCabe was nervous. The weather, he thought, was a safe topic. "A cold morning," McCabe said in greeting.

"I'll warm it up for you," said a Black and Tan, and then he torched the store.

"I'll warm it up for you . . . ," Mary repeats that line every time she tells the story. She laughs, and her audience always laughs with her. This was apparently the only sign of wit anyone in Ballylongford ever detected among the Black and Tans. It wasn't much wit, but then Bally regarded the British as a slow and stolid lot, and any wit was remarkable and memorable.

Trinity College's agent, James Welply, reported the loss of McCabe's store, which was actually a cottage that McCabe rented from Trinity, to the bursar of the college soon afterward. "Destroyed by crown forces, 23 February 1921," was how he put it.

In Mary's telling, the burning of McCabe's store never stands alone. She links it to everyday life after the Troubles subsided. Mary says McCabe got a new store. Then, for some reason no one can now recall, he led a horse through the new store and into the yard out back. It was a courtyard, fenced by the walls of surrounding buildings. The horse barely fit through the doors to get there, and once there the horse up and died. Then the horse swelled as dead horses will. It swelled so much that McCabe could not drag it out through the store. The dead horse was not good for business. It grew worse for business every day. The stench filled the store. The stench, soon enough, filled Ballylongford. The dead horse became the village's understandable preoccupation. There was no way to move the horse. They had to butcher it, cutting off its legs and removing each stinking, putrescent piece through the store. This everyone thought was hilarious. It was the funniest thing that happened to McCabe since the Black and Tans burned his store.

In Mary's stories McCabe has a knack for living through tragedy without becoming tragic; he has a talent for staying rooted in the everyday, but history has ironic twists of its own. McCabe had children, and his children had children. His grandson Jerry McCabe went to school in Ballylongford. My cousins knew him. Jerry McCabe became a *garda*—an Irish policeman—at a time when the Troubles seemed far away. In 1996 he was guarding an armored car when a splinter group of the IRA killed him in a botched robbery attempt. He, too, like Eddie Carmody, would lie dead in the road.

5

Erected by His Comrades in Arms to the Memory of Lieut. Eddie Carmody, Ballylongford Co. IRA. Murdered by British Crown Forces on Nov. 22d 1920.
— Memorial to Eddie Carmody, Ballylongford, County Kerry

When Sara tells her stories, she has no need of a history of the Irish war of independence. She does not think about these things historically. The English did terrible things because they were English. That was their nature. You could recognize them as English because they did terrible things. Irish martyrs died at the hands of the English. The killers were always English, no matter that they were sometimes, in fact, Welsh or Scots or Ulstermen. The Irish resisted because they were Irish. They were rebels. That was their nature. If they failed to resist, they were traitors.

What is important to her is not explaining why the Troubles returned but recognizing when they returned. The Time of Troubles was about dying at the hands of foreigners or traitors. Eddie Carmody died and revealed the Troubles. Although no one died in the kitchen in Ahanagran some seventy-five years ago, Eddie Carmody showed that the threat of death was present.

But I am a historian, and, listening to Sara's stories as an adult, I get stuck on Eddie Carmody. Right at the start of her stories,

I can see that she is heading for places where I will lose my bearings. I can see her using Eddie Carmody to split time, to divide the everyday and the Time of Troubles. To her Eddie Carmody is a hero who exists only in the moment of his heroism. He is like the relic of a saint; his bleeding body attaches Sara and Mary to the Troubles. He is transcendent. He is a very Catholic revolutionary.

I am a historian. I don't believe in transcendence. There is only the everyday. I know that memories have histories, so I begin to craft my own history of memories. Eddie Carmody was once more than a body bleeding on the road. It is I, not my mother, Sara, who wants to see him before he lies dead in the road. I try to see him when he was just the son of a big farmer. It is hard to do this when all accounts of his life are written in the light of his death.

I move outside my mother's memories. I move into history. We each take our positions.

Compared to my mother's memories, my history is flat and its authority tentative. It is derived from what the English reported and the Irish witnessed. It is derived from things created at the time and things remembered later. It is at times uncomfortably close to a collective memory.

In Ballylongford in 1916 neighbors were not yet ready to kill one another over politics. There were, to be sure, Irish Volunteers who were in touch with The O'Rahilly before he died in the Easter Rising. But the Volunteers played cards with the local constables. The local constables did not regard the Volunteers as dangerous. When the British in Dublin went through The O'Rahilly's papers and found correspondence to Volunteers in Ballylongford, they forwarded the names to the constables. But these men were the constables' neighbors, and the constables refused to arrest them. The Volunteers blustered and drilled, but the constables couldn't imagine them as violent revolutionaries. After the Easter Rising the constables warned the Volunteers to destroy whatever correspondence they had from The O'Rahilly. This was not yet the Troubles in Ballylongford, when some of these neighbors would try to kill the constables.

Eddie Carmody was an Irish Volunteer and later an Irish Republican Army man stealing shotguns from the countryside, but such operations still merged with the dancing, drinking, and talking, the everyday life, of the countryside. There were signs—indeed in hindsight prophecies—that people expected the Volunteers, and the IRA after its founding in 1919, to leave everyday life and history and move into the Time of Troubles. Canon Hayes, then the parish priest in Ballylongford, linked Carmody, or someone like him, to the hallowed martyrs of centuries of blood and slaughter. In a sermon that Eddie Carmody himself supposedly heard, and that Sara's parents, Jack and Margaret Walsh, might have heard, Canon Hayes said he would not condemn the men who stole the guns because they were fighting for the freedom the Irish had sought for the last seven hundred years—three quarters of a millennium. The common standards by which the taking of guns was theft were, Canon Hayes implied, not applicable. The Troubles had standards of their own.

Canon Hayes saw the Troubles on the horizon; he and others welcomed them. Liam Scully, who had lived in Ballylongford, moved to Limerick later in 1919. He was killed in an attack on the Kilmollack police barracks in 1920. The earlier, neighborly relations between the Volunteers and the constables collapsed. With the rise of the IRA, things became more serious. The IRA began shooting constables, and Black and Tans sought to kill the IRA.

In April 1920 IRA men from Ballydonoghue killed Sergeant McKenna and wounded two other Ballylongford constables at Gale Bridge as they returned from Listowel with the monthly payroll. It was not the Ballylongford IRA men who killed McKenna, but that made little difference.

The Black and Tans, as the British auxiliaries to the Irish constabulary were called, came in strength to Ballylongford soon after. The IRA gunmen were shooting constables. Like Sergeant

McKenna, some constables died in ambushes. Some resigned in fear for their lives. Others resigned because the IRA threatened their families.

The British refused to acknowledge that this was a revolution; to them the IRA men were criminals. The British government had recruited the Black and Tans in order to buttress a constabulary that had no stomach for this fight. Sara Walsh says, and her generation firmly believes, that the Black and Tans were the scum of English prisons. The uniforms they wore were supposedly prison uniforms. In fact, the Black and Tans were mostly British ex-soldiers, World War I veterans unable to readjust to civilian life. The Black and Tans were men who needed a job, men who missed the regimentation. To people in Ballylongford, some of them seemed to miss more than that. In Ireland they could and did murder and kill and loot in the name of suppressing murderers and robbers. They wore khaki uniforms with the black-green caps and belts of the police. In Limerick a group of them went on a drunken spree breaking windows and assaulting civilians. The people of Limerick dubbed them the Black and Tans after a local pack of hounds.

Ballylongford became a center of rebel activities. In November 1920 when the IRA learned of a Black and Tan operation against Ballylongford, they ordered the Bally company to cache their arms, disperse into the countryside, and not carry out any action until they got direct orders from their high command. It was on November 23 that District Inspector Tobias O'Sullivan and four or five lorries of Black and Tans and police arrived in Bally.

Until that day the IRA men fighting the Black and Tans still lived the everyday life of the countryside. On the evening of November 23, 1920, Eddie Carmody, unarmed and mistaking this November day for everyday life, came to Bally for a game of cards. There were drunken Black and Tans in the streets firing their guns indiscriminately. Eddie Carmody and other Volunteers made their way out of the village. They were hiding near the Doctor's Cross when they mistook some Tans for Volunteers from Carrig. They revealed themselves, and the Tans opened fire.

Brian O'Grady, another IRA man, heard the shots. He was hiding in a tidal creek nearby. He knew someone had been wounded or killed. Four or five minutes passed. Then, there was a shout, "We have got O'Grady," a burst of rifle fire and a cheer. They had not got O'Grady; they had got Eddie Carmody. The four or five minutes of silence had been the last moments of Eddie Carmody's life. Although wounded in the first volley, he managed to get over the wall. The Tans found him there. The second round of shots killed him.

Within a few years, stories embroidered Eddie Carmody's death in ways that linked him not only with his comrades in the IRA but with the valiant dead of long before. He was supposedly taken alive to the barracks and, in pain and agony, tormented in an attempt to get him to reveal his comrades. He, of course, refused, as Irish patriots always refused.

That Eddie Carmody was almost certainly dead when the Tans dragged him back to their barracks matters little. They took his body and threw it into a room on the first story of the barracks where they stored turf for their fires. In some later stories this becomes an outhouse. The Carmody family retrieved his body the next morning.

The Tans had removed Eddie Carmody from everyday life. They made him a person of the Troubles. Eddie Carmody became part of the litany of revolutionary dead that Dorothy Macardle listed in her book *Tragedies of Kerry*. She attached each name to its place, the list building in Homeric cadences: Young Scanlon murdered in Ballybunnion, Carmody in Ballylongford, and Houlihan in Ballyduff; Frank Hoffman of Tralee, Bill McCarthy of Lixnaw, and Joseph Taylor of Glencar. Three crosses in the field in Gortaglanna with the names of Padraic Dalton, Padraic Breathnach, and Diarmuid Lyons. A cross on the road from Castleisland to Tralee: REMEMBER DENIS BRODERICK WHO DIED IN DEFENCE OF IRELAND, MAY 24, 1921. And each reader knew that the list stretched back centuries; each reader knew that each place was sanctified by the death.

The ancient struggle raged all around Sara and her family in 1920 and 1921. The IRA assassinated District Inspector O'Sullivan in Listowel. The Tans burned Collins's creamery, timber yard, and public house. The IRA organized the North Kerry flying column and struck back. By February 1921 only one main road remained open in Kerry. The flying columns could appear anywhere. The IRA cut the roads, digging trenches across them. A ten-mile journey by automobile or lorry often took four or five hours.

For Ballylongford the worst came in February 1921. The Sixth Battalion of the IRA set up an ambush in Ballylongford on February 22. They killed one Black and Tan and badly wounded another. The next morning the Tans took their revenge. Several lorry loads of them entered Ballylongford. They burned houses and beat the inhabitants. They burned fourteen houses on Well Street. They were not particular about whom they burned out. This was when they burned McCabe's store. They also destroyed a small cottage owned by Trinity College and inhabited by Johanna Carmody, a widow with six children, three sick with bone disease. The house was derelict, dangerous to live in, but she squatted there. She was so poor she hadn't paid rent since 1917.

After the Black and Tans burned Ballylongford, they moved through the whole district, looting and beating as they went. It was probably during this time that they entered the house in Ahanagran and beat Margaret Walsh. Sara was a little more than one year old.

This is the context of Sara's stories of Eddie Carmody's death and the Black and Tans' beating of her mother. But as necessary as I think such a history is, it is also partial and insufficient. I know this every time I visit the place Eddie Carmody died.

Eddie Carmody died just outside Ballylongford near the Doctor's Cross. The plaque is in Irish and English. It was ERECTED

BY HIS COMRADES IN ARMS TO THE MEMORY OF LIEUT. EDDIE CAR-
MODY, BALLYLONGFORD CO. IRA. MURDERED BY BRITISH CROWN
FORCES ON NOV. 22D 1920. The date is apparently wrong. Dates
don't matter; time is not the same in the Troubles.

Except for the plaque, there is no longer any sign of the Troubles at the Doctor's Cross. Everyday life goes on all around the
plaque. The doctor's house that gave the crossroads its name is
gone now. The government has built a row of public housing
where the gate to the doctor's house once stood. There are barking dogs in front of the cottages. There are children on bicycles
in the road. When a car honks to pass, they spread out into a
line and throw out their arms so they become a slowly moving
roadblock.

But at the Doctor's Cross, I know I am missing something. I
am swallowed by the everyday. The children on bicycles, the
barking dogs, the resurgence of daily life cannot touch Eddie
Carmody any more than any history that I write can touch him.
There can be poems about him and plaques commemorating his
death. There can be memories and stories of Eddie Carmody,
but it is hard to imagine a history of Eddie Carmody that will
be true to Sara's understanding of him as a martyr of the Troubles.

Sara keeps her memories unshaken. I can narrate all this as a
history, but Eddie Carmody and Sara's memories have slipped
away from me. I contextualize them only to see them slipping
over the border.

Fighting in Bally died down after March 1921, and following
the truce of July 1921 the peace came. The Black and Tans
withdrew. There was, however, more killing. But neither Sara
nor her brothers and sisters talk of this killing. There are no
stories because the killings had become a civil war, and the heroes of the revolution were killing one another.

The Black and Tans were gone by the end of 1921. Sara
Walsh was barely two. The Irish Treaty of 1921 gave southern
Ireland home rule and brought the withdrawal of the Tans. The
Troubles were ending.

Sara says she recalls that there was a parade in Ballylongford when peace came and she was allowed to go. Everyone was carrying a torch or candle. She was then not yet two.
How could she remember? She says she remembers all the
lights.

6

There is a fort in the field at the back of our house and it is circular in shape, and it is surrounded by trees and furse. Lights were often seen in the fort and music was heard there.
   —Sarah Dee, "A Fairy Fort," Ballylongford Girls National
      School, c. 1937. Department of Irish Folklore,
      University College, Dublin, box S 402, pp. 127–128

Ahanagran, the place Sara Walsh came from, was unlike any place she would later live. It is important to realize that.

The past made it different; the land made it different; memory made it different. I would once have said history made it different, but my uncle, Johnny Walsh, Sara's youngest brother, disabused me of that.

Johnny now lives in the townland of Guhard, next to Ahanagran. O'Connor's castle, Carrigafoyle, is clearly visible from Johnny's fields. A large square tower with a walled courtyard at its front, it bears the wounds of batterings it took centuries ago. English cannons blasted a huge hole in its front so that now it opens as if it were an ancient tunnel. The collapse of this front wall took four floors with it so that, until you are nearly at the top of the battlements, the spiral stairs in the rear lead only to landings that open on empty space. Even in ruins, it is still the largest building for miles around. It is less than a mile from Johnny's house. He has passed it a thousand times and more.

He has wondered about it not at all. When his sister Sara, attempting to find history in memory, asks him who destroyed O'Connor's castle, he is torn between exasperation and hilarity. His eyes become lively as his body grows still.

"How the hell should I know who destroyed the castle, Sara!" he says, and the pair of them dissolve into laughter, the kind of laughter they shared as children. When she asks him about old people they had known before they themselves somehow became old, he is incredulous. He says: "For God's sake, Sara, they're dead." The very idea of seeking information about the dead makes Johnny erupt with laughter. He tries to hold it in, but his body shakes like an old building when a train passes. "What's the use of being ignorant," Johnny says, "if you can't show it?" The statement, like so much Johnny says, is double-edged.

For Johnny his card game is worth all the history in the world. The dead are of no concern to the living. He knows all he needs to know of the place in which he lives. He has lived here his whole life, and what he doesn't know he doesn't think has hurt him.

When Johnny remembers, he wants to remember what brought him pleasure. He remembers the long trip to a wake near Dublin years ago, the trip where Sara and Gerard had to pull him away from a wedding reception he had joined uninvited in a hotel in Castlebar where they had stopped for lunch. This is a habit of his. He joins any celebration that does not throw him out. Oh, he remembers the wake well enough. "I'm enjoying it still," he tells Sara. The good times are what Johnny chooses to remember. "We had a good time," he says. "Isn't that what life is for?"

Johnny and North Kerry have little interest in history as I know it, but North Kerry is as tangled up in its past as any place that I have ever seen. Johnny and his friends are in love with language. Talking is their native art, and what they talk about is mostly one another. When they talk, they get stuck in the paths of the past as fully and as unintentionally as the famous cow that once started up the ruined stairs of O'Connor's castle and found itself in the castle's tower. Cows cannot go downstairs, so, when this cow began to climb, it could not go backward. Both history and this Kerry cow could only go forward on a course the past had created. Ballylongford is in the same predicament as the cow. It is no more able to extricate itself from its past than the cow was from the castle.

Johnny and his neighbors might acknowledge the point, but they would insist that what matters about the past, whether you are a cow or the village of Ballylongford, is not what is gone and forgotten, but what remains as fully in the present as the ruined castle of the O'Connors. The past is a set of ruins, of ghosts on the roads, of paths worn across the fields by feet long dead. The exact order of the creation of these things, or even who created them, does not much matter. What matters is how all these remnants relate to one another in the present.

I have been slow to understand this, but, even though I appreciate the case for memory, I will still take the side of history. History values what is forgotten, hidden, what was recorded at the time in stone or on parchment or paper or on the land itself. History is most interested in what makes no immediate sense because this is what most clearly distinguishes the past from the present. It values most what is least altered. History loves chronology. History sorts and orders events by date. Historians assume relations between things that happen during the same period in the same place.

Kerry, and the thousands of places like it, will have none of this. These places believe in memory. Kerry wants to rework not just the story but the very facts themselves to meet the times. Kerry wants a past that meets the demands of the present; it wants present events and past events to connect and even to merge. Kerry is inventive: it will alter the cut of the past to fit present fashions. For Johnny, what is forgotten remains forgotten and best left undisturbed. The past around him is past enough.

But Sara Walsh grew up in a world of stories no longer told. The stories have been largely forgotten, and it was the stories

that helped to mark each townland as separate. They marked
the landscape as clearly as its hedgerows and ruins. To walk
through the landscape that Sara Walsh walked through as a child,
to see Ahanagran as she knew it, you must know the stories.
The hedges, fields, houses, and wells, the ruined monasteries
and castles: these were available for any eyes to see. But to see
them is not what it was like to inhabit the place. The landscape
does not speak to strangers.

Nor is it enough simply to hear the stories. These stories did
not float free. They were set in a landscape. To move across the
land was to move through its past. The landscape was a set of
stories as much as it was fences, fields, and buildings. To know
the landscape was to know the stories. To become part of the
place was to know both landscape and stories. To know, it was
necessary to listen, work, and travel.

The stories once formed a map of the place, a mapping of the
place's past as well as present, but in Ahanagran, in North Kerry,
it was as if the map was constantly being ripped up and pieces
carried off. The stories were uneven across the landscape in part
because they were unevenly remembered. And sometimes those
who remembered best were those who left.

The stories current today in Ahanagran are, by and large, not
the stories of Sara Walsh's childhood. They have changed over
time. The old tellers of tales died or departed; their listeners
forgot the old stories or took them away when they themselves
left. Sara Walsh herself retains only a small stock of the stories
she was told.

Because the stories were embedded in and defined the landscape, the death of the stories was a small death for the land
itself. The land did not die, of course, but it was orphaned and
rendered at least partially mute until reinvigorated by new stories.

The national school that Sara went to and hated provides the
only key for recalling the stories as they were told in the 1920s
and 1930s. Although it was a place alien to the stories, the school
preserved them. The irony is that only history can recall a world

once held in memory. Stories are not just about the past, they have a history.

These stories, once so intensely local, became national in the 1930s. Leaders of the Irish Free State set about constructing a "true" Irish culture, distinct from the English culture they felt had contaminated their country. By the mid-1930s rural people had become the designated keepers of the national memory. They were the repository of true Irishness, and the Irish Folklore Commission gathered rural stories, particularly those from the west of Ireland. And so schoolchildren, people the Walshes knew—their neighbors the Dees, their cousins the Hollys—wrote down the stories they had heard from parents and relatives and neighbors. These stories, the common stock of the townland and those around it, became the property of the Department of Irish Folklore at University College, Dublin, which now preserves them. The stories remain frozen, taken out of memory and deposited in history.

To get some sense of the Ahanagran my mother knew and moved through as a child, I went to the archives with her in 1995. University College, Dublin, is several miles and architecturally many centuries from Trinity College. It looks like an American state college. The archives are understaffed and open only a few hours a day, but the people in charge know the materials well. The archivist, a woman with the dark, almost blue-black hair of the black Irish, brought us the ledgers into which the "best" stories had been transcribed as well as the original copybooks in which children recorded their assignments. We looked at the copybooks of the Ballylongford school and some from Tarbert, Astee, and Listowel.

By chance, the first one my mother opened was that of her cousin Teresa Holly. Teresa eventually left the country and moved to Chicago, but the stories her father, Patrick, told her and she wrote down remained behind in the archives. Sara handled Teresa's old copybook as if it were a living thing. She was seeing, I thought, Teresa as she had been in 1936 in Ballylongford.

What she read in 1995 were stories not as adults told them but as children heard them. Although Sara Walsh was sixteen and on the verge of leaving Ireland in 1936, these were the stories she had heard. No longer a child, she read them again, the writings of children who later grew old as she did.

These stories join the other stories she has held in memory. Now there are two sets of stories rejoined after more than sixty years: one has lived in memory, the other has survived in the archives. The people who live in Sara Walsh's memories had once heard and told these stories. Only in this archive in Dublin can we recover many of the stories she heard as a child in Ballylongford.

In Dublin these stories are out of place. When they were alive in memory, they were part of the land itself. They were about the land and its features. They were the landscape people moved through.

Because people departed and people forgot, the places Sara came to know were unevenly stocked with stories. A farm did not just have fields. It had particular fields. In the Walshes' case, on the farm Sara came to know first, the fields fell into two groups. The lower fields east of the house toward Ballylongford and the upper fields west of the house bordered by Dowd's Road.

The house and the haggard separated the two sets of fields. The haggard contained a hay shed where hay and tools were stored and was surrounded by a hedge where Margaret Walsh put her clothes to dry after washing them in the ditch by the road. The fields, too, were hedged, but they seem to have been as poorly stocked with stories as with cattle. Too many Walshes had left; too many stories had been carried away.

Their neighbors' fields were more particularly named and more full of stories. The children from the archives, old people now, become my guides. At the Hollys' farm, where Sara spent so much time, there were fields known by their shape and location, as on the Walsh farm. Teresa had learned them from her father, Patrick, and she recorded them in her copybook: the three-cornered field, which had three corners; the parkeen field, from the Irish word for field, *páire*, with the diminutive suffix *ín* (pronounced een) added; and the long field. There were fields known by utilitarian names that had survived their original use: the pound meadow, named because long ago cattle had been impounded in it. There were fields known by their current use: the new field, which had once been a garden and now held cattle. There were fields defined by their history: Griffins' field, which was once used by the Griffins, who were now gone. And there were fields defined by natural (or supernatural features): the fort field, where someone had successfully defied the fairies and cut the trees ringing the fort, and the well field, named after a holy well that moved about the Hollys' farm.

At the Dees', the next farm down toward Ballybunnion, Sarah Dee has copied the names in her book. There was (in the Irish spelling of the 1930s) Páirc-na-cré, the field of the earth, where once there had been a great garden; the rotten field, where one year the hay rotted; Doran's field, where once a cottar named Doran lived, and, when he died, his house fell and all that remained was his name given to the field. The Hannons' field was rented by the Hannons before they fled the townland in the famine of the 1840s. And so the names continued through the long field and the pound field and the river field and the stable field and the fort field. And so it was on farm after farm.

These everyday names with hints of the stories embedded in them merged, as in the well field at the Hollys' farm, with fuller and more spectacular stories. There were several holy wells near Ballylongford. Each holy well was specific and different in the way each saint might be different. Holy wells were anchored in place, or rather most holy wells were anchored in place. The holy well on the Hollys' farm was exceptional even for a holy well because it took offense so easily and decamped so readily. Other holy wells might dry up or withhold their healing. The Hollys' well just got up and left. It had once been on the farm of Patrick McNamara, but one day a woman had gone to the well and drawn water to wash clothes. When she finished washing, she threw the suds back into the well. The holy well disappeared from Patrick McNamara's and reappeared in a field at Patrick Holly's, which thereupon became known as the well field.

The other holy wells in the neighborhood stayed put. They not only fixed themselves in the land, but they were a hook that snared time, twisting the past, present, and future into a temporal rope that people could depend on. Most holy wells were connected to a far older, Celtic past, but they acquired the story of a saint or martyr whose life came to explain the well's power. The most famous holy well near Ballylongford was not in Ahanagran but nearby at Tobar Naomh Eoin on John Dillon's land near Astee. Bridget Lyons of Astee wrote in her copybook how, during the time of the penal laws, when the Mass was outlawed, St. Eoin was saying Mass when the priest hunters came along. The people grew fearful, but St. Eoin told them not to be afraid. When he finished saying his Mass, he mounted his horse. It rose into the air and came down atop Cnoc an áir (Knockanore Mountain, which lies between Astee and Ballybunnion).

St. Eoin explained the well's power, and it was on days connected with St. Eoin, or St. John, that the well manifested its power. You could not go to Patrick Dillon's well on just any day and expect the water to cure you or grant your request. You could not go with just any request. Wells had specialties. There had to be a convergence of the specific human needs that the well specialized in, the saint's day of the well's patron, and the physical space of the well itself. Then, and only then, in this convergence of need, time, and space at a single point would its miraculous powers be displayed.

When Sara was a child, her mother was one of those who came to Tobar Naomh Eoin on the Saturday before May Day, the first Saturday in May and just before St. John's Day. She and other supplicants "made the round," going three times around the well saying the rosary. If the water bubbled as they prayed, it meant their prayers would be answered. They drank the water that flowed from the well in a little stream and left behind pieces of string, medals, and holy pictures. People, they said, were cured there. It was particularly recommended for sore eyes.

A holy well, such as the one at Tobar Naomh Eoin, domesticated the supernatural and put it to use, but this demanded proper care and local knowledge—the correct needs, the correct acts, the correct days, the correct place—preserved in stories.

In a place where talk was so thick, Sara often heard the world before she saw it. When as a small child she sat in her own house and watched the road and listened to the stories, she was already moving through narratives of the world. The farm in Ahanagran then and now makes one aware of movement and its meanings.

The house fronted on the road, keeping all who passed within its sight. The new Irish building codes demand that a house be set back. But after the old house burned in 1995, Gerard insisted that the rubble be bulldozed into a nearby pile and the new house be built on the same site as the old. The county council granted him an exception. Every movement still has a meaning, and the new house is also an eye on the road.

To front on the road was to see and create stories, but it was also to be open to stories. The world of neighbors and movement came in to Sara Walsh before she ever moved out into it. She had only to learn to listen. She learned very well.

She inherited a knowledge of the world that had depth and rootedness to it. It was a particular and local knowledge, largely useless anyplace else. When she grew older and moved out into the fields, roads, and lanes, she already had a head full of stories, which she gradually associated with the places to which she traveled.

It is these stories that the old copybooks preserve. The stories tell of things that the eye could not always see. In a land so poor, there was a conviction that riches lay not on the land but beneath it. To hear the stories, each attached to a particular place, North Kerry was full of treasures. Stephen Lavery heard from his mother, who had been told by a distant relative, then an old lady, how once a gentleman had come to this relative in Ballyline to request a spade to bury his gold. Two men named Scanlon and Moran followed him, lost him, and then searched on the O'Briens' farm in Ballyline. When they were digging, a bull roared out of the hole and frightened them. And no one has looked for that gold since.

These underground bulls were a menace to Kerry treasure hunters. John Pratt had dreamed of treasure in a field under a hawthorn tree on Carrig Island. His dream told him he needed holy water from six churches and he must search at midnight. He had to go as far as Limerick for the holy water. He and his friends had dug until they found a flagstone. When they removed the flagstone, out rushed a bull. Fire flared from the beast's mouth and nostrils. It was easy to lose one's wits in such circumstances, and John Pratt and his friends had. Some ran and some fainted. None thought to sprinkle the bull with holy water. If they had, the treasure would have been theirs.

Little was what it seemed in this landscape. Nothing was reliably only the here and now. The holy well at the Hollys', like the fairy forts and Guyney's Hole, were places where other times and other dimensions intruded on the everyday world. People and things from the past resurfaced there; miraculous things happened. The landscape made part of the everyday miraculous.

A person had to exercise care in this landscape. Children my mother once knew listened, remembered, and then recorded in their copybooks what their relatives and neighbors had told them. Between Ballylongford and Ballybunnion there was an enchanted village that appeared from beneath the waters once every seven years. To see the village was to die, but even here there were opportunities because sometimes the horses of the enchanted village would come at night and graze the fields of farms near the shore. A farmer near the site of the village noticed the grass eaten out in his meadow, so he stayed up to find out why. At about two o'clock a great number of horses rose from the water and came into his meadow. He picked up a lump of mud and threw it at the horses. He hit one with the mud, and although the others ran back into the sea and disappeared, he kept the horse he hit. It became a powerful animal.

The fairies lived in this landscape, and the dead sometimes walked among the living. The fairies are not leprechauns. The fairies are the Tuatha Dé, who lived in Ireland before the coming of the Gaels. In medieval Irish mythology, the Gaels and Tuatha Dé came to terms and divided Ireland between them. The Gaels received the world above the ground. The Tuatha Dé retired underground. The mounds in Irish fields are fairy forts. The Tuatha Dé lived in forts all around Ballylongford.

The children Sara Walsh grew up with did not necessarily know the history of the Tuatha Dé, but they knew all about the fairies as living parts of the landscape. They heard and retold the stories about them. Dan O'Brien, then seventy, told his grandaughter, Maura Ahern, that the fairies had a fort on the Laverys' farm in Ballyline, a townland about two miles from Ballylongford. It was round like all their other forts and surrounded by whitethorn and blackthorn bushes. The fairies sometimes entertained there. John O'Brien had eaten with them once, and Peter Scanlon had been taken in there on a May Eve—which had once been the old Celtic festival called Bealtaine—by the good people, as the fairies were sometimes called. In the fort there was the fairest music Scanlon had ever heard and the grandest supper he had ever sat before. As Scanlon sat down to eat, he recognized one of his greatest friends, a man dead for more than a year. Eat all you want, he told Scanlon, but do not drink a drop, for, if you do, you will die. But Scanlon did not heed the warning. He ate and he drank, and he came home early in the morning and went to bed. He never got out of the bed alive.

The fairies on the Laverys' farm in Ballyline were unusually agreeable as fairies went. They had allowed Scanlon's friend to warn him; and John O'Brien had feasted with them and lived. These fairies remembered and reciprocated favors. Long ago, in the time of Sara's grandparents, Patrick Lavery was cutting hay in his meadow when he saw a broken griddle in the ditch of the fort. He took it home, fixed it, and placed it back on the ditch. When he cut hay on that field again, the griddle was gone, but he found a loaf of bread the fairies had left in thanksgiving. Patrick did not take the bread, and the next day it, too, was gone.

The fairies had three forts in Ahanagran in the 1930s. There was a fort on Richard Mackessy's farm about a mile from Ballylongford. They also had a fort on the lands of Jeremiah Dee just down the road from the Walshes, and a third one on the Finertys' land. All the forts were circular. Some people said the Danes had originally built them. But Danes were rarer than fairies in North Kerry, so crediting the forts to the Danes did little to demystify them. People said underground tunnels connected the forts. Many people were said to have entered the tunnels. Few had ever come out.

The fort at Richard Mackessy's farm had a wall of earth and stone; people saw lights there and heard music. The stories passed on around evening fires made their way into the copybooks. Carl Kavanagh told his daughter Nellie how once John Kavanagh had seen an image glittering in the bushes. He looked at it for a long time, but, when he turned away, it vanished. And once a man named Dan Lyons met a crowd of people marching up and down the road opposite the fort. They played beautiful music. These stories about the forts came to be as much a part of Mackessy's farm as the fairies.

The fairies issued from their forts; the dead marched forth from graveyards and churchyards. In North Kerry ruined churchyards and monasteries were the favored graveyards.

The Aghavallen churchyard was less than a mile from Sara's house. It was just beyond the Doctor's Cross, where the road leads up toward Carrigafoyle Castle. It has long been a graveyard. Patrick Holly, Sara's uncle, told them how, long ago, two men hunting had let their hounds in and, when the dogs raised a hare, one of the men beat it to death with a stick. The hare cried like a human. Shortly after, the man's hand began to rot. It was the hand that had held the stick. And shortly after that, the man himself died. If you got hurt in a graveyard, people said, the wound would never heal.

Stories like this were always firmly attached to a particular

place, but they traveled easily through time. Mrs. Ahern, a shop-
keeper in Ballylongford, told her grandchildren the same story,
but instead of locating it in some indefinite past, as Patrick Holly
had, she said it had happened in the 1930s. The man with the
rotting hand had consulted the best surgeons in Dublin. It did
him no good. "There was something unearthly in that hare."

Night was when the greatest slippage occurred. At night
graveyards leaked their dead. There are no nights darker than
Kerry nights when the days have grown short and the clouds
cover the stars. It is as if parts of the present world have been
erased. Fissures open, and the dead walk through them.

There were places of known danger in the night. Galvin's
Gate, as everyone knew, was haunted. Even as a middle-aged
woman, Sara would not willingly pass Galvin's Gate at night.
But with all signs of the world erased, the past could leak into
North Kerry at virtually any point. A man named Edmond Ahern
going home from a card game was surrounded by a host of people cowled like nuns. They escorted him without a word until
from fright he jumped in a ditch. They passed on, and he saw
them go into Gad Church Yard. When he arrived home, he discovered that a large stone had fallen from above his door, and
he could not remove it. A man on the road from Listowel was
stopped by a young woman in white who so frightened his horse
that he fell from the horse car and fled home without the horse.

Why the people cowled like nuns and the young woman in
white appeared the stories did not say, but often the dead
walked to do what they had failed to do in life. They came to
pay debts. Priests returned to say Masses they had promised to
say but had failed to perform.

The fairies and the dead who walked those Kerry nights were
in some sense the lucky ones. Many of the children who told
those stories in the national school six decades ago are now dead,
but most had no opportunity to slip off to inhabit the Kerry
night, to consort with fairies or become ghosts, because many
did not die in this place. They died far away. The Kerry nights
will never be theirs.

Sara Walsh and most of those she grew up with would never know so dense a world again. No place would ever speak to them as this one spoke. For all its poverty and pain, for all its gossip and small grievances, it would leave them with a sense of loss no matter how good their reasons for leaving. Sara would never be tied so tightly to any place again.

7

I was about [four] years old when my dad went to America. We were going to lose our land and him working in America was our only hope of keeping it. —Sara, remembering her father's departure

ara Walsh was three or four (the dates of such things are hardly exact) when the fairies took Richard Mackessy's pony. Richard Mackessy had noticed his pony missing the evening before. The whole family had searched, but they found no sign of it. Richard Mackessy went to bed thinking the pony would be back by morning. But it did not come back, and he resumed the search. That is when he found the pony caught in a tree within the fort. The pony was held fast between two branches.

Why the fairies would put the pony up in the tree, no one said, but the fairies around Ballylongford seemed to have an affinity for horses. In Ahanagran one fear had to be balanced against another, and fear of the bailiffs coming to seize cattle for debts owed landlords or merchants could overcome fear of the fairies, particularly if the bailiffs feared the fairies as well. In an earlier time, some local men had spent the night in Finerty's fort protecting the cattle from bailiffs, but at about two in the morning they heard a great noise and saw a pack of hounds followed by men on horseback. They had ridden all around the fort before galloping off in the direction of another fort and disappearing.

The pony up the tree was, perhaps, a fairy joke, but even if fairies trifled with you, it was best not to trifle with fairies. On the Dees' farm there had once been a servant boy who was fencing a gap in the meadow. He entered the fairy fort to cut bushes. A thorn pierced his leg. He got blood poisoning and died two days later. People said it was because he had cut the bushes. And at a fairy fort in Beale, two miles from Ballylongford, the father of Thomas Collins had decided to plow up the fort and till it, but when he started to plow, his horses immediately fell and broke their legs. No one interfered with the fort thereafter.

It was roughly a year after the fairies had put Richard Mackessy's pony up the tree that Jack Walsh left for America. "My dad went to America in January 1924 to earn money to save our farm," Sara remembers, "we were not able to pay the rates." Sara was barely four. The rates were the poor rates, the taxes on the land that the Walshes struggled so hard to get and expand. If Jack did not pay them, he would lose his land.

There is no causal connection between emigration and fairies, of course. But there are connections. Both existed in the same place at the same time; both sprang from a common past. And each, in its own way, represented the forked alternatives of Irish country life. A person who left Ireland left behind the Tuatha Dé.

Because the fairies came from the people who had inhabited the country before the Gaels, the fairies of Ballylongford and its surrounding townlands had lived there longer than the Irish. The fairies were embodiments of the past and the place itself.

Emigration, just as much a product of the local past, represented an opposite prospect. The fairies had gone underground into the land itself; the emigrants went out of it. Those who left were absences not lingering presences. They were those who could not or would not stay. Ahanagran produced more emigrants than fairies.

When Jack Walsh left in 1924, his troubles were not unusual. It was a bad year generally in Kerry. In January 1924 the sheriff with a posse of soldiers seized cattle across North Kerry for nonpayment of rents, land payments, and rates. The Farmer's Union was reorganizing in Ballylongford. J. J. Galvin was elected chairman. The farmers wanted protection and relief. They claimed, *The Kerryman* reported, that the values set on their land by the Land Commission were "highly unjust and unbearable."

Jack Walsh was the last of his siblings to emigrate. Having no land had caused Jack Walsh's brother and his sisters to leave Ireland; his hope of keeping the land caused Jack Walsh to leave. The desire to keep farms was part of the great irony behind so much emigration. Jack Walsh carried the secret so many emigrants carry: he didn't leave to change things. His leaving was a desperate attempt to keep them the same. Jack Walsh left for America because he wanted to be an Irish farmer.

To save the farm, he left his wife, Margaret, with one baby in the grave, five young children, and another child growing in her womb. The day Jack left, Margaret Walsh stood crying among her children. She had no idea how long he would be away.

For Sara, a small child, that was for a time the end of it. Seventy years after it happened, she still remembers the leaving and its cause, but the memory is of her mother watching her father leave: "I remember my mom crying the day he left. That is my only memory of that day. I did not remember my dad at all."

The pony the fairies put up the tree and the departure of Jack Walsh happened almost contemporaneously in the same place, or so at least the stories say. These two stories tell of things that once happened alongside each other. Fairies and emigrants existed side by side. Ponies did not end up in trees every day, but then neither did fathers depart for America that often. The things these stories commemorate did not occur in separate realms. People who saw fairies still had to pay the rates.

The past is a set of connections that once ran only laterally or backward. They could not run forward because the future had not yet happened. But remembering the past forges connections among what happened then, what happened afterward, and what exists now. The older connections, the connections of things that simply happened simultaneously in a single place, become attenuated and lost. They are hard to restore. I can only guess at the connections that once existed among such stories. But I think it is necessary to put Richard Mackessy's pony back up that tree.

 **8**

And in this parish you, and your fathers before you, knew what it was to starve because you did not own your own land—and that has increased this unappeasable hunger for land.

—John B. Keane, *The Field*

In time, Jack Walsh became only an absence. His leaving tore a hole in Sara's life so large that forever after it would be his absence rather than his presence that would define him. He never could fill the empty space he had created.

Sara grew up without her father. She did not forget him, but by her ninth birthday, the time she had lived without him was greater than the time she had lived with him. Unlike her brother Johnny, who was in her mother's womb the day Jack Walsh left, she could always call up some picture of him. She could imagine his face, but a picture was not a presence, and the spaces Jack Walsh had occupied became vacant.

It is hard to recover the sense a four-year-old made of her father's absence. She did not know then that her father would be gone for years, that his absence would come to define him. Sara thinks of it now, after a long and full life; distance may give perspective, but distance also alters everything. It is hard to recover something as small as a four-year-old's pain and confusion across so many years.

It is even harder to recover what Jack Walsh thought. He never said what he thought, or, if he did, no one remembered or recorded it. He acted from his own memories and hopes, but those memories are gone. And Sara's mother, Margaret, I think, resented the farm too much to talk of it and the hold it had on them. Less willingly than Jack, she had made herself hostage to this land. That was done. She told her stories of other, better places, not of this green farm, with its smell of manure and burning turf and its soft yielding earth that rarely could support the cattle or the people who tended them. The land had the texture of a thing not yet fully formed, a thing perhaps never to be fully formed.

All I can recover is the history. And I think that is enough, because I think his going and all that followed was about land and history.

Jack Walsh never explained his attachment to the land. There are only his actions. To risk so much, to do what he did, there had to be a deep passion, something beyond the easy rationales, the simple "rational" choices that some economists think explain the past but that only explain their own preference for a simplistic world of simple people. The land in any economic sense was a bad bargain. The Walshes survived as a family in Ahanagran because Jack Walsh's father, William Walsh, married Ellen Carr and obtained land and raised children. The family's hold was tenuous. The farm was a lifeboat that could support children until they grew up. Then only one could remain: the farm could not be divided. The others sought safety elsewhere in the world. The eight of William Walsh's eleven children who preceded Jack Walsh to Chicago could testify to that.

Why not let it go, this land that had meant poverty for three generations? Why not just let it go? Accept the failure. Admit it was always a bad bargain, this work that yielded so little return.

Jack Walsh never explained. Whatever the answer, only history can give it. It is an important answer because it shaped Jack Walsh's life, his wife's and his children's lives. It is a history that shaped Sara Walsh's life, even though she never knew the events of this past. More than memory shapes the past, and history is more than a collection of memories. I must construct this patch of family history without reference to memory, for there are no memories of it in the family, at least not memories that I have heard.

It is odd. My mother has told me everything I know about this farm, but I am the one who ends up trying to explain to her how it drove her father's life, how saving it destroyed the heart of her parents' marriage, how it shaped her own life. And I end up thinking that a grandfather I do not remember meeting probably, in the end, regarded the land as worth the cost. Keeping the land was his achievement. My guess is that he thought it a good bargain. It is the arrogance of historians to presume to think such things, to believe their own best guesses, but believe them I do.

I make my guess, in part, because Kerry's writers make this passion for land one of their themes. John B. Keane, the Irish playwright who comes from Listowel near Ahanagran, has one of his characters, the Bishop, speak of the varieties of hunger. Eventually, the Bishop comes to the "hunger for land":

> And in this parish you, and your fathers before you, knew what it was to starve because you did not own your own land—and that has increased this unappeasable hunger for land. But how far are you prepared to go to satisfy this hunger?

Keane talks about death from the lack of land and the willingness to kill for land; these things had happened in Ahanagran and the surrounding townlands. There were witnesses of the famine of the 1840s still alive in Ballylongford when Sara was a child. Her sisters had memories of the violence that swirled around the land.

People had starved within a short walk of the house in Ahanagran because they had no land. The oldest people in the neighborhood of Ahanagran had witnessed it. John Ware was eight years old in 1846 and living on Carrig Island close to the castle of the O'Connors that Cromwell's troops had destroyed. Trinity College then owned the island and leased it to middling landlords, who rented it to peasant families. The potato blight—a new fungus *Phytophthora infestans*—appeared in Ireland in 1845. It was the smell you noticed first, people said. There was a foul smell of rot when the vines were still green, and then the vines withered and turned black. The people around Ballylongford called it the black scab, and it virtually destroyed the potato crop in Kerry in 1846. By that fall there was trouble. A huge body of people—five or six thousand—marched on the workhouse in Listowel shouting "Bread or Blood" and demanding food.

When a few of the potatoes escaped infection in 1846, the peasants cut out the eyes for seed and ate the remainder. Those who had scavenged this seed actually had high yields. It did them no good. They were tenants, and the landlords demanded the crop as rent. John Ware said the landlords took potatoes from families who then starved.

When John Ware was 101, he still claimed to remember well what happened the next year, in 1847. That was the worst year. One hundred people left Ballylongford. Those who stayed ate turnip greens and green oats and barley. In desperation they ate grass and seaweed. They died. There were twenty-one occupied houses on the road from Lenamore to Moher in 1847. A year later there were three. In 1848 the crop failed again all across Ireland. The British government turned the old barracks into a workhouse for the poor. They sent yellow meal—cornmeal— into the country, and from it the people made bread to live.

The potato blight was a sentence of death or exile to millions. Those with farms of twenty acres or more and cattle pulled through. The renters of small plots on which to grow potatoes and cabbage starved. By the late 1840s emigration had already reduced the population from eight to seven million people. Now another million died, mostly of disease brought on by malnutrition. Two million more fled that sentence in the decade following 1845; most often they went to America. As the number of ships carrying people from Ireland increased, the cost fell. Three pounds would buy passage on one of the "coffin ships." The very poorest could not afford even the coffin ships; they died where they lived or on the road. The population in the Baronies of Clanmaurice and Iraghticonnor around Listowel, of which Ahanagran was a small part, dropped from seventy-nine thousand in 1841 to fifty-two thousand in 1861. One out of every three people died or fled.

The great famine initiated mass migration in the west of Ireland. Each generation that followed learned the necessity of holding land. The land consolidation and market farming that had begun in the north and east before the famine spread to the south and west after it. Potato plots became pasture. The smallest holders were evicted. In 1850 the Crosbies leased from Trinity College the estate of Rusheen that contained part of Ballylongford and all of Middle Ahanagran. They evicted forty-seven smallholders that year. The undersheriff came from Tralee to enforce the evictions. Land that had provided potatoes for the Irish now provided meat and butter for English tables. Sporadic bad weather and poor crops harried those who held on through the late nineteenth century. Hunger pinched again. The population continued to fall. Between 1880 and 1926 the population of Munster, which included County Kerry, fell by one-third. Munster during these years had the largest number of emigrants of all the regions of Ireland.

Behind my guess that John Walsh thought the land worth the price he and his family paid are reasons beyond Keane's literary claims of a common passion for land in North Kerry that sprang from the famine. I guess because long before Jack Walsh migrated, he took great risks for the land.

Jack Walsh knew the violence that rose up from this land. He had known that violence most of his life. There is a story, a story made from a flash of memory, that suggests the power the land held and the trouble it brought. Mary, Sara's sister, says she remembers lying in bed in front of a window. There was a blast, a shotgun blast, and the front window exploded into the room where she and her twin, Nell, slept. The noise of the blast resounded and glass flew over and around the two girls. They were hysterical with fright.

As Mary tells the story, the blast came in retaliation for Jack Walsh's cutting hay for the Hickies, the landlords who lived at Killelton. The Hickies' tenants and the rest of the neighborhood were boycotting them either over the terms of their leases, over the terms of purchase, or for their holding on to land instead of releasing it for the tenants to buy. No one would cut the Hickies' hay. It would rot in the field if the neighbors had their way. But Jack Walsh cut it fom them. He did it, says Mary, because he was a good man always ready to help a neighbor. In retaliation one or more of the landlords' tenants shot out Jack Walsh's window.

I don't doubt the story, just Mary's coloring of it. Given the times, this was likely more than the undeserved punishment of a Good Samaritan. Mary says it happened when she was between two and four. It could have been in 1918, for there was trouble by then, but it probably was in 1919 or even 1920, when there was far greater trouble.

The shotgun blast is testimony to the power of the land. His need for money to support his farm, to pay his rates, tempted Jack Walsh to violate codes he knew he should not transgress. The power of the land brought his neighbors to punish him so that they might gain or keep land of their own. It had been this way for Jack's whole life; he had seen his father on the other side of these struggles.

Jack Walsh knew, I think, the particulars of these struggles for land in ways his children and grandchildren do not know. They no longer survive in memory. The passion for the land remains in my uncle Gerard, but if he knows the family struggles to obtain this land, he never has told me or my mother.

For the Walshes this struggle began when Ellen Carr married William Walsh in Ballylongford on March 1, 1870, and the tenants on the farm in Ahanagran were now Walshes rather than Carrs. When Ellen Carr married, she dangled near the end of a long chain of landlordism. When the British took the census of 1851, John Carr leased the farm from agents of Pierce Crosbie. Carr was also by then a petty landlord himself, for he had two subtenants. Pierce Crosbie, to whose representatives Carr paid rent, was the holder of the estate of Rusheen and himself a tenant of Trinity College, which had in 1597 inherited both the confiscated lands of the O'Connors of Carrigafoyle and the forfeited lands of the Earl of Desmond. At each step up the chain, a landlord claimed part of the revenue from below. What was left went to Trinity College. In a small way, Trinity College was the end result of the labor of those generations of Catholic Carrs and Walshes. The center of Protestant learning in Ireland was built in part from the rents of Catholic farmers.

When Ellen Carr married William Walsh, she linked him to the chain of landlords and tenants—overwhelmingly Protestant at the top of the chain, overwhelmingly Catholic at the bottom. She was only twenty. He was twenty-six.

By the time Jack Walsh was born in 1880, Ahanagran was a battlefield in the Land War. In May 1877 Trinity College had increased the Crosbies' rent on the estate of Rusheen to £1,234. The increase came as Ireland slipped into an agricultural depression. Landlords tried to pass rent increases on to tenants; tenants failed to meet their rents. By 1882 William Hickie on the neighboring estate of Killelton complained that most of his tenants were four or five years in arrears, and he appealed to Trinity for relief, saying he could not pay his own rent. James Crosbie, who had inherited Rusheen, was in worse circumstances. Neither got relief.

William Walsh, along with the other tenants of Rusheen, fought the Crosbies and Trinity College. They used the tools of the poor: withholding rent, the boycott, the threat of violence. Fighting the powerful demanded solidarity among the weak. The eviction of a tenant meant opportunity for an ambitious neighbor to acquire more land or for a landless man to acquire a farm. To control such temptation, the neighborhood resorted to boycotting, a word that derives from this Irish struggle for land. Men who crossed the collective interests of the neighborhood became social lepers. Those who failed to observe the boycott would themselves be boycotted. In such a local world, to be cut off from all aid, all social intercourse—to lose the talk and conviviality that were the only salves to a hard life, to lose the condolence of sociability—was a serious thing. When the policy of ostracism broke the resistance of Captain Charles C. Boycott, the English agent of a large landowner, the practice took his name.

A traveler reporting on the countryside around Listowel explained the tactics that had caused Captain Boycott to break. A boycotted farmer "finds himself no longer able to sell his goods, buy the necessaries of life, have his horses shod, corn milled, or exchange a word with a living soul within a radius of fifteen to twenty miles of his house; his servants are tampered with and induced to leave him, his tradespeople shut their doors in his face; people come and play football in his oat fields; his potatoes are rooted out; his fish or cattle poisoned; his game destroyed." No wonder that on the estate of Rusheen the farms of evicted tenants remained empty and unworked.

Crosbie and other landlords responded with more evictions and seizures of livestock. Some local tenants gave up and left for America, others escalated the conflict. Ideally, the boycott was peaceful, but it could easily shade into cattle maiming, haystack burning, and shootings. At nearby Killelton, the seat of the Hickies, where some forty years later Jack Walsh would make the mistake of harvesting hay, people came from all over North Kerry for a Land League Hunt. They came to kill hares and other game on the Hickie property. The animals that tenants were forbidden to kill became the symbols and objects of their rage. They killed the hares "to let the landlord know that he had no more power over his tenants." The whole of that part of Kerry, an agent of the college reported, "is—to put it mildly— disturbed." A group of tenants set upon Crosbie and beat him. By the mid-1880s there was what Trinity's land agents described as an organized attempt under the auspices of the National Land League to drive Crosbie out.

Crosbie was the smallest and most vulnerable of the local landlords. The plan was to refuse to pay rent until Crosbie could not meet his own rent and then, when the college revoked his lease, to demand that the college charge the tenants only what it had charged Crosbie. By eliminating his middleman's portion, they would effectively reduce their own rents.

I know of this struggle only because this plan, in part, succeeded. William Walsh was a tenant of Trinity College, and, by this breaking of a link in the chain of landlordism, Trinity College became aware of William Walsh. The refusal of William Walsh and the other tenants of Rusheen to pay rent bankrupted Colonel James Crosbie, whose family had held Rusheen for three centuries. Trinity took over direct supervision of the estate in 1886.

Just as the rents of Rusheen had helped in a small way to build Trinity, so the rebellion of the tenants of Rusheen brought them in a small way to Trinity's attention. Now Trinity preserves them in history. I sit in a reading room of the Old Library, at the opposite end of the building from where tourists line up to see the Book of Kells and look through the muniments of Trinity College. There I find William Walsh and eventually his son, Jack Walsh. History is all that remains for William Walsh and his fellows, for they and their rebellion have largely passed out of the living memory of Ballylongford. There is no family memory of William Walsh's struggle. If there is a local memory of it in Ballylongford, I never have heard it.

By 1886 Crosbie had lost his lease, and the college hired William Sidney Cox of Limerick to act as land agent for Rusheen. On the advice of Cox, Trinity refused to reduce the rents to the level they had charged Crosbie for fear of encouraging similar actions on neighboring college estates. They instead offered to cancel the arrears on payment of a half year's rent and grant a twenty five percent temporary abatement on the judicial rent set in 1882. The tenants held a meeting and rejected the offer. "They think," Cox reported, "that the College should be satisfied with same rental that was paid by Colonel Crosbie." The tenants were, in a statement repeated over and over by agents of the college in one form or another for the next twenty-five years, "an exceedingly bad lot and I apprehend trouble."

The college threatened to secure writs and seize property unless the rents were paid. They threatened Timothy Sullivan, who seems to have led the protest. They threatened David Sullivan and Michael Enright and John Kennally and Thomas Bambury. They threatened William Walsh. By then Walsh was, as the college described him, in "embarrassed circumstances."

The college and its tenants reached a compromise on rents at the end of 1887, but even reduced rents were more than the farms could yield if they were to provide any kind of living to their occupants. The estate of Rusheen came through the Land War, as these struggles were called, in miserable shape. It appeared, the agent reported, "very impoverished," the fields understocked with cattle, the houses and farm buildings "dilapidated" and "wretched." The old arrears disappeared, and the tenants began to accrue new debt. The reports grow monotonous. The year 1897 was "exceedingly bad," and 1898 was "disastrous."

The tenants descended into insolvency. By 1913 the accumulated rent due on the Walsh farm alone was £455; it was, in total, nearly seventeen years in arrears. For all practical purposes, the Walshes had ceased to pay at all following William's death in 1902.

The estate of Rusheen had long before become a losing proposition for Trinity. Its agent complained in 1904 that the estate was "the most troublesome and difficult property to manage that I know of." Seizing what stock there was only resulted in pauper tenants, who could pay no rent instead of little rent. Jack Walsh owed more than any tenant in Middle Ahanagran except Jeremiah Dee. In 1911 the college had got a process served against the Walshes, but there was little property Trinity could seize. Evictions were pointless: new tenants could not be found at existing rents. The farms could not be operated at a profit. Trinity evicted the Dees, but then it seems they were allowed to stay on as caretakers.

The various Land Acts gradually provided the means for tenants to buy their land and often for landlords to get generous prices. In the case of Rusheen, Trinity had forgiven the arrears, and the Land Commission had advanced the purchase price. The price was high—£323—but still less than the arrears. Jack Walsh got the farm, but the interest alone on his loan came to £11 a year.

Acquiring the farm was Jack's great success and his great burden. He bought the farm betting that it could be operated at a profit. For three generations, Carrs and Walshes had labored under the threat of losing this land they worked but did not own. They lived under the threat of dispossession. Now Jack Walsh saw the chance to enjoy the full rewards of his own labor.

It was a false hope. There was, after all, the debt he had incurred to buy the farm and the interest of about 3 percent on the debt; there were also the rates on the land, as the taxes were called.

And as Jack Walsh realized that achieving his greatest ambition had only created a new way to lose everything, he was tempted to violate rules that he knew all too well. He had grown up among poor men on poor land fighting the powerful. His father had been one of those poor men. Their only hope lay in solidarity and the ruthless punishment of those who broke ranks. Jack Walsh had witnessed the tactics as a child. Accepting work on a boycotted farm was a serious thing. Jack Walsh knew that.

But things had changed. The Land Acts and later the Congested Districts Board redistributed land. Famine and emigration depleted the ranks of laborers and cottars, people who rented an acre or less and who lived in one-room huts with what animals they owned. Things had changed, but this had not: to assist a landlord against his tenants, no matter how small the act, still brought retaliation. The old resentment against those with too much land burned still, but it was no longer always clear how much land was too much.

When shotguns shattered the window, when his daughters screamed in terror, Jack Walsh knew the message and why it came. How could he not know it? But to have gained the land, to have received the spoils of generations of struggle, and then to lose it—he could not lose it. So to keep the land, he turned, in a small way, against the very struggle that had given him his land. This betrayal brought retaliation. But he could not pay the rates; he could not pay his debt.

So to keep the land, he went to America. He departed in 1924 with his wife crying in the road and his children gathered around her. Except for one visit back home, he would be gone twenty-three years.

Sara was four years old. She knew none of the history that drove her father to America. She knew only its outcome.

9

Tim was a father to us after Dad left, and I remember Tim more than I do my dad.　　　　　　　　　　　　　　　　—Sara

To take his place in Ireland, Jack Walsh left his nephew Tim Walsh, and his wife, Margaret. Tim, the son of Jack's sister Kitty, who had gone to America in disgrace, lived in the house with Margaret and assumed the role of a hired man. He was much more. "Tim was a father to us after Dad left," Sara says, "and I remember Tim more than I do my dad."

But most of all it was Margaret Walsh who took Jack's place. She expanded, absorbed Jack's loss, and filled the void her husband had created like a balloon that grows from an exhaled breath. In Sara's memories and stories her mother lives more fully than her father. In emigrating to America he lost his voice and took on the silence that defined him. She knew only a child's love for her parents. With her father gone, she turned that love into a fierce attachment to her mother. Sara would never abide a harsh word said about her mother. When two boys from Astee called her mother an old, gray hag, Sara and her cousin Eileen Holly grabbed sticks and chased them down the road until the boys took to the fields. She did not get her revenge, but if she met those boys now as old men, I have no doubt she would reach for a stick again.

If Margaret Walsh ever heard the taunt, it must have stung.

Margaret Walsh in her forties looked like a peasant woman and dressed like one in a black dress and shawl common to Kerry. In the towns, the shades and weaves of these dark shawls marked status and taste. But in the old pictures they all look dark and indistinguishable. Sara remembers black as the uniform color of women's dress in the countryside. The shawls might have been originally black, or they might have grown black from dirt and wear. She does not remember her mother ever washing her shawl.

As Sara grew older, she identified her mother with Ireland. When Sara left, she remembered her mother as Ireland. America existed as the place her father had disappeared into. Ireland was where her mother remained. Ireland became the simple life, the point of departure for her own complicated life's journey into a vast and unknown world. She retains that image of herself and her life's trajectory to this day. "Ireland was poor, but we were happy there," she says.

The problem is that her own accounts of her mother in the years after her father left create the openings that allow history to infect her stories, to subvert and complicate what memory tries to portray so cleanly. Margaret Walsh kept in the house a photo taken of herself at about the turn of the century. In it she is a pretty woman in fine clothes. She passed that picture on to Sara. It was a memento of something past; now she could be taunted as a hag.

I saw the photograph as a child. I had never met my grandmother, and the photograph meant nothing to me. It was from long ago. I presumed, if I thought about it at all, that the picture had been taken in Ireland. My grandmother lived in Ireland; she was a character in my mother's Irish stories. As a child, I did not know my grandmother had been in New York, that she had emigrated and returned. This was not one of my mother's stories. She told me only recently, as we wrote this book.

Margaret Walsh left Ireland and returned. Such returns, such travelings back and forth, complicate Sara Walsh's life and stories and history itself. Long before Sara ever reached America, America had entered Ballylongford and Ahanagran. The Irish and Americans both stress the sea between them and the sea change from Kerryman or Kerrywoman to Yank. In her stories Sara now emphasizes the differences between Ireland and America, but differences do not eliminate connections. Ireland and America were different in the way partners in a marriage are different; and as in a marriage, it is the connections that matter as much as the differences. The connections are everywhere apparent. Sara's father embodied the connections. For Jack Walsh, Ireland always remained not only visible but tangible from America, just as America had been visible and tangible from Ireland.

As Sara grew up in Kerry, she gradually recognized the possibility of America. The Ireland of Sara's childhood never stood alone. It stood always in relation to America. America existed as a presence in the people who had returned and the memories they had brought back with them and in the things relatives who had not returned sent back across the sea.

In Sara's stories things arrived from America. Her father sent money to pay the rates, to help support the farm, to pay accounts at the store, eventually to put aside funds for a dowry for Mary, Nell's twin sister.

Most of what arrived from America was sweet and satisfying. Packages from the States hinted of wondrous lives led by Irish who had become Yanks. When Sara was seven, a parcel arrived from New York. Her other aunt Hannah, her mother's sister, had sent her a dress for her first Communion.

"It was so beautiful," she remembers. "I had never seen anything that beautiful, and it fit me. Also in the parcel was a pair of shoes, black patent leather, which I claimed, even though they were much too small for my big feet. But they were worth the pain and blisters. I felt like a princess. I will never forget that day I felt like a princess in Bally."

What those shoes replaced, at least for a day, were nail shoes—hobnailed boots—big, heavy shoes with nails protruding a quarter inch from the bottom so as to save wear on the sole. If Ireland was nail shoes, then New York was patent-leather shoes that pinched and blistered but shined and made a seven-year-old Irish girl feel like a princess.

America created absence even as it created opportunity. America was possibility: the Land of Opportunity, the Land of Promise, the Land of Liberty, the land of the free and a place where anyone who was willing to work could make his fortune. America was also deep regret, for, in the best of imagined worlds, no one would want to go there and no one would have to go there. Ireland would suffice.

Because of America, Sara Walsh came from a family of cosmopolitan peasants. The Walshes are cosmopolitan still. My relatives have played musical chairs with America for three generations now. Those left with no place to perch in Ireland go to America or, less often, to England. So many have gone that their own departure could never have been a surprise to them, but that didn't kill the pain of leaving or the deep longing they carried for home. Into my mother's generation, although Ireland was by then free, the Walshes thought of themselves as exiles banished from "Holy Ireland" by English injustice and greed.

This America subverts Sara's insistence on the poor but happy Ireland of her childhood. Her mother Margaret's leg subverts such insistence even more. Margaret Walsh told her daughter that she wished she had never returned from New York. Life was good there. The real emblem of Ireland was Margaret Walsh's sore and infected leg. One night, a long, wet, and dark night of the Irish winter, Margaret went out in a fierce storm to check on the animals. She tripped against a bucket and cut her shin. The cut never healed. It ulcerated and became a running sore, and that sore oozed pus and blood for years until antibiotics reached Ireland. Margaret spent her days in pain, limping through her work.

The doctor, whose name was Walsh, couldn't do anything. He was ten long miles away in Listowel in a land full of tuberculosis, where people seemed to die young. The hospital, where Sara's cousin John Martin Holly died in his teens of meningitis, was ten miles away. Ten miles could be a week's wait, as it was when Sara's brother Gerard pushed her into the fire and burned her leg so badly she bears the scars on her shin still. The rusty bucket, the doctor ten miles away, the festering wound on her calf—these were the Irish realities of Margaret's farm.

Dr. Walsh would at least be sober when he came. It was not always true of those who succeeded him. Dr. Ross was drunk when the tinker was dying. Tinkers, or travelers, as they are called now, were native Irish, poor transients who traveled by wagon and were regarded as gypsies all over rural Ireland. My mother's family was poor, but they owned land. Socially beneath them but physically all around them lived a handful of the once numerous cottars subsisting on badly paid farm labor and the dole. And beneath everyone were the tinkers. All property missing, all wash vanished from a line, all things untoward, undesired, and unexplained in a village and the townlands were laid at the door of the tinkers.

The tinkers sent for Dr. Ross during his weekly trip to Ballylongford. He came. He had been drinking, but he was always drinking. Alcohol was as much a part of his practice as his stethoscope. He took out his stethoscope when he came to examine the tinker.

The tinker was on a low bed, and Dr. Ross had to lean over to listen to the dying man's heart. Gravity and drink conspired against him. To the dying tinker it must have seemed that the stethoscope had tethered them together, that his heart was drawing the doctor in, that they would tumble into death together. Once he began to lean, Dr. Ross fell victim to gravity. He fell slowly with the weight of drink and the solemnity of a man concentrating on controlling his senses. He fell on top of the tinker. The story my mother tells ends with the village's laughter. It freezes the drunken Dr. Ross helplessly sprawled on top of the dying man he had come to help. It is how Ballylongford remembers him.

These stories—of Sara's burned leg, of the dying tinker, and of Margaret's ulcerous wound—are all linked. The moral of the

story of my mother's leg is the distance from a doctor's care.
The moral of the story of the tinker is the ineptitude of the
doctor when he did arrive. The moral of the story of Margaret
Walsh's leg is that this ulcerated wound would have been healed
in America. These were all stories of Irish backwardness. In
the light of America, Margaret Walsh's wound marked only her
ability to bear up under things that there was really no need
to endure. Even courage can lose its meaning in situations
where courage should be unnecessary. Sara tells the story with
the implicit knowledge that America could have healed her
mother's leg.

But standing against this America that shone so brightly, this
America that still stirred Margaret Walsh, was Tim. Tim was "a
great working man." That is how Sara's brothers Gerard and
Johnny remember him. He was very strict with us, Sara says.
"He kept us in line." The years have weighed heavily on their
memories of Tim. They compress him; just as under the weight
of earth and time ferns become coal or diamonds, so Tim, once
so lanky and flexible, becomes rigid and crystallized. He is now
the sum of his most basic qualities: wise, a good working man.
Only a phrase or two to set him apart from all those around him
who must have had some wisdom or work of their own.

He was a father to them, so they all say, and maybe that is
what held him there. Tim would seem a more likely candidate
to join that vast exodus from Kerry than most of those who left.
Why would he stay? He would never get land or a farm, and
thus he would never marry. He would work and take care of his
uncle's children. He could not fail to see that.

Taking care of them was, I think, his joy, but it was also a
burden and a sorrow. There was something bitter between Tim
and Margaret Walsh that Sara never knew or won't say. After
Jack left, they shared a house but spoke only when necessary.
That silence at its worst became the weather of the house, seep-
ing like cold and damp into everyone. But the bitterness remained silent. It did not become words to infect the children
and turn them against Tim. When Tim died, years later, long

after Jack and Margaret were gone, he had been living with Sara's brother Johnny.

So why not America? Maybe because his mother was in America. His mother had left him and, as far as he apparently knew, forgotten him. Maybe her presence barred the whole continent to him, just as his presence had barred Ireland to her. But maybe it was only because he was such a good working man, because he could weave sugan—as the Irish call strands of woven straw— and make the ropes into the seats of chairs, because he could thatch a roof better than any man in Ahanagran, because he could cut turf with the best of them. What use were such things in America where there was neither sugan nor thatch nor turf?

Tim's persistence, Sara's father's departure, her mother's longing, all of these things defined America in terms of Ireland and Ireland in terms of America. For a child like Sara, America was known without really being knowable. It was known the same way that the world beneath the fairy forts was known. People vanished into them; occasionally some returned. Things were different there, but no one who did not become a fairy could ever really know it.

But this, again, is my historian's guess. In Sara's memories America and Ireland exist as simple contrasts. American abundance, Irish poverty; American progress, Irish backwardness. But she wavered between them because there was a final pairing: American sadness, Irish happiness. "Ireland was poor, but we were happy there," she says. "I found that people in America were not happy. It was not the land of milk and honey that I was led to believe it was, at least life on the Southwest Side of Chicago was very different."

10

More things went on in Holy Ireland than in Old New York.
—Mary Bambury, Sara's sister

There are three stories that interlock. They are the stories of, first, Bridget Scanlon, the madwoman on Dowd's Road, second, Sara's own mother, Margaret Hegarty, who became Margaret Walsh, and, third, Sara's uncle Tom Hegarty, who married Bridget Lynch. Each began before Sara was born. Each is about choice and consequence. Each is about being a woman involved in North Kerry. Each story seems to be about love, but they are all really about land. Land was far more important than love in North Kerry.

Bridget Scanlon

When Sara Walsh was a girl, Bridget Scanlon lived off Dowd's Road in a house shared with her brother Eugene Scanlon, whom everyone called Euge. The Scanlons were distant relatives of the Hegartys, Sara's mother's family. They were distant enough that romance was possible between Bridget and Margaret Hegarty's brother Tom.

When Bridget Scanlon fell in love with Tom Hegarty, property eventually became an issue. But for the relationship to get so far as property meant that Tom must have given her some encouragement. And when to her at least marriage seemed a possibility, property intruded. Tom had a farm to maintain and sisters to marry off. He needed to marry a woman who would bring a fortune, as a dowry was called. His bride's dowry would help improve the farm, and part of it would probably benefit his sisters by giving them a start on fortunes of their own.

The farm was in Guhard, not far from Ahanagran. The Hegartys had held the farm for a long time. In 1825 a Lyon Hegarty rented ninety-five acres from Barry Gunn, the landlord of the townland of "Gohard" in the parish of Lisselton. None of it was arable land, and only fifty-one acres were fit for pasture. The rest was bog and mountain. William Hegarty may have been Lyon's son or grandson. I don't know. William Hegarty married Ellen Scanlon, and they had a family of four daughters and four sons on their Guhard farm. Sara's uncle, her mother's brother, Tom, would inherit the farm.

Along with the farm, Tom would inherit the obligation to keep the farm and to help marry off his sisters. People with a farm could not risk it on love. A woman might be pretty and capable, but if, like Bridget Scanlon, she had no fortune, she faced desperate choices. She could stay and live a celibate life, dependent on her father and, after him, her brothers. She could endure demoralizing poverty. She could face the *drochshaol*, the bad life. Or she could choose America. What was certain was that a man with a farm would never allow his son to marry a woman who brought no dowry. Love would always yield to a fortune. This remained true into Sara's generation. Her sister Mary brought a fortune to John Bambury. Her sisters-in-law Sheila and Josie brought fortunes to their marriages to her brothers.

Bridget Scanlon could never command a dowry. Bridget Scanlon could only bring herself, and in another time and place herself might have been enough, for she was a brown-haired, good-looking country girl. But Bridget Scanlon was poor, and she must have seen her chance in life disappearing as Thomas (as everyone but Bridget knew he would) chose a fortune over her love. Maybe Tom Hegarty loved her. She certainly loved him.

She tried to prevent the marriage. There was a scene in front of Tom and his family. Bridget's love came only to bitter feelings between the Scanlons and Hegartys.

Tom married another Bridget, Bridget Lynch, as anyone who thought about it knew he must. The match was arranged in the usual manner with a broker and negotiations between the families. Bridget Lynch brought a fortune with her. Eventually, Bridget Lynch became Sara's aunt.

Bridget Scanlon, who might have become Sara's aunt, became a spinster. She retreated to her brother's house off Dowd's Road. And, over time, she went mad. Losing Tom Hegarty might have driven her mad, losing what she thought was her chance in life, but in North Kerry there is so much psychosis and schizophrenia that there is no telling the cause. Bridget went mad and lived in Dowd's Road with her brother.

Bridget and her brother Eugene became the other half of Ireland, the dry and barren half. The Scanlons, like the Dowds who lived across the field from them, never married. In the half century following Tom's rejection of Bridget, they aged and withered among the grass and cows and rain until eventually the last of them died.

There was, Sara noticed as she grew, a tension between her mother and Euge. Euge as a neighbor and distant relative visited them regularly, bringing an apple to split among six children. He told his stories by the fire. But there was a tension beneath the stories. Euge, perhaps, thought of his mad sister as he sat by the fire of Tom Hegarty's sister.

Another woman bore Tom Hegarty's children. Bridget Scanlon stayed home, aged, and died, submerged in a current of madness.

Margaret Walsh

Margaret Hegarty was Tom Hegarty's sister and became Sara's mother, and she was not as different from Bridget Scanlon as she once might have seemed. Margaret Hegarty faced Bridget

Scanlon's choices. She, too, had no fortune. Margaret Hegarty chose America.

She left Ireland because there was no place for her there. Two of her brothers also went to America, as did her sister Hannah. America beckoned to her; it was a place that made marriage and family possible. There a woman could work in order to marry. Women went disproportionately to America. It was a predictable thing. In Ballylongford the stories treat this matter-of-factly. A story of a drowning would begin by saying that a family in Rusheen "were a large family. . . . All of the girls went to America and some of the boys." All the girls going to America was a predictable thing.

Margaret Hegarty migrated around the turn of the century, and at that moment history takes her. She leaves, for a while at least, the realm of stories. Without fully passing out of Irish history, she moved into American history. The groove she was following is worn deep by hundreds of thousands who preceded her and hundreds of thousands who would follow. The feet of women created this particular groove. If they had passed by land instead of sea, it would have stood out like old wagon wheel ruts on the Oregon Trail. Between 1885 and 1920 roughly seven hundred thousand Irishwomen migrated to the United States. The vast majority, like Margaret Hegarty, were single, young, and worked for wages in the new country. Many came alone, although friends or relatives awaited them in America. America offered them a life with something to remember at its end besides frustration, poverty, and disappointment.

Margaret Hegarty went to New York, and she went into domestic service. She became a maid. So common were Irish female servants that they received a generic nickname: a Bridget. Swept up in this stream of Irish immigration, Margaret became a Bridget, lost in the work of cleaning up after the middle class and the rich. She created what would be her fortune by making beds, by hand washing clothes piece by piece, and by mopping the floors of those who never doubted that they were better than she and that their lives, their ambitions, and their welfare mattered infinitely more than those of the woman who cleaned their messes. She lived among their orders and condescension, and what she distilled from it was her savings and her pleasure in the life of New York.

But this much could be said of many women. The truth is that in America Margaret Hegarty becomes historically invisible to me. In New York she existed only in aggregate. The lives of these Bridgets flow together in the census, where they are measured and mixed and added and averaged. Real lives never add together. An average income or an average life span means nothing in lived experience. One person's success does not balance another's failure and create a new person halfway between them. Only statistical lives can be summed and calculated and averaged. Only on the census could Margaret Hegarty be reduced to woman worker, or more specifically, Irish-born woman worker.

I can only see Margaret Hegarty in the aggregate in the census, but this is, in its way, revealing—the way odds on a bet are revealing. Odds don't guarantee the outcome, but they do create a realm of probability. I can know Margaret Hegarty was not unique. More than half the Irishwomen workers in America were in service. In the United States only Swedish and African American women went into domestic service at rates comparable to those of the Irish.

The life of service, then, was familiar to her and predictable without being desired. Although Margaret Hegarty left a life of service gladly, she had not felt mistreated. She thought the family she worked for had treated her well.

There is only one moment in her long passage through America when Margaret Hegarty stands out distinctly. One day during her years of service, she went to the Schloss Studios on Broadway at Ninety-eighth Street. She was well-dressed; she stood in front of a formal backdrop with an urn and columns. She smiled and faced the camera at an angle. She did not look like a maid. She did not look like a peasant girl from a poor farm in Guhard. There were no urns and columns in Guhard. And that was the point. The photo was a record of what she had gained since her departure. The photograph was to be sent home. The photo-graph is a record of what she gave up when she returned.

And she did return. The vast majority never returned. Her brothers did not return. Willie Hegarty married in the States and died in an accident. Eugene never did marry and died in Chi-cago. They became just names, people who vanished into the United States. Her sister Hannah married in the United States. She sent things home. Margaret herself came home and brought back her own fortune. And the money Margaret brought back was fully her own. There is a sense, of course, in which any farm girl's fortune was her own. It was the final return on the labor she gave her parents—the messages run, the turf stacked in the haggard, the fires kept going, the animals tended, the cooking and cleaning, the mending—for which she received at the time only her room and board. But this accounting imposes a modern economic logic on households that calculated in very different ways.

This much is history. I construct it from census data and from what scholars write. I construct it from a faded photograph. But Margaret Hegarty also survives in memory. On her return to Ireland, Margaret Hegarty moved out of the parade of Bridgets, out of the stream of American emigration and domestic work, and back into the more singular world of her Irish existence. She moved into the realm of stories and memories. She told stories, and the stories are remembered. But the stories are not all of a kind; these stories and memories conflict.

Sara Walsh remembers her mother's stories as stories of regret. There is no romance in them. She longed for New York. She said her life was good there. She carried traces of America in her speech and her heart. She often spoke of New York and how much she loved it. When her children did not come quickly out of the rain, she would say to them, "What do you think this is, the Fourth of July?" Margaret Hegarty wished, her daughter Sara says, that she had never returned from America. She regretted the return, and her stories made her a person of regrets.

But if she loved it so much, why did she return? There were

other stories told by her mother that Sara Walsh did not hear until years later. These were stories of romance.

When Margaret Hegarty married Jack Walsh, it was a love match, or so the only people old enough to remember say. There is one set of stories that tell of a joyful and triumphant return. These stories that Margaret Hegarty once told her sisters survived in the stories Maud Murray, her niece, told nearly a century later. In these stories, Margaret returns with a fortune and marries for love.

Maud Murray, who died as I finished this book, was a very old woman who never left Ireland; she remembered her aunt's return vividly because Margaret brought home with her a roll of superb cotton that she gave to her sister to make dresses for her nieces. Maud Murray remembered her father driving several times up and down the main street in Listowel in a horse and trap to show off his girls and their new dresses to best advantage. For Maud the return of Margaret Hegarty in the glory of those days sparked memories that burned across nearly a century. Maud remembered her own girlhood triumph, and so she remembered her aunt. That day in Listowel in the horse and trap was bathed in the light of her aunt's beauty and success. Maud's triumph seemed to her but a reflection of Margaret's.

Jack Walsh may have met Margaret even before she went to America. He may have been what brought her back. She left New York even though she was happy there. Something must have brought her back.

They married at Ballybunnion by the sea near the mouth of the Shannon on a Wednesday, February 7, 1914. Shrove week was the preferred time for marriage, and Wednesday, the sayings said, was the best day for marriage: Monday for health, Tuesday for wealth, Wednesday, the best day, Thursday for losses, Friday for crosses, Saturday no luck at all. Margaret was thirty-two years old. Jack was thirty-four. Marrying late was the only birth control Ireland knew.

Although her daughter would not know it for years, Margaret Hegarty had confronted all the fated cruelties of Irish life. She had emigrated and then returned, and she had married for love. America had given Margaret Hegarty a fortune of her own, earned by her own labor in New York; it was a small fortune to be sure but still a fortune. It was a fortune that gave Jack Walsh hope of keeping the farm. He bought the farm in 1912. He married early in 1914. He needed the money to pay his debts, but it still could have been love. Maybe America allowed Margaret Hegarty and Jack Walsh the luxury of love. If so, in time, America would exact its price.

If she left New York for the love of Jack Walsh, there is significance in her never telling that story of her romantic and successful return. The stories of romance were ones Margaret Hegarty told her sisters before her children were born. The stories Maud remembers are stories Margaret told in the first flush of happiness, when everything she tried seemed to succeed and when she probably never doubted that her marriage, too, would succeed. Then she had just returned from America; then people remarked on her beauty and the fine things she brought back with her.

Maud Murray's stories of Margaret Hegarty's triumph and of a love match are now nearly as old as the century, but Margaret's daughter, Sara, never heard these stories until 1995. She had to wait three-quarters of a century to read them in a letter from a cousin. They confuse her. "I always thought it was an arranged marriage," Sara says. "Didn't you know," she asks Maud, "that my father went to America?"

Margaret Hegarty got all that poor Bridget Scanlon, mad in the house beyond the last Walsh fields, had wanted: a husband, children, and a farm. America had allowed her to achieve this. And how bitter it became. America had given her a fortune and a husband and a farm. And the farm claimed the fortune, and then America claimed the husband. She became a prisoner of the farm that her husband worked in America to save.

Margaret changed her stories. The stories she told her sisters vanished. The stories she told her daughter Sara were full of regrets. We tell different stories at different times in our lives.

Our angle of vision changes. Our experience reveals consequences we had not imagined. What had once seemed a moment
of victory later seems a bitter trap. We edit our memories. We
choose to forget. We forge the same memories into different
stories.

Tom Hegarty

In Guhard, Margaret Walsh's birthplace, her brother Tom Hegarty, who had romanced Bridget Scanlon, married Bridget
Lynch. He inherited the farm from his father, William, who died
in the 1920s. Margaret's mother and Sara's grandmother, Ellen,
lived on with her son and his new wife for a while. Sara would
often ride her bicycle to Guhard on messages.

"Message" in rural Ireland is an all-encompassing term. Going
for groceries was a message, borrowing baking soda was a message, carrying news or making a request was a message. Messages were freedom of a sort, far better than staying home and
cleaning the house or caring for the animals. Sara usually took
her time so that she came home when the chores were done.

Sara went with a message to her uncle. Guhard was in the
hills above Ahanagran, and she was, she says, "tired indeed"
when she arrived. Her aunt Bridget was sitting at the table when
she entered the house. Bridget was silent, but her whole body
was shaking. Her face was contorted. Sara told her that she had
a message. Aunt Bridget just sat, her face twisted. She kept shaking. She said nothing. Sara ran to find her uncle to tell him
something bad was happening.

After she found him, she bolted for home. Normally she would
have stopped and climbed to the top of the hill behind the
house, where there was a panoramic view of the River Shannon
and Ballybunnion on the North Atlantic. The common and the
everyday had turned strange. People she had known her whole
life had taken on the appearance of nightmares. And she pedaled
with all the speed she could muster down the steep hill from
Guhard. The bicycle careened out of control. She could not slow

herself, and she went down on her face, her hands and knees smashing into the ground and then sliding along the gravel. Her mother had to pick the gravel from her wounds piece by piece. She sat there frightened and in pain. She told her mother what she had seen, but neither while her mother picked out the stones nor afterward did Sara ask why her aunt had shaken and her face had become twisted. Nor did her mother offer an explanation. In those days, she says, we didn't ask questions.

Years later in Chicago, Sara saw a neighbor of her aunt Bea's go into an epileptic fit. Someone, she can't remember who, gave the fit a name, and she realized that it was what she had seen in Guhard.

This memory of Guhard remained so fixed because it was mysterious, a thing without explanation, and yet, paradoxically, there were few things that people did without commentary. Life in Ballylongford was lived as annotated text. Things happened; they were described, and they were commented on. Ballylongford was a small village, and gossip ran like a stream through its streets. In a place so poor, there was often nothing to share but talk. Much of the talk was wonderful, and its cadences brighten Sara's life yet, but much of it was cruel and vicious and meant to wound. Talk was the solution in which the horrible things were preserved and kept for inspection.

Because Bridget was an epileptic, it became too difficult for her to care for Ellen, her mother-in-law, as Ellen aged. And so Ellen moved in with her daughter Mary, who had married another John Walsh, in Pollagh. Sara continued to visit her there, but Ellen grew confused, longed for Guhard, and eventually died.

This was sad but predictable and certainly no sin. Sara's uncle Tom and aunt Bridget had a son, who will go unnamed. They, in turn, aged, and he, in turn, married and inherited the farm. This was long after Sara had left Ireland.

His parents continued to share the house, but the family disintegrated. The son drank, married, and then lost his wife, I do not know how. He, so the story goes, shut off his own father and mother, Tom and Bridget, from the kitchen by partitioning the house. He shut them up in one room with a door to the outside. They lost access to the kitchen. They could not get food. He was depriving his own parents. Tom died of a heart attack collecting sticks to start his fire. And then one day Bridget fell into the fire in that closed-off room during an epileptic fit. The son had come only when he smelled her burning flesh. Gangrene set in; she died shortly thereafter in Listowel hospital.

In 1981 I went with my mother to what had once been her grandmother's and then her aunt and uncle's house. The house was still standing, but the roof was gone. There was a small stream running through the building. It came in the back door and out the front. The table where Aunt Bridget sat that day my mother saw her shaking in the kitchen was still there a half century later, but two legs were missing, and it had tumbled down.

By then the son of Tom and Bridget also had died in this house. As the story goes, he had died a drunken wreck and in wrecking himself had wrecked the house and nearly wrecked what remained of his family. After his mother's death, he had continued to drink. The drink had distracted him from farming, and the drink had distracted him from cutting turf in the bogs. And when winter came, there was no turf to burn. To keep warm, he had begun burning the house and its furniture. He had burned most of the wood that the house contained, sparing only the table, a chair, and a bedstead. He had stripped the interior wood and burned it on the hearth. The cold and the drink and the sickness got him before the winter ended. He died in bed.

This is a story told widely around Ballylongford; it is a story my mother and others have told me. But it is a story that seems different in print. My mother recoils from it, and although she has told it numerous times, she wants it stricken from the record of her memories.

The story, as told in whispers, is about people everyone knew, but in print the story seems at once less malicious and more cruel. The story whispered in Ballylongford is gossip whose principals were well known. There is no malice in placing the story on the page, but that makes it seem all the more cruel. I, the teller, have no connection with those who enacted it. Why must I tell it? I tell the story because it is true, because it was told to me, because it seems necessary to evoke the place from which Sara came.

The story is one of the occasions when we clash, my mother and I. Her memories are hers, and she wants the right to edit them as she wishes, even after they have spilled out on the page. History seems to her an unnatural act. Why is it necessary to tell these things? "Have mercy," she tells me.

"And should I edit out the stories of the Black and Tans," I ask her, "because it might give offense to their descendants?"

This seems to her mere sophistry.

"And if I edit out what might be offensive to my family," I ask her, "how can I have any standing to give offense to anyone's family? Do I take out everything that might give anyone offense?"

My mother's memory serves the present. Its loyalty is to the people she may see next week or next month and to whom she will have to explain herself. She is thousands of miles from Ireland, but she is among them yet.

My history, too, is for the present, but its loyalty is to a past. I recognize that this past is in part my own construction, but that seems all the more reason to hew to the rules of my craft. By making the private public, I risk hurting people, telling what they do not wish widely known, in the service of a dead thing— history. To my mother this seems cruel precisely because it is done without malice. It is like shooting a bystander to test a gun. In this, she is closer to her brother Johnny. These people are dead, let them lie. Let the evil be buried with them, or, at least, let it only be talked of among ourselves.

It is one of those moments when the tensions within this book, the contest of history and memory, seem so strong that the book itself must die.

That old house where Sara's aunt Bridget sat in better times once stood on the far borders of a child's world. It is good, perhaps, that she and her aunt Bridget could not see the future.

But now, when the future itself has come and become the past, that house shows the difficulty of remembering the past.

My mother's family were not people to flinch before the future. They knew the deep currents were always there, just offshore: madness, regret, death, and America. You could not flinch before them, even if they caught you. You could not give in. Giving in brought only derision. But for all their stoicism and endurance in the face of the future, they sometimes recoil from the past.

There is a set of stories that Sara's generation of Walshes and Hollys tells that, when I first heard, I did not understand. They are suicide stories, and the butt of their humor is the suicides, those who cannot bear their Irish lives. The stories surprised me because I did not think Irish Catholics would either commit suicide or joke about it. Sara remembers quite a few suicides, and the stories about them are still told. The stories shocked me because of their refusal to grant sympathy. I did not understand that the suicide's fault was less weakness than the breaking of solidarity. In these stories my relatives treated the hardness of life as tenants treated a landlord: a powerful adversary whom people must, at all costs, resist. They must never break ranks. Suicides broke ranks. They betrayed those around them.

The geography of suicide lay along the river and its tributaries. Drowning was the preferred means of suicide. It was more considerate to kill yourself outside, for in Kerry they believed that, if you killed yourself in a house, then your ghost remained forever upsetting the future tenants.

In Chicago a half century after leaving Kerry, Sara's cousins Teresa and Danny Holly and her brother Bill all have stories about the suicides. The stories are of a kind. Teresa tells of Marcie Callaghan from Bally, who marries and moves to Tarbert. A neighbor comes to her with a tale of woe. He is very, very down. He is going to drown himself near Tarbert Island.

"I'm going to drown myself," he tells Marcie.

Marcie listens and follows him to the door. "Good luck to ye, Bill," she says.

Which reminds Sara's brother Bill of another story of a man who went down by Old Man Clancy's to drown himself. Old Man Clancy listens to his troubles and his plans to end them.

"Ye'd better hurry," Old Man Clancy tells him. "The tide is going out."

Which reminds Danny Holly of a man who was walking up the road from the Strand. He was all wet.

"What happened to ye?" a passerby asks.

"I was out there, ye know. I was wanting to drown meself."

"And a fine mess you've made of it, too," the lad says.

In the stories the suicides are reduced to a type and granted mock solicitude. The stories are generic. You need to have lived there to know to whom they apply. Those who come from Ballylongford remember and judge, but understanding the judgments demands local knowledge. "More things went on in Holy Ireland," Sara's sister Mary says, "than in Old New York." But these should be the things, they all think, of memory and stories and not the things of history. I do not come from there.

11

On the way back home we went into a field that had cabbage growing and stole some to eat. It was a difficult day in our lives.
—Sara, on a message she went on with her brother Gerard

She was trouble, her brothers say, although they say it fondly. With no father and a mother who suffered and endured, Sara grew up with an impatience about her. Or so her brothers say.

But Sara denies it. She pictures herself content in a world to which she imagined no alternatives. Her stories undermine her denials. In them she assesses the world, discerns the place she is expected to occupy. She sees how individuals, neighbors, families, whole classes of people rub against one another, giving off tremors like tectonic plates. She measures them like so much seismic activity. From their friction and in the upheavals, she discerns her place.

Many of her stories contain implicit criticisms of how things are and judgments about the rightness and wrongness of things. It is a habit I recognize. To her children she preached endurance and acceptance—"things could be worse"—but her stories imply that things could be better.

She wanted to leave, her brother Johnny says. She always wanted to leave. But she denies it, and Gerard, her older brother, thinks about it a minute and then supports her.

She avoided work, her sister Mary says, while I, Mary, who

had to do everything, now suffer in my old age with a bad back. The doctor, Mary says, blames her bad back on too much youthful work. And Sara laughs at her sister's criticism and shakes her head at Mary's virtue, but she admits she loved the messages and would never hurry back from them. The messages taught her the variety and fine distinctions of the countryside.

Many of Sara's messages involved food because food defined neighborliness. Tea and bread were what she carried as a girl to the workers cutting turf in the bog or waining the hay, as they called gathering the hay in the fields and placing it on carts. Bringing or going after food begins many of her stories. She would, for instance, go to the Dowds for baking soda or sugar. The Dowds lived on Dowd's Road—a lane really—which lay beyond the Walshes' last western field. The road was not much more than a quarter of a mile long. It ran between the hedgerows and took her past Guyney's Hole, where, so the story went, a horse had drowned. Guyney's Hole is little more than a deep spot in a ditch between the road and the hedge. Travelers passing by had claimed to see that ghost horse rising up alongside the road. Sara was terrified of Guyney's Hole, but it never occurred to her to measure the hole until years later on a trip back from the States. There wasn't enough water, she says, to reach a horse's knee.

The landscape was thick with such stories from the past, but the Walshes' neighbors lived their lives to make it thicker still. She rode a bicycle on messages, which became the basis of stories she still tells. Stories clung to her old bicycle like barnacles. She defined herself by the stories she knew. The stories she told established her relationships with others. Whoever she became lay within the lines marked out by the stories and the relationships. There is no locating her without the stories, without the relations. She can be found only by triangulation.

Including the parents, there had once been seven Dowds, but the parents had died and so had the eldest son, Tom. Molly had emigrated to Pittsburgh. That left Bill and Sis and Bridget. They grew old together, sitting in front of a turf fire, Bill leaning back

so his chair balanced on two legs with its back against the wall.
He would smoke his pipe and spit across the room at the fire.

Sara loved the Dowds. They would give her the run of the
house and let her climb the ladder into the loft. Bill wouldn't
say anything. In a country full of talk, he exhausted his conversation in the morning on the way to the creamery. "Morning,"
he'd say, "fine day." The actual condition of the day never mattered to Bill. They were all fine days.

Bill had land and did not marry, which seems a mystery to me
but not to my mother.

"It seems strange he didn't marry," I say. I think that in Ireland land ensures marriage.

"That's because you didn't know Bill Dowd," she says.

She has a fondness for the Dowds, but a woman would have
to have a desperate passion for staying in Ireland to resign herself
to evenings of watching the spit fly by linking herself to a man
whose conversational range was three words.

Sara's messages were repetitive, performed over and over
again like the prayers on a rosary. One trip blended into another
until there was just the message to the Dowds. In this respect,
messages were like the trips to school. They were so plural that
they became singular.

The school journey was typical of everyday life. It was repetitive, known and familiar. She traveled with her sisters, Nell and
Mary, her brothers Gerard and Bill, and a gang of cousins—the
Hollys. Johnny did not come. He was too young. Incidents stood
out only as variations on a theme. There was no narrative of
everyday life. There was only a description. But that is not exactly right, for the descriptions themselves were stories.

Sara describes the journey to school from memory—what she
saw, whom she saw. School lay to the east, toward Ballylongford,
and as she traveled she moved through the raw, living stuff of
stories. To hear her describe the journey is to hear her pass
places from which stories pour out. In memory she moves
through that landscape still.

There were on the road fronting her house three cottages im-

mediately to the east. The children had to pass them when they
went to school. Kate Bodie was the Walshes' nearest neighbor
on the Ballylongford side.

Kate Bodie embodies sex in Sara's stories. Sex is present elsewhere—it is whispered even about the lives of people old and
single and seemingly as celibate as the stone walls. And sometimes sex appears more openly. The story of Kitty O'Brien and
Timothy Reidy can hardly be told, of course, without sex. Sex
pushes Kitty from Ireland. But sex does not define her. Even
Tim Reidy with his rag on every bush is not simply a function
of his desire. He was the creamery manager and not just the
seducer of local girls.

But Kate was defined by sex. That and her singing and her
good humor are all there is to her in Sara's stories. Kate had
several children, and each of them had a different father. Kate
gave herself away freely, but she kept her sanity, her good nature, her fine voice, and a pride of sorts amid the disapproval of
the townland. She had a good heart, Sara remembers, but a good
heart did not prevent Sara's mother from warning her children
to stay away from the Bodies. They could not stay literally away.
They had to pass the house daily. They would peer in and see
Kate as she sat singing to herself by the fire. She had, Sara says,
a fine voice. Even much later, when Kate was old and Sara visited her bringing a bottle of brandy, Kate reciprocated with all
she had left, a song.

It was not really Kate Bodie that Margaret Walsh feared. It
was her son Dick. Sex, it seemed, permeated the Bodie cottage
itself. Dick, Kate's oldest son, was no more able to contain himself than Kate. He had already begun his own career of fathering
children. Margaret Walsh did not want her daughters near him.

Kate finally did marry, and, when she did, that became a story.
She was, the story goes, on the way to church with her husband-
to-be, who, like her son, was named Dick. His wedding suit was
not up to Kate's standards.

"You should at least look decent," Kate said, pronouncing the
first *e* in decent as a long *a*, as the Irish do.

"Ah, Kate, you're none too decent yourself," Dick replied.

Beyond the Bodies the children passed the Finucanes and moved from sex to madness. There were three Finucanes, all quite mad. When the Walshes and their cousins the Hollys walked to school, Mick Finucane would often be out in the road in front of the cottage waving his arms at the moon that lingered in the winter morning's sky. His sister was also touched, but she would usually stay inside. Mick's brother, the third of the mad Finucanes, was the only one that scared them, for he would just sit or stand and look at the passing children strangely. If he was around, Sara and the others would rush by or else avoid him entirely by cutting across the fields to the old Muddy Road.

The route across the fields to the Muddy Road was a shortcut to Bally, but it took them by two horses that frightened them only slightly less than the last of the trio of mad Finucanes. The Muddy Road got its name because high tide pushed the river up over it. It led toward even more madness. In Bally, Sara says, there were all kinds of crazy people. Mane Haley lived between Sullivan's Empire—as Sara called the Sullivan's general store and other enterprises—and the forge. Mane Haley would come out with her wild hair and mad eyes and scare them as they went to school. She lived with a man called The Ducker; they eventually married on the advice of the parish priest.

Farther up Ballyline Street, on the way to the police station, there was another crazy woman. She fascinated Sara because, unlike the others, she was unknown, although you could see her with her face always pressed to the window. To be unknown in that village was far stranger than to be crazy.

To a child's eye this world seemed given and eternal, and Sara sometimes remembers it as a place on which a pervasive poverty imposed equality. This was, however, a world that was new, and it possessed distinctions. In a half century, Ballylongford had been stripped of its landlords, most of the cottars, and many smaller farmers. It was a narrowed social world but the stories Sara tells of her travelings near and through the village reveal lingering distinctions.

Sara knew that the Bodies and the Finucanes, like the families on the dole in the cottages in Rusheen Park, were below her. It was not that they were mad, promiscuous, drunk, or poor—or it was not just that. They were beneath her because they had no land. Sara Walsh knew she was poor, dirt poor, but her family had land. And to lose that land would be to become in some way like the Bodies and Finucanes.

Not everyone with land was equal. Her best friends were her cousins the Hollys. But the Hollys had better land than the Walshes. Everyone knew it. They could support more cows and send more milk to the creamery. Sara always felt that the Hollys thought better land made them better people. She smelled a slight condescension as distinct as the pervasive odors of burning turf and cow dung that hung over the countryside.

The quality of the land may have been behind the tension Sara always felt between her mother and her aunt Hannah Holly. Hannah was the only one of Jack's sisters to remain in Ireland. She, too, had once left. Unlike her sister Kitty, who had left in shame, Hannah left with honor. She had become a nun and gone to England to live in a convent and work among the Irish there. But Aunt Han came to doubt her vocation. She left the order; she left England; she returned to Kerry. In 1912 she married Patrick Holly, a widower with one son. She would bear Patrick ten children.

The Hollys lived very close, and although the Holly and Walsh children were like brothers and sisters, there was always the feeling that the Hollys were a little bit better than the Walshes. The Holly farm could maintain a family without a man leaving to find work. Margaret may have resented this. Sara thinks so, but all she could detect at the time was the tension between her mother and aunt, not the source of the tension.

The fault did not lie in any quality of Hannah's that a child could detect. Hannah was a good, gracious, and sweet woman, but it would not have taken much of a slight to create tension. The poverty of the place made distinctions small, but that made people all the more sensitive to them. The people of Ahanagran were touchy. Like most touchy people, they were elaborately polite, for offense once taken was not forgotten. Sara Walsh herself learned to watch for the small marks of disrespect and condescension. She marked them with stories—the slights received, the revenge taken. The stories mark the social order.

There were some stories best forgotten, but because the land itself formed a set of stories—things that had happened *here*— erasing stories sometimes meant altering the land itself. Around Ballylongford, the people desired that not only the landlords but what they had created and built on the land should be rooted out and destroyed.

The year Sara Walsh was born the last of the old landlord families were still present. Early in 1919 the IRA commandeered an automobile from Boland's garage and drove out to Killelton House to seize whatever guns they could find.

Killelton House belonged to the Hickies, once one of the great landlord families of North Kerry. To get to the house, visitors had to stop by the gate, where there were two lodges, one for the gardener and the other for the washerwoman. She was the one who usually opened the gate.

Killelton House had been the center of a vast estate that included fishing rights on the Shannon, but these had ebbed away until only the great house and the surrounding land remained. Colonel William Scott Hickie lived there. He or his father had witnessed a legal document for William Walsh in the 1880s. Hickie, at about the time of the IRA visit, had hired Jack Walsh to cut his hay, and Jack Walsh had got the shotgun blast from the Hickies' tenants in retribution. The Hickies were Catholics—unusual among the Anglo-Irish gentry. Colonel Hickie was an ex–British Army officer and as gun crazy as any of the rural gentry. He owned enough guns to stock a gun room. Hickie sat in Killelton House among the decay of his family's fortune and treated the IRA men cordially. He produced a bottle of wine and insisted they take a glass. They drank and smoked and talked.

The raid didn't produce much besides talk. The police had already confiscated most of Hickie's guns. The IRA got what was left: a pistol, a shotgun, and a .22-caliber rifle. Hickie discussed the revolution as if he was discussing a horse that would race at Listowel. The revolution, Hickie thought, would place, not win. Hickie said the Irish would get dominion status within the empire but they would never get a republic. When the colonel's daughter, Constance, tried to drive down the new avenue leading to the house from Carrigafoyle Castle, the IRA men standing guard detained her. She became angry and hostile, but she later apologized. At this point, it still seemed a particularly voluble and genteel revolution.

The IRA visit was merely a moment in the Hickies' decline. The IRA men, who praised the Hickies as a "good Catholic family," left Killelton and went their own way. When the colonel died, the servants established squatters' rights to the house. They eventually paid Constance £500 for it. They gradually demolished much of the house for building materials. One of the Moriarty families who had been the Hickies' servants turned part of it into a cabin. The Hickies had also built two chapels at Astee. They survived no better than Killelton. Both were demolished and the Hickie memorial tablets thrown into the graveyard. The local people wanted no monuments to trigger memory. They wanted to see the land as if the years of rack rents and evictions had never happened. The old order was changing even as Sara Walsh thought the countryside timeless.

But the decline of the old elite meant the rise of a new. There were new resentments. Food marked neighborliness, and it marked the places neighborliness did not extend, where class or distance or old animosities blocked its reach. Food was a signal. The Galvins lived nearby and were Irish farmers like the Walshes, but the Galvins were not neighbors. The Galvins were, in the village's eyes, rich. They were the society of Ballylongford. Many things marked the Galvins as wealthy and different, but the mark in Sara's stories is biscuits. They ate biscuits, or cookies as we call them, on ordinary days. She was sent there once with a message. Mrs. Galvin was sitting by the fire having tea and eating biscuits. Sara had never seen a biscuit such as the one she was eating. "I remember they were in a round tin box. That was the first time I saw such a box. She did not offer me one biscuit."

Sara never tasted the Galvins' biscuits, nor did she get their apples, although her cousins did. One day, a day still clearly remembered after half a century, on the way home from school, she, her cousin Danny Holly, and other children from Ahanagran decided to steal apples from the Galvins' orchard.

The thieves climbed the trees in their bare feet, and Sara fell. In falling, she cut her feet. It was her bleeding feet that gave her away. Danny Holly told Sara's mother what had happened. And one confession naturally begot another. Her mother made her go to the priest immediately and confess again. Such confessions need not involve the Galvins. Sara still regrets she got no apples. She still recalls that others did and that they did not get caught.

My mother still refers to cookies, candy, and fruit as treats, a child's word still resonant for a woman in her seventies. Treats, she says, were rare. And treats were rare because "we and all our neighbors were very poor."

When Sara Walsh stole, she stole food, but stealing a cabbage was different from stealing an apple. She would not steal from neighbors, and stealing the apple, a luxury, was a mark of social distance—a child's sense that the Galvins by virtue of their class were not really neighbors. Stealing the cabbage, an everyday food, marked her sense of how physical distance limited the sway of neighborly obligation. She would never have stolen a cabbage from a neighbor's garden, but that day she had gone with her brother Gerard on a message near Ballybunnion. Ballybunnion, facing the North Atlantic at the mouth of the Shannon, was a long distance to go with a message on a cold, wet winter's day. Much farther than Ballylongford or Astee or her grandmother's house in Guhard.

We took the ass and trap. When we arrived at our destination very cold and hungry, we gave the family the message; they didn't offer us even a cup of tea. On the way back home we went into a field that had cabbage growing and stole some to eat. It was a difficult day in our lives.

Not even a cup of tea, not even the expected solidarity of the poor: they had passed beyond the world of neighborly obligation. And so the neighborhood paid the toll. They stole a cabbage. Two wet, cold, hungry children in the rain dividing raw stolen cabbage. It was a difficult day.

Food marked the divisions and connections between people, and food marked the divisions and connections of the year. When Sara was a child, sweets marked class: in her eyes the rich were people like the Galvins, to whom eating treats marked status rather than a particular occasion. For everybody else the calendar remained divided, its days marked by the food you ate. Sweets meant it was Christmas. It was the only time they were sure to appear.

At Christmas there were currants in the bread. Christmas was the highlight of the year, the standard of all my mother's comparisons. To mark how exciting bringing in the hay was, she tells me it was as exciting as Christmas, even though there were no sweets. For the men haying was backbreaking labor, but for children it meant riding the hay carts.

Food also marked the station. The station was the saying of Mass in a private home, and it was a great occasion. It was a practice nearly two hundred years old in the 1920s. It had evolved from the days of the penal laws, when fugitive priests, from fear of detection, had to celebrate Mass in church ruins and bogs and glens. The Masses had moved into homes, and then the homes had been divided into groups with each home hosting a Mass twice a year.

With the building of churches and the freedom to worship, the practice had changed but not disappeared. By the 1920s the stations involved a group of five neighbors. The Mass was rotated so that each family would host the priest once every five years.

White marked the station. The neighbors would whitewash the entire house, outside and in. They would even whitewash the cow stalls, the pigpen, and the stables. The table would be covered with white cloth. And on the table would be currant cake and raisin bread.

In the sentences with which she remembers such a day, Sara Walsh uses words that appear few other places in the stories she tells or the letters she sends me: "great joy," "very solemn," "very special," "celebrate," and "honor."

And then she turns back to food. She remembers the menu, not just cakes and breads but eggs, tea, and rashers of bacon in a room that usually held live animals not the flesh of dead ones. And when the station passed, the whitewashed house stood as the best-kept house in Ahanagran.

Although the Mass was a great honor, the priests do not occupy a high station in Sara Walsh's stories of Ballylongford and Ahanagran. There were good priests, but she gives bad priests prominence of place. The good priests were generic. They were the good-natured and honored priests of Irish jokes:

> Another tale I remember was that of a farmer near Bally who was digging potatoes when the priest came by. The priest said, "Jack, what kind of a crop have you?" The farmer said, "To tell you the truth, Father, I left them to God and God left them to me and between the two of us we have nothing."

The bad priests were particular. The priests of Ballylongford—the Fathers Alman, the young Father Alman and the old Father Alman—were honored, but they were not good-natured, and they were not loved. The priests were lords of a petty fiefdom. They acted like no ordinary person acted. When a priest walked the streets of Ballylongford, everyone stepped out of his way as if he was God Almighty. When old Father Alman left Bally on Sunday to say Mass in Astee—a suburb of Bally, Sara's cousin

Thomas Holly now calls it—he went on horseback. If he ran into a storm, he took shelter in the nearest house, and he would bring the horse in with him. It is a detail that astonishes my mother even now: "He would bring his horse in with him."

It was not as if animals were strangers to Sara's kitchen; it was precisely because they weren't that the priest's actions took on added meaning. The presence of the horse perverted an accepted logic. The kitchen often stank of urine from the straw by the stove, where calves and bonives (as they called young pigs in Ireland) were nursed through the first week of life in the winter. And Sara, who is not romantic about such things or sentimental about animals, says simply that the animals were family, connected to us the same way we were connected to the land. In the same way that the land sustained them and killed them, they sustained and killed the animals. But they no more would have brought a horse into the kitchen than they would have brought in a cow.

The horse spoke to another equation. Its presence didn't humanize it and make it like family, it demeaned the family and made their home seem a stable. It reduced farmers to the level of cottars, whom commentators often equated with their beasts. The horse was part of an equation that reduced people to animals, and it was factored by a man who supposedly saw these people as all having souls equal before God.

These priests were not the Father Flanagans that the movies portrayed when Sara was a young woman. There was no mercy in them. Old Father Alman, in Sara's memory, was the meanest man who ever lived. When a girl got pregnant and she had no husband, old Father Alman would announce her name aloud from the pulpit, as if, with all her trouble, she needed to drink a full draft of shame. And Tim Walsh, in church each Sunday, would have his own beginnings thrown in his face in the shaming of another. My mother carries the resentment of it still. It was not very Christian, she tells me.

Other priests—the missionaries—would come once a year for a week of services. Mostly they preached. They preached always of sin. Margaret Walsh would take her children, and they would sit through a week of sermons. The priests told the countrypeople what sinners they were. Poor farmers, Sara says, who never got off the farm except to go to Mass or the creamery. She carried those sermons with her to America, and when she saw Chicago and the possibilities there were in the world for doing wrong, the sermons seemed odd and laughable. To call those poor people—those women who never left the farm but to go to Mass—sinners, she thinks, didn't make any sense.

All these stories are judgments on the world. All these stories imagine different possibilities. There was an impatience about Sara.

12

The horse that earns the oats never gets them.

—North Kerry folk saying

ven as a child, then, impatience was part of Sara, as well as the willingness to judge and then mask the judgment. Open defiance never became her habit. She did not choose between the deep conservatism of the place (accepting that things are as they are) and the ancestral willingness to rebel (acknowledging that things should be different). She incorporated both; she played them both, sometimes at once.

She learned, too, very early the endurance and resistance of the place. They did not expect justice, but they always knew what justice would be. "The horse that earns the oats never gets them," they would say. "The less you do, the more you are thanked," they would say. She remembers these sayings. She embodied them, made them her own.

There was a price. She learned to cast herself as victim. This is a habit that comes at considerable cost, for it involves inevitably an acknowledgment of defeat and subordination. Being a victim is an admission of the inability to control the circumstances of life. But victims claim a lesser power. After all you have done, they say, we remain. Do your worst. We will see who can endure. We will see that all you gain from your power is another challenge. These were the public stances of the people she came from, the stances against outsiders, but they were also their personal stances.

There is a story about Gerard and fire that predates by more than sixty years the story of the fire in 1995 that destroyed the house in Ahanagran. In this earlier story Gerard pushes Sara into a fire burning in the hearth.

Sara had said something. She mocked him, perhaps, or challenged him or refused some order or request. She does not remember what she said. Whatever it was, it was not out of character. She was standing by the fire. Her mother was not there. Her father had already gone to America. She was standing by the fire, and she said something to Gerard—an insult, a taunt, a refusal to do his will, neither of them can now remember. He was older but not much older. She must have had her back to him or else she turned to run, for, when he shoved her, one of her shins touched the coals in the hearth.

She screamed. Sara remembers that. She screamed, and then she cried, for the pain was very great and she was only six years old. The burn was serious. The scars are there still. There must have been a moment when the flesh hissed, when the smell of sizzling flesh filled the room. She could only cry because the doctor was in Listowel. It took, as she recalls, days before he came. She lay in pain awaiting his coming, and she lay in pain after he left. She endured.

This is a snatch of memory; it connects to other forgotten things. In 1981 my mother, Sara, took my brother Stephen and me to the old national school she had once attended. By then the school was abandoned and vandalized. My cousin Maggie, who is Johnny's daughter and who teaches Irish, came with us. There were pages of an old ledger lying on the floor. Stephen picked one up, and we looked at it. It was an attendance roll with the names in Irish. There were dates on the ledger, 1925 and 1926, marking the students' entry into the school and their attendance. I asked my mother, "Weren't you in school then?" She was, and we looked through the loose pages, searching for her name in Irish.

We found two pages with her name—Sorcha Breatnach—on them. I have one now hanging on my office wall. Except for the names, virtually everything else on the page was in English. It continued to be the language of daily life as it had been for two generations, ever since it had supplanted Irish as the dominant language of North Kerry. The ledger gives the date of my mother's admission to school (June 1925), the number of days she had attended that term (112), and her age (six years, six months). Following her name are various hieroglyphics, which seem to mark attendance, but if they do, then my mother missed school frequently. She was gone two entire weeks at the end of one month. Those were the weeks, Sara thinks, after Gerard pushed her into the fire.

So Gerard and the fire link with the school and Sara's absence for two weeks. In return, the ledger dates the fire story. It does so through that Irish name. The Irish name was a marker left by the burst of nationalism following independence. Sara Walsh became Sorcha Breatnach.

But the irony is that the school that did the translating was probably the most alien of Sara's childhood experiences, and the name it gave her was alien, too. For the truth was that Sara did not have an Irish name, and so the school made one up for her.

Down the hall from my office, I have a colleague, Robin Stacey, who is a medievalist; Robin reads Irish. She leads me through the naming of my mother. Sorcha, when pronounced in Irish, has no hard consonants. It is pronounced as Sorha and thus sounds like Sara, and so they called her Sorcha. The word means light or bright or brightness in Irish. It seems to be a reinvented name. A century or more earlier it was a common Irish name, but it had long been Anglicized to Sara or Sally. Sara's childhood nickname was Sal. As for Breatnach, Robin tells me, it is a "syncopated adjectival noun deriving from Bretain, 'Britain,' and means British or Welsh person." In Ireland, Walsh is pronounced Welsh and is probably a variant spelling of a name denoting an origin in Wales, and so Breatnach is a literal translation. To emphasize my mother's Irishness, the teachers called her Sorcha Breatnach: bright Welsh person.

Sara hated school and feared the teachers. School meant more

resistance, more endurance. The school that sought to invent
Ireland, to record its stories, to teach its language was for her
the most alien part of her world. It was to be endured and resisted. For her, the countryside was Ireland; the school was alien.
For her, the spoken English of the stories was Ireland. Even
though English itself had once been the language imposed by
the schools, Irish now became the language the school imposed.
Sara associated it with boredom, violence, and the unaccountable
demands teachers made on her.

The teachers did not intend this to be so. There were good
teachers as near as Listowel, but Sara Walsh did not know them.
School divided everything that normally went together. The
school building was divided, and the classes were strictly segregated. The school enforced its ways with a ready violence. The
school had three teachers for the girls and three for the boys.
There was Miss Julia O'Connor from Listowel, who had a
brother in Tarbert. She was very mean. She once slapped Sara
so hard for failing to spell a word correctly that the red mark of
the hand stayed imprinted on her face for hours. A second
teacher, Miss Devan, lived near the school, very close to Fitz-
maurice the butcher, and was going with Mr. Moriarty, one of
the teachers in the boys' school. Every morning when Sara
reached school, she had to peel two large potatoes and drop them
in a pan of water so that they would be ready to boil for dinner
for Miss Devan and Mr. Moriarty. The third teacher was a nice
widow, Mrs. Boland.

Sara, who learned so quickly outside school, found school hard
and foreign. She would leave when she was eleven. Until then,
she endured. School was sitting and waiting to get hit. "School
was," she says, "school. . . . We didn't learn much." She remembers the smell of the outhouse. There were holes in the roof
where the odor escaped and the rain came in. She remembers
the odor and the constant wet. She remembers waiting for the
open fire to take the chill off the schoolroom.

She remembers that her name became Sorcha Breatnach. Besides that she remembers only snatches of Irish. She remembers

póg mo thóin, the ultimate everyday phrase of resistance. She taught me to say it when I was a child and harassed her to say something in Irish; she was immediately embarrassed and told me I was never to use it. I, of course, used it at every opportunity and remember it still. It is my only Irish. It means kiss my ass.

In making Sara Walsh Sorcha Breatnach, the teachers were inventing Ireland, making it anew from scraps of history. I imagine they believed that in renaming and educating her they were restoring Sara Walsh to her rightful identity. They believed, as all teachers believe, in the magical power of words. But Sara Walsh and her classmates had a different way of understanding their Irishness. They believed in memory and everyday life.

Sara was a small child engulfed by complicated changes. She was the raw stuff of nation building in a nation that in the end could not support her. There had never been a united independent Ireland before. The war of independence gave the new Irish Free State control of the national schools, and they set out to create a national history just as they had created a national present. They would distill from the Troubles a language, a history, and an identity. The schools would impose all of this on everyday life.

But what was supposed to be native seemed alien to Sara. She resisted what the teachers thought was her true identity and her true name. In school she perfected resisting and enduring. In that, she was true to the place that gave her birth.

13

Drifting about in the saddest of lives
Doing odd jobs for other men's wives
—Nineteenth-century Irish ballad

Sara was eleven when she left school. She left relatively
soon after her father came home in 1929. Jack Walsh had
been gone five years, and Sara hardly knew him. His
youngest son, Johnny, born after his departure, did not know
him at all and would not go near him at first.

Sara remembers remarkably little about the visit. All she knew
was that her father had vanished and now he had returned. He
made little impression on her. She remembers he brought sweet
American tobacco. So certain was she of the sweetness of America she thought it must be candy. She ate it and thought she
would die.

There is confusion as to why he returned. Sara thinks it was
for a visit. But according to Mary, Jack Walsh intended to stay
home in Ahanagran until he saw the checks from the creamery.
He then realized that he could not afford to stay. Mary's story
may be true. The documents I can find are only a flat record of
what Jack Walsh did; they do not speak to what he intended.

This is what I know Jack Walsh did. The previous January in
Chicago he had declared his intention to become an American
citizen. He was still, however, a British subject, and so on August

11, 1928, he had requested and received a British passport from the British consulate in Chicago. Great Britain and Ireland were still technically linked. The picture shows a handsome, square-faced Irishman, who looks younger than his forty-eight years.

He presumably would not have got the passport unless he was planning a trip. The passport was only good until February 1929. He either was planning to have finished his travels by then or was not planning to return to the United States. He made no provision for the document's renewal, nor did he obtain a visa to return to the United States.

In February 1929, with his passport about to expire, he was in Ireland. He got a renewal from the Irish Department of External Affairs with only six days left on the passport. But they renewed it only until May 11, 1929. They restricted the renewal because he had failed to produce "full evidence of nationality" and because he had declared his intention to become an American citizen. On February 9, at Cobh, the port for the city of Cork and the main embarkation point from western Ireland, he went to the American consulate and obtained a non-quota immigrant visa. He seems to have taken a ship back to America soon after that.

These documents are consistent with Mary's story. He came home intending to stay but at the last minute realized he must return. But the documents are also consistent with a man who cut things close. It is equally possible that he had always intended to return to the United States. He did not anticipate problems with the renewal and was confident he could get a visa in Ireland.

In Mary's story, Sara was the creamery girl who inadvertently brought the evidence that prompted her father's second departure. She took the can of milk to the creamery, stopping at Scanlon's well on her return to bring home a bucket of water for tea and cooking. Sara was the only girl to take milk to the creamery. It was another sign of her difference, and it did not please her.

The creamery check was small, and, Sara says, her mother was not a good manager. She was in debt to the shops in town. The farm depended on the checks Jack Walsh sent from Chicago. It could not be weaned from them. He stayed briefly, then he was gone again.

Other changes followed. When he arrived back in Chicago, Jack Walsh sent for Nell, Mary's twin, and in 1930 she, too, vanished into America. Nell seems to have left willingly. America had now claimed Sara's father and her sister as well as the vast majority of her uncles and aunts. Only her mother had returned to stay.

Sara left school because the family needed whatever money she could bring in. Working as a servant girl meant that her own family would not have to board her. They would save the cost of supporting her and gain her wages.

Her first job was working for the Heaphys. Ballylongford was a warren of shops and pubs. The Sullivans, who ran what Sara always later referred to as the Empire—a grocery, a pub, a hardware store, a lumberyard, a feed store—were the giants of the village. The rest were small operations.

The Heaphys' shop was a room off the kitchen facing the street. Sara's mother shopped at Heaphy's. She would stop there after the 9:00 A.M. Mass on Sundays. Tim, Margaret, and four of the children rode in the pony and trap; two—usually Mary and Gerard—walked behind. They stopped at Heaphy's, and her mother got sugar, flour, and tea.

Because Margaret could not pay for all she bought, Sara went to work for the Heaphys. Sara took care of the Heaphys' children, helped in the store, and "did everything" from washing clothes to peeling potatoes. She cleaned up the shed where potatoes and flour were stored, and she cleaned up the yard.

For six days a week, her world shrank to the size of the Heaphys' place. In this narrowed existence she realized the full possibility of drudgery. She was a servant girl, and servant girl pretty much summed up the possible employment for young farm girls in Ireland in the 1920s and 1930s. It was a life no one desired. There is a nineteenth-century Irish song that, in the way of such ballads, manages to sentimentalize poverty, hatred, and exploitation:

> . . . This girl was poor; she hadn't a home
> Or a single thing she could call her own,
> Drifting about in the saddest of lives
> Doing odd jobs for other men's wives,
> As if for drudgery created,
> Begging a crust from a woman she hated.

Sara was poor, but she had a home, even if she saw it only on Sundays. Home was where all her earnings went. Home was her escape from the Heaphys. There was, to be sure, a woman she hated, but one can't really call Lil Heaphy "other men's wives" because Sara doesn't even remember Mr. Heaphy. He was, at best, a shadow cast by Lil. Lil with her children, a small stock of goods, and a large store of meanness dominated the house. She was a hard woman.

Lil Heaphy worked Sara from morning until night. Awakened before daylight, Sara worked all day. She went to bed long after dark, sleeping in the back bedroom. Lil was a hard woman, but these hours exaggerate her harshness. In the winter, daylight in North Kerry comes after 8:00 A.M., and sunset comes around 4:00 P.M. In the summer, on the other hand, daylight to after dark would leave little time for sleep.

Sara never forgot how Lil Heaphy drove her. Even now, when Sara tells the story of how one of Lil Heaphy's children nearly drowned in a swamp behind the forge while Sara watched the store, she makes sure to excuse herself from responsibility: someone else was watching the children. They pulled the child from the swamp, but it died at home in bed. It seemed to Sara that Lil Heaphy in grief and rage was glaring at her still and apportioning responsibility for the loss. When in middle age Sara first returned to Ireland in the early 1970s, Lil Heaphy was still alive. She saw her once or twice, but "I couldn't ever warm up to her," she says.

Sara worked for Lil Heaphy for four years. Her only escape, except for Sundays, was sickness. "I remember one time I got sick while working at Heaphy's. I got very, very sick. I guess I had a high fever because I could hardly navigate. I went home.

I walked home. I told her I was sick. My mother took care of me for a few days until I was better, but then I had to go back to work."

She left Heaphy's for a job in Listowel when she was about fourteen. She worked at a place called O'Sullivan's, and her cousin Eileen Holly worked at McKenna's on the square. O'Sullivan was a professor of Irish at St. Michael's College, and he seems to have insisted on the Irish spelling of his name, Mícheál ó'Súilleabháin, but Sara Walsh, who knew little Irish except phrases children pick up, called him O'Sullivan.

ó'Súilleabháin was a fine name for the college, but O'SULLIVAN'S is what it said above the store his wife ran to supplement his teaching salary. His wife was the world's second-meanest woman. And again, in addition to the store, there were children, a lot of children, to watch. The O'Sullivans did not permit Sara to eat with the family. She got whatever was left over. Mrs. O'Sullivan had a peephole to make sure hired girls gave nothing away free. For two more years it was work from early in the morning until late at night. She got to go home on Saturday night. Bill Holly would come to get Sara and his sister Eileen in the pony and trap and take them back to Ahanagran. They would return on Sunday night.

Sara's experience in Listowel was limited, but the town still represented an expanded geography. It marked the final expansion of the Ireland of her childhood. This was a walking world, a landscape that had extended itself as she grew. Guhard had been an early boundary of this geography. And now this southern boundary reached only as far as Listowel, seven miles from Ballylongford. On the north the boundary never extended beyond the River Shannon. The river blocked any further movement. On the west the immediate boundary was Ballybunnion and the Atlantic, but this was the most porous boundary of all. So many of her relatives and neighbors had moved beyond it that the real western boundary lay an ocean and half a continent away in Chicago. Ballylongford remained this geography's eastern border. Sara never visited the next village, Tarbert, although it was only about five miles away. Her North Kerry was a small world of family, neighbors, and work. There was no place within it where she could not leave at noon and be back in her own bed by evening.

The O'Sullivans confined her from Monday through Saturday, but for part of Sunday, after Mass, she was free. It was as if for an afternoon she could live a different life, altogether free from the gaze of Mrs. O'Sullivan.

Pollagh came to be one of her favorite places in this world. Pollagh, southeast of Ballylongford, was where her grandmother Hegarty had died and one of her aunts, her mother's sister, still lived. Sara had fallen in love with Pollagh during her school years. She would go to Pollagh on messages during the long daylight hours of the Irish summer. It was on those bicycle rides that she first saw Tim Sullivan. He was about five years older than Sara. He would stop and talk to her when she went by his house on her way to her grandmother's.

When Sara worked for Lil Heaphy, Tim Sullivan would come by the Heaphy's store for groceries after he took his milk to the creamery. Sara used to think she liked him, but he was entering young manhood and she was still a child. When he came in the store, he wouldn't bid her the hour of the day.

Later, when she went to work in Listowel, she and Eileen Holly would ride their bicycles toward Pollagh on Sundays. They went just to see Tim. When they came near the Sullivans', Sara would get off the bike and walk slowly past the house. When she saw him, both she and Eileen would jump back on their bicycles and ride off. Sara was too shy to speak to him.

The rest of the ride toward her aunt's, for by then her grandmother had died, was through the bogs, which she always found beautiful and lonely. It was in the bogs that the banshee would cry in the night when someone was about to die. Pollagh itself was along the River Galey. "The banks were a long, perfect square in the fields. I would sit on the banks and watch the river flow and the crystal-clear water and the crystal-clear air. My mind was also clear. I knew nothing of the world. My world was Bally and the surrounding farms. I had the innocence of a small child. These were great years."

She had mastered a small geography of childhood, and in hindsight those years, although poor, fatherless, and filled with drudgery from eleven on, were, nonetheless, "great years." Emigration would give Sara a freedom from this tight world. But it was a freedom that she did not want. Emigration was, she says, not a choice she made.

14

When Sara thought of America in the early 1930s, she thought of Mick Mac. Like Sara's father and mother, Mick Mac went to America and returned. And like her father, his return was brief. America reclaimed him. Mick Mac was Michael McNamara. Once a neighbor and a figure of everyday life, then a creature of the Troubles, he became a Yank. A decade of Mick Mac's life had grasped all the possibilities open to most of those born in Ahanagran. After that, he mostly drank.

Michael McNamara, a hero of the Troubles, was not readily recognizable in Mick Mac. It took me a long time to realize that the Mick Mac of my mother's stories and the old man, dying and drinking, whom I barely remember meeting when I was a teenager in California, was Michael McNamara. His story was one of those the national school children gathered in the mid-1930s.

Padraig Ó Cuilinn was fourteen when he wrote in a careful hand in his Collins' School exercise book the story of Michael

McNamara. He may have heard the story from Patrick Holly, Sara's uncle, for he credits several of the stories he told to him. It was November 23, 1937, when he wrote the story down, but already the Time of Troubles had retreated back to long ago, and he made Michael McNamara older than he was:

> There were many Heroes in this locality long ago and the best of which I heard about is Michael Mcnamara. He had some escapes from the Black-and-Tans. One day he was going along the road with his gun and the Tans came on without his ever seeing them. When they were right behind him, he stood, thinking, he would be shot in the spot, but they past him by without noticing him at-all.
>
> Some people say that he used to wear medals and he was a very holy man and that is what saved him. He is now about 56 years of age and is living in America.

Michael McNamara came late to the fighting. He joined the Sixth Battalion of the IRA six weeks before the end of the war. He may have been active before this. Mary says he was there the night Eddie Carmody died, but, then, to be truly of the Troubles in Ballylongford, it is necessary to be there the night Eddie Carmody died. After the truce with the British, the IRA split. Some, like Michael McNamara, remained loyal to the new Irish Free State; others rejected the treaty with the British. Once comrades, now under separate Free State and Republican banners, they fought each other, tortured each other, and murdered each other.

Michael McNamara went to America. Mick Mac came back. He reappeared every few summers in Ballylongford as if he had taken a pledge to drink it dry. Mick Mac had become a Yank, and Yanks were different from any neighbors Sara knew.

Some Yanks were different because they put on airs. In North Kerry, where they are so polite to an American's face, they are still full of stories of returned Yanks. These Yanks lose, at least to Irish ears, their Irish accents. They claim to know what the

Irish do not know and to have forgotten all that marked them as Irish. In one story that Mary tells ("That happened," she always says), a returned Yank feigns not to recognize an ass. "What is that long-tailed bugger in the corner?" he says.

Mick Mac did not put on airs, but neither did he act fully like a Kerryman. Mick Mac would sleep late and be just going to the pub in the afternoon when Sara's school was letting out. He must have kept close the memories and hungers of being a child in Ballylongford because he would wait every day by a shop that sold candy—sweets, Sara still calls them—and buy the children a fistful. It was, Sara says, Christmas in July.

From there, Mick Mac went to Kelly's pub and drank away the afternoon and evening. And when the pub closed, he would take the dark road home. He went along it singing, but Mick Mac could not sing. His songs were a fluctuating roar. He sounded like an inebriated lion coming down the road.

Mick Mac was a friendly drunk, and he would stop at any house that might let him in. Lights attracted him, and so Margaret Walsh covered the window so he would not see the kerosene lamp. A glimpse of the light and he would bang on the door, roaring his presence and waking the children. Margaret would not go to sleep until he safely passed her house.

Sara does not know what drew him in that one night. The window was covered, and her mother had strung a makeshift clothesline across the room hoping to dry some wet clothes. Mick Mac pounded on the door, bellowing louder than ever, waking the children. Margaret opened the door to silence him, but he strode cheerfully in. Sara, up by now, remembers him taking off his coat as he walked into the room. He had his coat in hand, swinging it out from his body, when he hit the clothesline. He felt the rope more than saw it. He turned when his body struck the line. His turning pulled the ends loose, and as he continued to turn, swinging his coat, the line wrapped around him. His body was like a reel spinning the line in. And as the line came in, clothes fell to the floor. Mick, turning and spinning with his coat still in hand, trod all over them.

With her children amazed and laughing, Margaret's work went down in this drunken, roaring wreck twirling through her house while holding his own coat. "Mick, God blast you," she screamed, "and get out of my house." And she drove him out into the rain and dark. He was back the next night.

Mick Mac was the strange possibility of America. That possibility was all around Sara as she grew. When Sara played with her cousins the Hollys, she knew that their mother, her father's sister, was the last of that generation of Walshes in Ireland. The rest were in America. Her own father was gone to America. Her sister Nell was gone. Her own mother had gone and come back. You could feel, see, and hear America on those farms, in the absences as well as the presences.

America and North Kerry existed only in relation to each other. The distance was illusory. Each presented possibilities the other lacked, and each compensated for the other's shortcomings. North Kerry's exploitation and stunted possibilities might be escaped in America, and North Kerry itself was sustained by American dollars sent home. The misery and loneliness that haunted many of those in America were soothed by dreams of a return to Kerry. To the Irish of North Kerry, America, and Chicago in particular, was closer than Dublin. There were more intimate connections.

Yet, even with the farm failing, with so many gone, with herself a servant girl and no fortune, Sara says she didn't think she would go. Maybe Mary would go first. She was older. But because Mary was older, she would have first claim on any fortune her father might earn. Gerard, too, was older, but Gerard was most likely to get the farm, and certainly the farm needed his labor more than hers. Sara was next. She paints herself as oblivious, but emigration must have crossed her mind.

15

He was the only car around. He was the big shot.
—Sara, on the man who took her to Dublin for her passport

These are things that Sara admits and remembers: She hated the work. She hated the work on the farm; she hated taking the milk to the creamery; she hated the Heaphys and the O'Sullivans. There was her impatience and her willingness to judge and to imagine something better. It seems to me that six years with the Heaphys and O'Sullivans and the prospect of more would have made a person glad to go to America.

And there is Johnny, who says she was ready to go.

But she denies that she wanted to go or imagined she ever would have to go. She loved Pollagh and Guhard; she loved her mother; she loved the deep familiarity of Ahanagran and all that surrounded it. She was a peasant girl, a servant girl, and she knew nothing else.

Gerard, who is older than Johnny and Sara, says the loves outweighed the hatreds.

She did not want to go. She says Johnny is wrong. She says, "That was the only life I knew. I didn't know glad or anything else about it. That was the way things were, and you accepted them."

It has been more than half a century since her departure, and the three of them cannot recall her leaving without churning up the feelings that followed the event itself. And more than that, these original feelings have leaked out and mixed with the feelings aroused by the numerous acts of remembering again and again over half a century. There are only contradictory accounts of what she felt.

It is her memory that she did not want to go.

She casts the story of her going as a descent from innocence to knowledge. But she has told me enough to make me think this innocence was, at best, comparative. The suicides, the fact of Tim, her aunt Kitty gone to America, the death of Eddie Carmody in the road, the killings, her father vanished, the absences of others who had gone, her mother's pain, the hardness of Lil Heaphy, the meanness of Mrs. O'Sullivan: Sara knew something of life.

The innocence was only, perhaps, that she expected help and comfort from kin and friends of kin.

In 1936 Jack Walsh sent for her. On July 23 he went to the Cunard White Star Limited offices in Chicago and paid $82.50 for a third-class ticket. He paid $8.00 for her head tax and $18.20 for railroad fare from New York to Chicago. The total was $108.70. He kept the receipt and mailed the tickets to Ireland.

Sara came to America because Ireland could not support her and her work in America might in a small way help support the Irish farm. Her wages in Ireland were not enough. The bills at Heaphy's had become bills at Wallace's, the general store. Margaret was no better a manager than she had been in 1929. Jack sent back money to pay the rates and to pay for the groceries. He was twelve years gone, but his work was still necessary to support the farm.

Emigration gave Sara a freedom she did not want. Emigration, she insists, was not a choice she made. It was her mother who told her she was going to Chicago to live with her father, whom she did not know, and her sister Nell, whom she had almost forgotten. She did not want to go, but she did not protest. She was sixteen, and, in the paradoxical way such things happen, she was denied any choice in determining her life, and at that moment her life became her own.

The journey to America, the central pivot on which all Sara Walsh's stories turn, began in self-imposed silence.

To get a passport, she had to go to Dublin. There was a man named Coughlin who had a car because his employer had given it to him. It was the third car my mother had seen. There had been cars in Ballylongford at the time of the revolution, but they had largely disappeared. The first car she remembers belonged to the priest in Ballylongford. She saw it only from the outside. She had got to sit in the seat of the second car, and this was a great favor and thrill, although the car never moved. The third car eventually took her to Dublin; it was Coughlin's.

The story of the ride to Dublin is not a story my mother has regularly told. She only told it to me a few years ago. Her account was brief and undramatic. She remembered Coughlin as "a very good friend of my mother's, and my mother was a very decent woman." It was the car that made him who he was. "He was the only car around. He was the big shot." She slips back into Irish phrasings when she talks about it. Usually her English is Americanized and unaccented. "The car belonged to the man he worked for, somebody in Dublin, I think. At that time there were no cars in Ahanagran, but, when he came home, he'd stop by and talk to my mother and bring us little sweets, candies."

"He will take you up, and he will bring you back," her mother told her. And so he did, on November 3, 1936, the day Sara got her immigrant identification card at the U.S. consulate in Dublin. Only a little distance after leaving Bally, he had reached for her, tearing her dress. She had begun to cry uncontrollably. He had left her alone. She remembers pinning together the torn dress; it was her only dress.

On the way back, as if he had meditated on his desire and reassured himself of her helplessness, he tried once more. She screamed and cried again, and once more he stopped. When she got home, she never told anybody. "I was afraid to tell my mother, because you didn't talk about such things. And nobody ever knew anything about it. . . ."

This then was a story without an audience. The man who tried to rape my mother was a family friend and remained so until her mother died. Even if Sara had told the story, her mother might not have believed her. Her own brother didn't believe her when she told him years later. She had to have children and the children had to be grown before she found an audience.

Coughlin attempted to rape her, and his attempt changed the trajectory of Sara Walsh's story, for it makes the trip to Dublin, the capital of Ireland, the first sign of her transformation into an outsider. She was moving into spaces where her family could not protect her. Moving beyond the small, sheltering gravity of home, moving out toward America, stripped her of protections she did not even know she had until they disappeared. Suddenly, in the midst of Ireland, she encountered unpredictable violence. Coughlin of the car probably would not have dared rape without the convenience of a victim soon to depart forever. She was prey; there would be other predators. This new vulnerability was different from the exploitation that she was leaving and that she took for granted. A girl on a lonely journey between outposts of family separated by an ocean and half a continent, she had become more vulnerable than she had ever been in her life.

The story of the emigration is memory now, and parts of it I have heard for years. Much of the story always seems to take place in the present tense. Tim drives the trap that will take her to the railroad station in Listowel. He holds Sara's arm to keep her from getting out. Her mother and her sister Mary are in the road; they stand with their hands stretched above their heads toward the heavens as if they are praying, keening as if my mother had died. "I tried to jump out and go back to my mother," she says. "I knew I would never see her again, and I didn't."

It was November 1936. Tim put her on the train at Listowel. It was her first train trip. It was a long trip on a cold train from Listowel to Cobh.

When the train arrived in Cobh, she became one of many. She was one emigrant in a long line of emigrants walking to the *Laconia*, the ship that would take them to America. It was a long walk, and it was raining and cold that November day. Her mother had given her a pound so she could get a bed to sleep in, because the boat was not sailing until noon the next day. As the line of people moved on, someone came and asked who had money for a bed. She gave the person her pound. She was shown into a large room in an old building with several mattresses on a cement floor. There were no blankets. She just stretched out on a mattress.

An old woman came and poked her awake with a stick. She awoke from a dead sleep. She couldn't tell how many hours she had slept. The old woman told her to go outside and wait for the boat. She waited in a new line for what seemed like an eternity to board the boat. It was still dark and raining and bitter cold. No one knew the hour because no one had a watch.

It was years later, she told me, that she read a story about emigrants from Ireland and how one cruel scheme they were put through was paying the pound for a night's sleep and being awakened, sometimes less than a few hours later, and sent back into line to wait for the boat with the explanation that it was loading time. The beds were then rented to another group from the long line, and the same cruel scheme was repeated again and again.

As the boat left Cobh, she watched with all the other emigrants as Ireland, her "beloved homeland," disappeared on the horizon. She was sixteen. Ireland had become only memories.

PART II

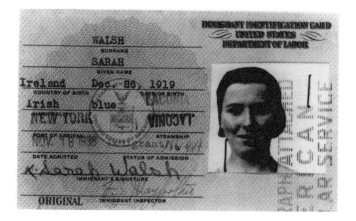

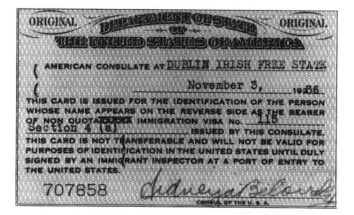

16

There is no doubt that in the course of a year large numbers of aliens presenting fraudulent proof of American citizenship gain lawful entry, due to the fact that it is a physical impossibility for the small number of immigrant inspectors to discover this class of smuggler, except in exceptional cases.

—Report of the Commissioner General of Immigration,
District No. 11, Headquarters at Detroit, 1924

Sara stood on the deck of the *Laconia* and watched Ireland recede. Twice, in 1924 and again in 1929, Jack Walsh had stood on a ship's deck and watched Ireland fade, become insubstantial, and then disappear below the horizon. And before Sara and Jack Walsh, there had been Margaret and Kitty and Ed and Bea and all the other Walshes seeing Ireland vanish.

What awaited Sara in America was in part the cumulative result of those earlier journeys. She would find in Chicago what her father had prepared for her in his dozen years there. What he had found was what his brothers and sisters had achieved in their many years in America. And what had awaited them was the world that other relatives and other Irish had helped make in Chicago. Her journey depended on their earlier journeys, and most particularly it depended on her father's.

Jack Walsh had not left under the same conditions as his brothers and sisters. Before World War I, America was largely open, at least to Europeans like himself. In 1921, however, Congress had passed "an Act to limit the immigration of aliens into the United States." It had established quotas for immigrants entering the country, and although Great Britain, of which Ireland was legally still a part, had a relatively large quota, the number of immigrants desiring entrance was larger still. Under the quotas, 20 percent of a nation's annual allotment could enter the United States in any given month. Once 20 percent had been reached, all immigrants from that country arriving during the remainder of the month were detained and deported. From July 1, the beginning of the fiscal year, to November or December, ships would wait outside New York Harbor for midnight on the last day of each month to unload all their passengers under the new month's quota. But with 20 percent of a country's quota being filled every month, annual quotas were often reached by November or December, five or six months after the beginning of the fiscal year. Leaving in January 1924, Jack Walsh had virtually no chance of legal entry under the quota. As a result, he had not gone directly to the United States. He had, instead, landed in Canada.

The treaty with Britain that ended the revolution in Ireland and established the Irish Free State did not sever all ties between Ireland and Great Britain; Jack Walsh was still a British subject entitled to a British passport. The passport from a country he hated would get him into Canada. A long train ride would take him to Windsor, Ontario, and from Windsor a three-or four-minute ferry ride would take him to Detroit. From Detroit he would go to Chicago. He would be an illegal immigrant.

That was apparently the plan, but something went wrong. It was no easy thing to get caught at the Canadian border, and he counted on that, but it seems to have happened. There were immigration inspectors at the end of the ferry ride and a detention room. Representatives of the Detroit and Windsor Ferry Company said the inspectors detained those who looked suspicious. Jack Walsh looked like a foreign workingman; they detained him even though he probably claimed that he was only coming for a visit. They presumably culled him from the daily riders on the ferry, interrogated him, and shipped him back to Canada.

According to the family stories, at some point (it is unclear when) his brother Ed, a Chicago policeman, intervened to help him get into the country. Ed, a citizen and a cop, most likely just walked him across the border, past the inspection station. Jack Walsh's illegal entry did not prevent him from getting work. Being illegal didn't matter to him if he could work. He only needed a job that could provide the money necessary to save the farm; he could then return to Ireland. He became a carpenter. Jack Walsh, to whose children cars were exotic, built garages.

This is the account of immigration that family stories preserve and that my own research supplements; it is not, however, the story that immigration documents record. Jack Walsh filed two documents in regard to his immigration. The earliest document that I have is Jack Walsh's declaration of intention to become a citizen. It is dated January 26, 1928, four years after he left Ireland. He claims to have entered the United States on December 1, 1927, by taking the ferry from Windsor, Canada, to Detroit.

These documents created a mystery: they leave unexplained Jack Walsh's whereabouts between 1924 and the end of 1927. He certainly seems to have ridden the ferry to Detroit on that December Thursday in 1927, for the Bureau of Naturalization has a certificate of arrival showing his date of entry. He had to file it later with his citizenship petition. He came now as a quota immigrant even though Congress, in the spring of 1924, had lowered the quotas and changed the criteria to exclude more eastern and southern Europeans.

In January 1928 Jack Walsh told the immigration officials that he was forty-seven years old and five feet ten inches tall and weighed 175 pounds. He listed his occupation as garage builder. He swore he was not an anarchist or a polygamist and that he meant to reside permanently in the United States and become a citizen.

Except for the date of his immigration and his intent to become a citizen, the document seems plausible. But the date of immigration leaves nearly four years unaccounted for. And as for his becoming a citizen, within a year he would be back in Ireland, where, according to the memories of his daughter Mary, he hoped to stay.

The second document is even more confusing. Five years later, in January 1933, he filed a petition for citizenship. Daniel Heafey, a streetcar conductor, and Denis Gleason, an unemployed welder, were his witnesses. He now listed his occupation as repairman.

It is hard for me to make sense of the petition for citizenship. I have a copy of it in front of me. Much of the information is wrong. He could not remember his wife's birthday. He left the month and day blank. He guessed at the year and got it wrong by three years. He gave the wrong date for his marriage, off this time by three days. He was wrong about the year his daughter Sara was born. All this is understandable. When Sara was a child in Ireland, the people she knew never celebrated birthdays. She had no idea of her parents' ages. But Jack Walsh was also wrong about more fundamental things. He was wrong about the number of his children. He failed to list his youngest son and namesake, Johnny, at all.

He swore that he had resided continuously in the United States since December 1927. This was not true. He was back in Ireland in 1929.

This man with no head for dates remembers to repeat one date exactly. It is the date he gave on his original declaration of intention to become a citizen: the date of his arrival in the United States, December 1, 1927.

How could a man who left Ireland for the United States in January 1924 not enter the country until nearly four years had passed? Either he had stayed in Canada for four years or he had restaged his immigration to mask his earlier, illegal immigration.

It is memory now that seemingly subverts history. Family memory says that the certificate of arrival, the declaration of intention, the petition for citizenship conceal rather than reveal. Jack Walsh may have stepped ashore at Detroit on December 1,

1927, but family stories indicate that he did so only to mask an earlier illegal arrival. These artifacts of the past, filed away and forgotten, preserve lies and misinformation. They deceive even when there is no need to deceive because the date of his marriage or the existence of his youngest son would not affect his eligibility to become a citizen.

But, look closer, and this subversion is not just the work of memory. History itself works at cross-purposes. It is not memory but marriage certificates and baptismal records that contradict the dates on the citizenship application. And the citizenship application is itself an artifact of memory, memorializing perhaps not so much lies as a misremembering. The document does not necessarily record the truth; it only records what he said in 1933.

This distinction is true of all records. They record only what someone said or saw or remembered. His own baptismal record lists his birth as April 23, 1880, but he gave his birthday as April 20. Surely he knew his own birthday. But, given what my mother describes as the carelessness about such things, maybe not. Or perhaps the day he was baptized, April 25, 1880, the priest misheard the birthday, or perhaps more than a century later I misread the priest's hand. There is nothing here that holds firm.

But above all, as a historian, I recognize that family memories challenge the seemingly plain meaning of the immigration documents: first arrived at Detroit, December 1, 1927. The stories cause me to check further, to try to place Jack Walsh in Chicago before December 1, 1927. There are no city directories for Chicago between 1923 and 1928. He is in the 1928 directory. He is a lodger at 1133 North Avers. He is living with his sister Nell and her husband, William, who was then a sergeant in the Chicago Police Department. So the question becomes: Could he have arrived in Detroit on December 1, 1927, and still have appeared in the 1928 directory? My guess is that he could not have. To get maximum sales, I presume the directory must have been available at or near the first of the year, which means the information had to be gathered and compiled earlier. Gathered, I presume, well before December 1, 1927. But this is surmise;

it remains only a guess, for there is no publication data for the directory.

From what I have, from this mix of memory and history, I can form a credible story. In 1924 Jack Walsh was caught crossing the border at Detroit and deported to Canada. He got word to his brother Ed, a Chicago cop, who came to Canada and smuggled him across the border. This was not hard. Testimony before the House Committee on Immigration and Naturalization admitted that many crossed at the Canadian or Mexican border without being subjected to any examination.

He was illegal, but he obtained work easily. He worked for several years building garages. But then in 1927 he decided he needed to regularize his residence, to become legal. To file for citizenship, he needed to prove legal entry into the country.

But why would he decide to become a citizen, this man who only wanted to save his Irish farm? Either he was planning to return to Ireland for a visit and needed to reenter the United States on his return, or he decided that he would have to bring some of his children to America. If he filed for citizenship, he could reenter as a non-quota immigrant. And if he became a citizen, his children under eighteen would get preference in the issuance of visas and be able to enter without regard to the quota. Eventually, he would both travel back to Ireland and bring over children. There were certainly advantages to filing for citizenship.

The Butlers, Nell and Bill, were active in Democratic politics. Perhaps they used political connections to get him admitted under the quota. At the very least, they could find someone to tell him the rules and how to turn them to his advantage. In any case, he restaged his entry, made it legal. It was December. Construction had slowed. He entered Canada and reentered the United States, this time legally. In January he filed for citizenship. All this makes sense, but it is only a guess. It is an attempt to reconcile memory and the documents.

❧ 17 ❧

Seventeenth to be slain on duty in three years, Policeman Edward J. Mulvihill was shot to death by an Italian gunman last night.
—*Chicago Tribune*, December 19, 1916

By 1933 Jack Walsh was on the South Side. He had got a job with the street railway. He repaired the streetcars.

It becomes easier to piece together Jack's life in Chicago. His daughter Nell was with him. He lived at 6320 South Talman Avenue. He was still living with relatives, this time at his sister Bea Mulvihill's house. He was still caught in the paths the past had worn. Things that had happened years before brought him to the place he was now.

Bea, baptized Brigitta, was sixty-one years old in 1933, eight years older than Jack. She had been born in September 1872. She had endured a hard life, and her tragedies eventually brought her brother Jack, and with him his daughter Nell, to live with her. Bea's husband, Ed Mulvihill, had been, like Ed Walsh, a Chicago policeman. Nearly all the Walsh sisters had married Chicago policemen. But by 1933 Ed Mulvihill had been dead for nearly twenty years.

I have heard several versions of Ed Mulvihill's death. My mother once told me that he walked in on a holdup and was shot. This had happened when his children were very little, only one and two. Another time my mother told me that he was a mounted policeman, downtown in Grant Park, and had been shot apprehending a murderer. It had happened, she said, before she arrived in the country. I could, however, find no mention of the death of a policeman named Mulvihill in the 1930s or the 1920s or the late teens, and I knew that no Chicago cop killed on duty goes uncommemorated. The only Mulvihill I could find in the City Council records was a sergeant honored for beating up strikers.

My mother checked with my uncle Pat O'Hara, her sister Nell's husband. Pat said he remembered the story differently. Ed Mulvihill had been shot on the South Side. He had been on foot patrol at Sixty-third and Damen. A woman had got off the streetcar. She had asked for protection from a man who was following her. He took her home, and after leaving her at her door, he started back to his beat on Sixty-third. A man confronted him, accused him of trying to steal his girl, and pulled a gun. He shot Ed Mulvihill, who died on the sidewalk. Pat couldn't remember the date, but he said that there was a plaque in the Loop at police headquarters honoring those who died in the line of duty. Ed Mulvihill's name was on it.

The plaque is indeed there. My stepson, Colin, who was a biologist with a postdoctoral fellowship at the University of Chicago at the time, went and copied the inscription on the plaque for me. The plaque gave the date of his death: December 18, 1916, long before Jack Walsh came to the country, before Sara was even born.

Ed Mulvihill's death was front-page news in both the *Chicago Daily News* and the *Chicago Tribune*. He was the seventeenth policeman killed on duty in three years. He was shot by an Italian, a Sicilian. Ed Mulvihill's dying was the most notable thing he ever did. Death was big in the *Chicago Tribune*. In the *Tribune* the story of his death was sandwiched between other deaths: metaphorical death—Mayor Big Bill Thompson's declaration of war to the death on the whiskey ring; death and sex—news of the death of the "Mad Princess" Clara Chimay, once famous and now long forgotten; and wholesale death—news of the war in Europe with its vast harvest of nameless dead.

Louis Delloiaconna a.k.a. Louis Iovena a.k.a. Louis Dovina a.k.a. Louis the Masher killed Ed Mulvihill. The *Tribune* unleashed its best newspaper prose on Louis Delloiaconna: " 'Louis the Masher,' known in the west side Italian quarter for a crafty gun toting Beau Brummel of the district, has been identified as the murderer."

The police freely gave information to the papers. The police thought Louis was from New York, but they weren't sure. He had lived at 700 Miller Street for only three weeks. On the evening of the murder Louis had borrowed an overcoat, one with a fur collar. "I want to make a mash with it," he had said.

Louis had been stalking Florence Ward for several days. She worked at the Sawyer Biscuit factory on Harrison Street. Louis told her that he loved her and wanted to marry her. That was on the Friday before the murder, and it was the first time she had ever seen him. On Saturday, Louis told her he would throw acid in her face or kill her if she didn't marry him.

On Monday, Florence Ward's mother went to meet her by now thoroughly frightened daughter when she got off work. While waiting, Mrs. Ward stopped Ed Mulvihill, who was walking his beat, and told him of Louis's threats. They were talking when Florence Ward came down the street. Louis was watching from a doorway; he moved toward her. Florence Ward's mother pointed out her daughter, and Ed Mulvihill ran toward the converging pair.

Louis the Masher saw Ed Mulvihill coming. He ran, turning into an alley off Sholto Street and Vernon Park Place. When Mulvihill reached the mouth of the alley, Louis turned toward Vernon Park. Mulvihill reached for his service revolver. Louis already had his gun out. He shot Ed Mulvihill, and Mulvihill fell. Florence Ward and her mother screamed. Ed Mulvihill, on the ground and bleeding, reached for the gun he had dropped. Louis ran past the patrolman; he stopped and fired three more shots. Ed Mulvihill died in the alley.

The police began arresting Italians immediately. Sergeants Yancey and Fleming arrested three who happened to be in the vicinity of the shooting. They arrested more in various parts of the Italian district. The police thought Louis was hiding somewhere among the West Side Italians. They planned to canvass all the houses in the area to find him. Captain Mullen was confident that they would make the arrest quickly.

On December 20 the police received reports that Louis Delloiaconna had been seen begging money on Maxwell Street in order to leave the city. Louis had displayed a dime, saying it was the only money he possessed.

After that Louis disappeared. The grand jury delivered an indictment for murder on March 29, 1917. Florence Ward, her mother, and Sergeant Yancey all appeared to testify. The clerk of the grand jury was named Frank Walsh, but he was no relation of ours. The indictment came in language, printed below, that would have bewildered both the immigrant murderer, Louis Delloiaconna, and the immigrant cop, Ed Mulvihill. It said that Louis Delloiaconna had

> in and upon the body of one Edward Mulvihill in the peace of the People of the said State of Illinois then and there being ½unlawfully½ feloniously wilfullu and of his malice aforethought did make an assault and that the said Louis Delloiaconna a certain pistol commonly called revolver then and there charged with gunpowder and divers leaden bullets which said pistol the said Louis Delloiaconna in his hand then and there had and held then and there had and held then and there unlawfully feloniously wilfully and of his malice aforethought did discharge and shoot off to against towards and upon the said Edward Mulvihill. . . .

The indictment described his death in a mistyped, misspelled, awkward sentence that probably took me longer to copy than it took Ed Mulvihill to die. It was a sentence nearly as incomprehensible as his death. And it was a sentence without effect. The state of Illinois took no further action against Louis Delloiaconna. The police never made an arrest. He never stood trial.

Ed Mulvihill's death stayed in the news, directly and indirectly, for a couple of weeks. The *Tribune* treated it with that distinctive mix of viciousness and sentimentality that has remained the hallmark of American right-wing journalism.

The inability of the police to catch the murderer helped initiate a campaign against Italians in general. A week after Mulvihill's death the *Tribune* ran a story with the headline: LITTLE SICILY'S MURDERERS GO ALL OVER THE CITY. Italians, the story said, were murdering one another at such a rate in Little Sicily, the area on the North Side between Chicago Avenue and Division and west of Wells, that even the Sicilians were abandoning the neighborhood and scattering across the city. As they migrated, they brought murder and robbery with them. Immigration officials were not weeding out criminals, the paper complained, the courts were not convicting murderers, parole boards released those they did convict, and the police were not devoting enough resources to stamping out the Sicilian Black Hand.

The *Chicago Tribune*—which proclaimed itself "The World's Greatest Newspaper"—editorialized that "Chicago is rapidly approaching the point where ordinary peaceful citizens will feel it safer to carry pistols than to trust in the police and the courts. If that point is reached it means anarchy. It will be reached unless official Chicago and legal Chicago administers justice more speedily and more adequately than it has done in the last few years." The *Tribune*'s writers frothed briefly, presumably restrained their desire to arm themselves, and then moved on to other things.

The newspapers sentimentalized Ed Mulvihill's widow and orphans as reflexively as they had demonized Italians. Ed Mulvihill's sons, Jerry and Billy, were eight and six when their father died, and it was just before Christmas. The family lived at 1341 South Harding Avenue then. Aunt Bea and her children were left in horrible circumstances. She had no resources except what she would receive from the Policeman's Benevolent Fund.

Ed Mulvihill's brother, Patrick, who was an operator at the Lake Street El station, set the tone of the stories. According to the *Tribune*'s reporter, Patrick said that "their daddy told them

before he went on his beat to make out their lists for Santa
Claus, but I guess they didn't know he'd be walking a beat with
Santa Claus before the night was out." "Walking a beat with
Santa Claus" was nice, but the *Daily News* was not to be outdone.
The *Daily News* played the altar boy angle. The boys would, the
paper reported, "carry out their father's last wish and serve the
priest at St. Finbarr's Roman Catholic church west 14th street
and South Harding avenue, as altar boys Christmas morning."

The case lingered in the *Tribune* as the paper started a fund
for the Mulvihill family. The fund cost the *Tribune* nothing but
a few inches of type. It allowed the paper to trumpet its civic-
mindedness. By Christmas Eve there were thirteen dollars in
the fund. Forty-two dollars more came in by the end of the year.
Bea Mulvihill moved out of her home on South Harding Avenue
and into her sister Kitty's house. And there, as far as the newspapers and their readers were concerned, the story ended.

Ed Mulvihill's murder, for all its transmutations in family stories, was real. The consequences of the death of this man left
the newspapers but rippled on through the years, shaping everything that followed for Bea and her two sons, Bill and Jerry.
Eventually, the death created a place in her home for Jack
Walsh.

The stories Sara heard, from Bea and others, are stories of
persistence and resourcefulness. They tell how Bea worked as a
scrubwoman, cleaning floors; they tell how she scrimped and
saved and eventually bought the house at 6320 South Talman
that Jack Walsh moved into in the early 1930s. The house was
only a few blocks from where her sister Kitty and Kitty's husband, Tommy O'Brien, had bought their new house on South
Mozart Street. The proximity of the families emphasized the
importance of family, the webs of mutual support.

But there is, I suspect, more to the story than this. Widowed
washerwomen did not buy houses in this neighborhood on their
wages. There must have been other money available to Aunt
Bea. Although I cannot get access to the records to be sure, I
presume she got money from the Police Benevolent Fund es-

tablished for cases like her own. And I suspect she got a widow's pension from Cook County, but these records, too, are closed. Illinois was the first state to provide for widows' pensions, the early precursor of Aid to Dependent Children. Widows' pensions in Cook County were meager, and the program required able-bodied women with only a few children to work. Like Bea, the majority of the recipients did so. The combination of aid and wages would explain the house more persuasively than only the thrift of a washerwoman.

"Jolly" is the word Sara uses to describe Aunt Bea. Aunt Bea, a widow with her Irish husband murdered, somehow remained jolly. She doted on her sons and worked hard for them. With the purchase of the house on South Talman, she had achieved a remarkable success. Her neighbor was a doctor, Dr. McCarthy, and her sons were the best friends of his sons.

Her boys and Dr. McCarthy's boys were both wild, but their wildness did not seem unusual or extravagant when they were young. It was a stage, people would say. And one of the McCarthy boys did become a doctor like his father. Aunt Bea could be hard on the boys, both the McCarthys and the Mulvihills. The McCarthys would tease her until she exploded, yelling and screaming at them. But the teasing was good-natured. They wanted the explosion.

Maybe once it seemed possible that despite their wildness the Mulvihill and McCarthy boys might become doctors or their equivalents. They did things together; there was no reason to separate them. Bill and the McCarthy boys went into business one Christmas. They offered a dozen Christmas trees for sale on a corner lot that had once been a gasoline station. There was now only a pit near where the pumps had been. When their first customer, a woman, came by, the McCarthy boys stepped aside, behind a row of trees, to let Bill make the sale. While the woman looked, Bill turned his back so as not to seem overanxious, and when he looked again, she was gone. Not gone in the sense of having left the lot and walked down the street but actually vanished. He had only turned his back for a moment. The

McCarthy boys came out from behind the trees. "Where is she?" they asked. The boys looked up and down the street. They couldn't find her.

They found her when they went back to the lot. She was unconscious at the bottom of the pit, where they had been throwing trimmings. They had laid out the trees to mask the pit, and the woman, absorbed in picking a tree, apparently had backed into it. It was not a good omen.

The woman was, as it turned out, all right. She didn't sue or even threaten to sue, at least in the story. To the McCarthys, the pit became just part of a rueful story. But to Bill Mulvihill, that pit might as well have been a metaphor for his and his brother Jerry's lives; no matter what they touched, someone ended up in the pit.

Bea's sons Bill and Jerry were twenty-three and twenty-five years old in 1933 when Jack Walsh and his daughter Nell were living with Bea. "Irish mafia" Sara calls them, but this exaggerates their accomplishments. They were small-time hustlers. They were no longer the altar boys whose father walked the beat with Santa Claus.

When Sara left Ireland, she thought she was coming to Bea's house on South Talman Avenue. That was the address she gave on entry. The stories of Jack Walsh and his sister Bea had converged on South Talman Avenue. It seemed that South Talman Avenue would be the place her own American story would begin.

18

"Good bye from old Sal."
—Sara's closing from a postcard written on the *Laconia*,
November 1936

There is only a single piece of writing in Sara Walsh's hand that survives from her voyage to America, indeed from that entire time of her girlhood. It is a postcard she sent to her sister Mary in Ahanagran. It is postmarked November 17, 1936, a Tuesday, the day the ship docked in Boston. It had been written the previous Saturday, November 14.

Dearest sister Mary & all,
    Hoping ye are well. I have wrote two letters to my mom. I have been terrible sick. We are not supposed to land in New York until Thursday. I am very lonely. Be good to my dear mom whom I adore. I will not forget her. We are having a terrible voyage. Every time the old boat tumbles, my stomach goes too. Hello Bill, Gerard, Johnny, Tim, dearest mother. I will write to ye all when I land. Good bye from old Sal.

She had been seasick for the first four days. The boat rocked and the water sloshed down stairways and hallways. Everything was crashing to the floors. The *Laconia* had endured one of the roughest crossings in decades. The worst of the storms lasted at least two days.

Sara doesn't remember how long she was at sea. When they finally landed, she thought she was in New York. She only knew she was in Boston when she saw a newspaper boy who had come on board and read the masthead of the newspaper. She did not know where Boston was. She had never heard of it.

She remembers that the newspaper boy was holding a newspaper high above his head that read LACONIA FEARED LOST ARRIVES SAFELY. She had never seen a newspaper boy or an American paper. Everything, she remembers, was a first—from the time she left home every experience was a new one.

The headline in the Boston newspaper my mother remembers seeing hints at how memory works. Remembering the headline that proclaimed the ship's supposed loss and successful arrival is a wonderful touch for an immigration story: believed dead and then reborn in a new land. It is a perfect symbolic headline, but, as far as I can tell, there was no such headline.

Sara Walsh did indeed go through a great storm, or rather a series of storms, as bad apparently as anything seen in the North Atlantic in a generation. Each ship that docked in Boston brought news of the terrors at sea. The *Importer* docked the same day as the *Laconia*. "We thought the end of the world had come," its passengers said. The freighter *Isis* sank, with the loss of thirty-nine lives. The *Tweedbank* lost her captain and two of the crew. Ships crossing the North Atlantic were severely damaged and delayed. Sara did not exaggerate the dangers of the storm.

But the rest of the story is the addition and subtraction of memory. The *Laconia*, unbeknownst to sixteen-year-old Sara Walsh, was always scheduled to stop in Boston before going on to New York. There was most likely a newspaper boy, but there was not, so far as I can tell, a headline. It is true that I cannot find all the Boston papers for that day, but, in those I can find, the *Laconia* is hardly front-page news, and there is no claim made that the ship had been feared lost. Indeed, the ship had been in radio contact and had reported it might be late.

My mother and I talk about the headline. She is surprised that

I cannot find it. And then it turns out that my father, who is now dead and who grew up in Boston, claimed to have seen it. But this is six years before my mother and father met. He would have had no reason to think twice about the *Laconia* and remember such a headline. He could not know that the ship carried his future wife. But later, perhaps, as my mother tells him of the first time she saw Boston with no inkling that her future husband lived in this city, he attaches some headline dimly remembered to the *Laconia*, giving himself a connection to the moment of his wife's coming to America. And my mother incorporates the headline into her telling, and, eventually, it is she, rather than my father, who claims to have seen it. But all this is hypothetical. I can only guess how the headline became memory.

The *Laconia*'s docking at the Cunard Pier in East Boston was, however, news. It was in the papers. The biggest news concerned an Irish immigrant, but it was not my mother. The emigrant was Mary Kathleen Duffy. She was six years old and from County Roscommon. Her father had emigrated to Yorkshire, for there was no work in Ireland. Her mother was dead. Her aunt and uncle in Dorchester, with no children of their own, had adopted her. *The Boston Globe* of November 17, 1936, turned Mary Kathleen Duffy into a little Shirley Temple at sea. "Mary," the *Globe* reported, "is the liveliest and most talkative child that ever stepped foot on our shores from the old country." Mary had "proved one of the best sailors on board and did not miss a single meal." Besides Mary, the *Globe* noted the arrival on the *Laconia* of Cunliffe M. G. Hoyt, a British official from the Gold Coast on his way to Trinidad, and John C. Plimpton, who had been in England for several months and was soon to depart "on a yachting cruise to the West Indies."

The newspaper challenges my mother's memory, but my mother's memory also reveals what the newspaper masks and renders invisible: Irish immigration, even in 1936, was not just heartwarming stories of a "six-year-old Irish lass" traveling, for all one could tell, in the company of colonial officials and men with yachts, it was also young women with third-class passage, wearing all the clothes they owned on their back and desperately struggling to keep those clothes unsoiled by their own vomit. It was Sara Walsh wondering what they were doing in Boston and where in the world Boston might be. Historical sources, like memory, tell only some stories.

19

Family Name: WALSH
Given Name: SARAH
Age: 16
Sex: F
Married or Single: S
Calling or Occupation: DOMST.

—From List or Manifest of Alien Passengers for the United States, November 18, 1936, New York

"I have no recollection," my mother tells me, "of time, as to how long we were docked in Boston, or why the boat had stopped there. I remember vaguely something about repairs from the storm, but I can't be sure of this. When we arrived in New York, there was great excitement. Everyone was pushing their way to the deck to catch a glimpse of the Statue of Liberty. I finally found my way to the deck, and I did get to see the statue. It was so big and so beautiful. It is engraved forever in my mind. I did not know at that time what it stood for. I had never heard of it. I had not heard of very much really. My education was fourth grade, that's all."

After the *Laconia* entered New York Harbor, inspectors from the Immigration and Naturalization Service examined and interviewed the immigrants among the passengers. By 1936 the government maintained Ellis Island largely for holding and deporting aliens rather than admitting them. The inspectors boarded the ships, checked passports, and pinned name tags on the immigrants. They examined them physically and asked them questions. Some people were sent to Ellis Island for further examination and detained. The diseased and mentally defective could not enter.

It was 10:10 on November 18, 1936, when the immigration inspector had asked Sara the final questions. After that she came ashore through the Cunard terminal at New York Harbor. The immigrants formed a separate line from other passengers. Sara remembers standing in line forever. Then she passed through a final checkpoint and entered America.

There is one artifact of that experience that exists separate from her memory of it. The inspector who asked questions recorded her answers. The resulting document is clear and legible except for his signature. It is a signature that had nearly flattened out from endless repetition. Written on documents hundreds or thousands of times a day, it had slipped into illegibility. I went into the records of the Immigration and Naturalization Service to find a typed version of his name. The inspector was Francis J. Maypother.

Sara could provide the important information that Francis Maypother and the United States needed to know about her in monosyllabic answers—yes or no. The inspector marked the answers in the appropriate line on his form.

Some of the questions were bewildering to Sara then and remain bewildering to her now. "Whether a polygamist," the form says. Are you a polygamist? Mr. Maypother must have asked. I read the question to my mother now.

"Was I a what?" she asks.

"A polygamist."

She hesitates over the phone. "What's a polygamist?" She is making sure she understands this.

"Did you have more than one husband or did your husband have more than one wife?"

"I was a sixteen-year-old Irish girl," she says.

The polygamy question, like the anarchy question next to it, was a relic of old American fears. Old hysterias from the late nineteenth and early twentieth century, when Mormons and anarchists seemed dangers to the Republic, had produced questions that remained on bureaucratic forms long after the national adrenaline had ceased to run. Codified and asked of every immigrant, by the 1930s they served to bewilder sixteen-year-old Irish girls on long November nights.

The form records her as a sixteen-year-old Irish girl. Her hair was fair, her eyes were blue. She stood five feet five inches tall, and her complexion was fresh. When they asked about her calling or occupation, she probably said servant girl. They put her down as a domestic.

She was healthy, and she had not come here to overthrow the United States government. She said that she had come to stay and she intended to become a citizen.

There are two answers on the form that catch my attention. When Maypother asked if she was going to join a relative and where he was, she gave her father's name, John Walsh, but she listed 6320 South Talman as the address. That was her aunt Bea's address. Between her setting sail and her arrival in Chicago, then, Jack Walsh had changed his plans. He had left one sister's house for another. She would actually live on South Mozart Street with her aunt Kitty.

And when Maypother asked her if she was in the possession of fifty dollars and if less, how much, she replied, according to the report, that she had fifty dollars. She had no such amount. Her mother had given her a pound when she left Ahanagran; she had been cheated out of that in Cobh. I ask her now, nearly sixty years later. She remembers the pound and would, she thinks, surely remember if she had a sum so large as fifty dollars. She says she had never even seen an American dollar.

"How did you know to answer that you had fifty dollars?" I ask her.

"I don't know. How can I remember answers I gave sixty years ago. All I remember is the lines. Maybe someone on the ship told me to say, yes, I have fifty dollars." But, then, she doubts it. She was too shy to have talked to anyone.

I read her the answers she gave on the form nearly six decades before.

"How much I'm finding out about myself," my mother tells me dryly.

Maybe Maypother was sympathetic to the terrified and tired girl standing in front of him. Maybe he just decided to enter the appropriate answers for her and wave her through. It was late on a Wednesday night, and the inspectors were notoriously over-worked.

Jack Hegarty was there to meet her. Jack was her cousin, the son of her mother's brother John. Jack was the unimaginable American future. He lived in New York, where he was a buyer for B. Altman's department store. He bought Oriental rugs and frequently traveled to Asia. Sara's mother had told her this, but Sara did not know what a department store was or what an Oriental rug was. She says that the Orient could have been a book for all she knew. "All I knew of the world," she says, remembering Jack Hegarty and her arrival in New York, "was the farm where I was born and the village where we went to Mass on Sunday, with one general store there, the creamery, and the half dozen public houses."

Jack Hegarty was short, and he was with a tall red-haired woman. They approached her. They were reading name tags. They read Sara's name aloud. Jack Hegarty said he was her cousin. He introduced the tall red-haired woman as his wife, Maureen.

Sara remembers Maureen vividly. There were no women like her in Ballylongford. She was at least three inches taller than her husband and very beautiful. Sara had never seen anyone with such beautiful clothes and fancy shoes, and she carried a purse. She had never seen a woman with a purse so big. Most purses she had seen in North Kerry were sewn from flour sacks to hold their few coppers.

The bag Sara carried was sewn from a flour sack. This was

her only baggage. The only clothes she owned were on her back.

The trip to Manhattan was her second ride in an automobile. The ride thrilled her. The city's lights thrilled her, but she was so shy that when her cousin or anyone else talked to her she never raised her head to reply. She had never imagined anything like New York. The cars, the buildings, the buses, the people, the lights—everything was new and frightening.

Jack and Maureen Hegarty lived in a high-rise apartment building. Sara had never ridden on an elevator before. "Her feet," she says, "had never left the ground before this day."

It was late, and they told her they were going to work in the morning and they would not be back until evening. They would leave food on the table for her.

When she awoke, she went to the window and gazed in amazement at the city below. She could not believe how high off the ground she was. She found cornflakes and bread and tea on the table and a note telling her the milk was in the refrigerator. She did not know what the word "refrigerator" meant. She saw a white thing, and out of curiosity she opened it. There was milk in it. She had discovered her first refrigerator.

She had never seen cornflakes. She ate them dry. They were, she thought, very good. She was very hungry.

She continued to look out the window at America. She thought to herself, "So this is New York, where my mother worked as a maid for ten years before returning to Ireland to marry my dad."

All of a sudden, she heard someone opening the door. She looked and saw a black woman. She froze in fear. She had never seen anyone with that color skin before.

Sara felt frightened and alone and homesick. The woman, an American, who was a maid like Sara's mother had been, said hello to her. She is sure that she didn't answer. Sara stood motionless, as if she were a piece of furniture. The woman proceeded to dust, sweep, and clean. If she had dusted Sara, she probably would not have moved. After what seemed like an eternity, the black woman left. "This experience," she says, "has stayed with me for fifty years and always reminds me of how ignorant [I was], and, indeed, I was a greenhorn from the auld sod."

That night, she remembers, her cousin Jack put her on a train for Chicago.

20

He was a stranger to me.
　　　　　—Sara, talking about her father, Jack Walsh

There was no flow to events. Everything happened in fragments. America came to her in pieces. One thing stopped; another began. She was on the ship. She was in New York with Jack and Maureen Hegarty. She was on the train to Chicago. This was how the future appeared. She participated, but she did not control it. She would need time to assemble these pieces. Like other young immigrants, Sara Walsh traveled in a shifting combination of awe, ignorance, fear, resignation, sadness, and hope. This was the usual emotional range of greenhorns.

On the train to Chicago she sat on the first empty seat she could find. It was in a middle car. She remembers having to go to the bathroom, but bathrooms were new to her and she was unfamiliar with running water. She was torn between the need to urinate and the fear that she would not know how to locate or manage the restroom. She would never have asked a person on a train where a bathroom was, let alone how to operate a toilet. When a child across the aisle said he had to pee, Sara's heart leaped. She knew what that word meant. She watched as his mother took him to the bathroom. She waited and then followed them.

She neither ate nor drank until she reached Chicago. She had no food. Jack Hegarty may have given her some American money, but she didn't know what the various denominations meant, and, in any case, she lacked the courage to go to a dining car. She was, she recalls, "so very thirsty and hungry." The train rocked on with Sara more absorbed in her hungers and discomforts than in America unfolding past the windows.

Chicago brought panic rather than relief, for, when the conductor called out Chicago, he said the train would make two stops. No one had told her there were two stops. She was simply told to get off the train in Chicago. She determined to take the first one. And the good Lord, she thought, was with her because waiting on the platform were her father and her sister Nell.

In a sack, Sara carried a piece of salt pork. She gave it to her father. It was her final Irish message. It was all she had brought him from Ireland. It was all the farm and his wife and children had to offer a man now more than a decade gone. Who knows what he thought as he looked at the meat, the product of the farm he worked so hard to keep. A daughter he barely knew, fresh from that farm, had handed him a token of the land that he had left so long ago and that every day he struggled to hold. I wonder what he thought.

But there is, in the end, no telling what he thought. Jack Walsh is the great black hole at the center of these stories of Ireland and South Mozart Street. Half a century and more later, sitting around a table at my uncle Bill's condominium, surrounded by people who knew my grandfather, I asked my uncle Pat O'Hara about his father-in-law, John Walsh, whom everyone called Jack. He laughed and started to talk, and the story, as always, was about someone else. I asked my uncle Bill, who arrived in this country in 1947, the year Jack Walsh left, and he talked about the White Sox. He talked about going to Comiskey Park with his father and his utter bewilderment at the game he saw and his father's enthusiasm for it.

When Sara saw her father, "he was," she says, "a stranger to me." But she can't recall that moment as she experienced it for the first time because she now knows all that followed. She knows her father loved baseball and he loved Sara's sister Nell. "Nell was the pet. My Dad loved Nell very much. He and I were never close. I couldn't get close to my Dad because he wasn't the kind you could get close to. And it's probably because I didn't know him. And when he went back to Ireland, I think he was the same way with the others. He never got close to any of them but Nell. He was crazy about Nell. Because Nell stayed with him. I left Chicago. He was very good to Nell." Except for Nell and baseball, there was, as far as I can tell from my mother's stories, no other love or enthusiasm in his life.

This, then, essentially is what I know about the life of Jack Walsh during these years in Chicago. He had got a job repairing the trolleys. He worked in the carbarns, first at Van Buren and Halsted then at Sixty-ninth and Halsted. He repaired streetcars, working outside in the bitter winters and the hot and humid summers. In the winter his hands would freeze, but the foreman would make him keep on working.

He managed to hold his job through the Depression. He worked on streetcars until he went back to Ireland. He left for work at six in the morning. He returned at six in the evening. Sara insists on that twelve-hour span, but the union—the Amalgamated Association of Street, Electric, Railway, and Motor Coach Employees of America, Division 241—had secured the eight-hour day by 1936. Presuming no overtime, that leaves four hours; an hour to work, an hour back, an hour for lunch accounts for three. I wonder about that last hour.

Jack Walsh was a union man—by choice or habit or necessity, I do not know. The union saw him through the Depression. Wages had been cut and hours reduced to spread the work. Men still lost their jobs, and the union solicited funds from those still working to help them. The worst was over by 1936. When Sara arrived, the union had restored the eight-hour day. It secured a four-cent-an-hour wage increase, restoring wages after seven long years to their pre-Depression 1929 levels of seventy-seven to eighty-five cents an hour.

On Sundays when the White Sox were in town, he took the

streetcar to Comiskey Park. Sometimes, once or twice a year, he would join other men from St. Rita's Parish and go to South Bend to watch Notre Dame play football. There is a picture of him and my uncle Pat and a group of men posing behind a bus. It is 1940. They are well dressed and smiling. There is a boy in knickers. Jack Walsh is in the front row. He kneels on one knee between two boys. The camera captures him on this wildly atypical day. Well dressed in a suit, overcoat, and hat, he is relaxed, about to leave the city. In the end the picture tells me nothing.

I ask Pat who the others are. They are men from the parish. Their names have vanished, and even on that fall afternoon so long ago, they rested lightly in Pat's and Jack Walsh's minds. They were casual acquaintances. They shared a bus on the way to a football game.

I can re-create the furniture, the surroundings of Jack Walsh's life far more easily than I can the life itself. I can re-create Halsted Street, where he worked and traveled to the carbarns on Sixty-ninth, much more easily than I can recapture him. During the late 1920s and early 1930s, there were furniture stores at Sixty-first and Halsted; from Sixty-second to Sixty-fifth, there was a mixture of clothing and shoe stores. These were branches of downtown stores: O'Connor and Goldberg, Florsheim, and others. There was a burlesque house, the Empress, near Sixty-third. At Sixty-ninth, where the streetcars intersected and Jack Walsh worked, there was a smaller neighborhood business district and several automobile agencies that sold Fords and Chevrolets.

Jack Walsh lacks the solidity of the things he moves among, of the streetcars he repairs. He is a vast silence. In a family in which everything, in the end, is reduced to stories, he yields few stories. "He was a very quiet man," Sara says, "he had very little to say."

There is no telling what he thought as she handed him her message.

PART III

21

When we lived on South Mozart Street . . .
　　　　　　　—Sara's phrase for opening her Chicago stories

My aunt Nell died at home in Chicago on a gray November day in 1994. She was nearly seventy-nine years old. My mother had flown from California to be with her sister, and when I called her at Nell's house, the number I dialed was the one she had memorized as a sixteen-year-old girl fresh from Ireland. Over the years some letters had been changed to numerals, but for my mother those seven numbers held fast across half a century and more. When she had first learned those numbers, her sister had been a beautiful young woman. And Nell, the gentlest woman that I had ever known, had scorned my mother—her sister—as a greenhorn.

The phone number that followed Nell when she moved is the last tangible link to 6420 South Mozart Street. It remains anchored to a past that now only my mother and my uncle, Nell's husband, Pat O'Hara, share. Except for my mother, the inhabitants of that once dense and crowded house are gone. When my mother went there in 1936, the small two-bedroom bungalow already held seven people. She made eight. For her, Chicago, the South Side, the Depression, and all those early years in America reduced to those eight people at South Mozart Street. Her stories begin with the same phrase, "When we lived on South Mozart Street. . . ."

By 1936 the house had become a fortress of sorts against the Depression and the troubles of rural Ireland; its inhabitants were refugees. Kinship and disaster brought people there. No one stands alone in Irish American families. You are born into a web of relations. By yourself, you are little more than a human dot, insignificant and indistinguishable. Connect all the dots, and there is family. You exist as a point in a set of relations. You may ignore or rage against your relations, the people who define you less by what you do or say or think or accomplish and more by who your parents are and whom you marry. In the end, you are still so-and-so's daughter and niece to so-and-so. When things get bad enough, you follow the lines to safety.

In my grandfather's family in 1936, the lines led to South Mozart Street, and the house belonged to Kitty and Tommy O'Brien. Kitty O'Brien was Sara's aunt, her father's sister. Kitty took in Jack Walsh and his daughters Nell and Sara. Billy and Jackie Ahern lived there, too. They were the sons of Kitty's sister, Lizzie. When Lizzie died, Kitty had taken them in. In 1936 Billy and Jackie were in their early twenties and still there. Saddest of all to those around him was Will Lynch, who had once been Kitty's sister Nora's husband. Nora was the most beautiful of Jack Walsh's sisters, and she had left Will to run off with another Irishman. She had divorced Will, something nearly unheard of in Catholic Chicago, and he had sought refuge with Kitty. A half century later, his name still brings a mixture of ridicule, pity, and fondness.

Sleeping eight people in that two-bedroom bungalow was, Sara says, "tricky." Tommy and Kitty slept in the large bedroom. In the other, smaller bedroom Sara's father and Billy and Jackie Ahern slept on three single beds. Will Lynch slept upstairs in the attic. A crude partition had been built up there and a light bulb rigged to dangle from the ceiling. Nell and Sara slept in the dining room. Every night they would move the large dining room table and its six chairs against the wall and unfold two army cots. Every morning they would fold the cots, stand them in a corner, and move the table and six chairs back to the center of the room.

Sixty years later, Sara still feels those cots with their wood frames and canvas sheeting. She remembers the nightly discomfort, the far too narrow expanse of the canvas. Each night she slept as if America were an army and she a draftee.

But then Sara remembers everything about that house, which across this distance seems as alive as the people who lived in it. The bathroom had a tub, sink, and toilet and enough room to stand up. A light bulb hung from the ceiling. Tommy and Kitty had a double bed in their room as well as a dresser and chair. They had their own very small closet. The other bedroom had only its three single beds. The dining room she knew by its heft and feel, every night moving the table and chairs. The basement had a still, but no one used it anymore, for it was 1936 and Prohibition had ended.

For my mother, South Mozart Street retains something of the wonder it held for a sixteen-year-old-girl from a small farm in County Kerry. But for her children, looking back, it contains a different kind of wonder. For us, the disorder of our own lives, which for years caused my mother such grief and brought such disapproval, pales before this house with its drinking, disease, and death, as well as its laughter and fierce pride. I am still surprised that my mother came from such a place. I am proud that she did.

22

It was terrible getting used to it.
                    —Sara, on her first months in Chicago

Sara found herself among strangers and those who might as well have been strangers. South Mozart Street was full of blood strangers: her father, sister, uncles, aunts, and cousins. They were all family; they were all Irish; they had all become Yanks. They would, she presumed, show her how it was done.

But from the first day—from the glances, the silences, the fleeting moments of exasperation at her awkwardness and ignorance—she had no sense that any of them but Will Lynch welcomed her. Her father, this quiet, reserved man, had sent for her, but he had received her like a person receives an expected parcel: pleased she had arrived safely, he turned to other things.

Her own sister Nell was ashamed of her. To Nell, five years in the country, her sister was a greenhorn. She was an unanticipated burden who suddenly appeared in Chicago to embarrass her with a Kerry brogue, the scent of an Irish farm, and an experience of the world that made flush toilets, elevators, streetcars, and automobiles exotic.

Sara was shy and ignorant, but she was not stupid or oblivious. She saw Nell's shame and recognized herself as the cause. From the first, Nell let Sara know the burden of kinship.

"It was terrible getting used to it," Sara remembers. "Nell

had been here for years, not that many years, but enough to be Americanized. And she was very critical of me. She didn't like the way I put on my shoes. She didn't like the way I combed my hair. And she didn't like the way I talked—my brogue was too thick. And she didn't want to take me to the Irish dances with her. Because she was very pretty, she was a beautiful girl, she had a lot of boyfriends . . . and I was young, younger than she was."

In those first days in Chicago, Sara and Nell took positions, who looked up and who looked down, that they would maintain for years. As Sara became beautiful, others forgot the contrast between the broad-faced sixteen-year-old peasant girl and her attractive twenty-one-year-old sister, who looked and dressed like an American girl. But Sara remembers. There are still touches of awe and tinges of envy when Sara talks of her older sister. Nell was, in fact, a beauty queen. She was a queen at one of the Irish festivals in 1935 or 1936 and was supposedly, although I can find no record of it, a runner-up in a citywide contest the year Sara came.

Knowing the notes and slips and changes in my mother's voice, seeing the pictures before me, I can, I think, recapture part of those moments, those early days. But it is a dangerous assumption. I can't be sure.

The picture of my mother is from her green card—the immigrant's identification card issued in Dublin and validated in New York on November 18, 1936, when she got off the ship. She stares at the camera, her mouth is neither a smile nor a frown, but she is attempting some expression because the lips are parted. Her mouth is open; it looks like a gash in her face. Her hair is short, greasy, and dirty from the voyage, and it lies combed back, really slicked back, on her head. Her forehead is broad, her face wide, her skin rough. She looks plain, as the Irish say. No one would give her a second look. I recognize her only in the eyes. The stare is neither glassy nor dull, nor is it conspicuous. It is seeing things. It is taking in everything. It is a look of disguised alertness. We knew that look as children. We needed to mask our movements, hide our intentions. We usually failed with her, but it helped us among the less discerning. And, imitating her, we tried to learn that look ourselves.

Nell is slender, her skin smooth. Her light-red hair is also short, but it is curled and frames her face. She smiles, her teeth are white, her eyes are large. She is made up; the lipstick and eye shadow are there, but they are understated. She looks as if she had stepped out of a magazine advertisement. She has the kind of beauty Americans mobilize to sell things. There is nothing haughty about her; she is wholesome; her beauty fills the room and touches all around her.

Sara tried in those first weeks to make sense of America. That everyone at 6420 South Mozart Street talked about the Chicago White Sox led her to believe that people in Chicago all wore white socks. When she asked her father, he laughed and everyone in the house joined in. When Sara remembers laughter at South Mozart Street, it always seems to be at her expense. During that first year, Nell and Kitty would often point at Sara and laugh. Sara longed for Ireland, her mother, and green fields.

During that first year Nell sought to avoid Sara; Sara sought to follow Nell. When they walked to Mass, Nell would walk ahead and then sit in a pew away from Sara. If Nell stopped to chat with friends, she made Sara keep her distance. Nell's rejection could only spur Sara to change, but her only example of successful change was Nell herself. And so she imitated Nell.

Nell's beauty was hardly uncultivated. She worked at it; she shopped with a dedication that amazed Sara, whose only shopping experiences were in the stores of Ballylongford and Listowel. Nell spent hours matching colors, searching for a purse to go with a pair of shoes. Everything had to be perfect. Sara started timing the trips. They took hours.

Nell's cultivation of beauty provided Sara with an example of how to be accepted in America. Sara learned to dress by following Nell and then, to Nell's outrage, borrowing and wearing the clothes that Nell bought.

Nell, who only wanted to be rid of her sister, found herself drafted as Sara's reluctant guide. In effect, Sara sought to disguise herself as Nell and thus as an American girl. Nell's embarrassment marked the differences between Ireland and America. When Nell was embarrassed, Sara changed herself accordingly. When she had changed enough, she and Nell reached an accommodation. They grew close.

Forming bonds was harder with the others. Immigration meant many things, but it didn't mean shedding the past. The past shadowed Sara's life as thoroughly in Chicago as it had in Ireland. The past could divide as easily as unite.

A common Irish past had brought her into this house, but parts of that past remained publicly unspoken. Those parts divided her from Kitty. The embodiment of that past was Kitty's son, Tim. On South Mozart Street no one publicly spoke of Tim or the past that had produced him.

Irish Chicago was in that way different from Ireland. Life in Bally was lived as annotated text. Things happened; they were described and commented on. Ballylongford was a small village, and gossip ran like a stream through its streets. In a place so poor, there was often nothing to share but talk.

Chicago was different. For all its crowding, South Mozart Street held its secrets. There was gossip, but it was a trickle and not a stream. In Ballylongford, Tim Walsh's origins were common knowledge; in Chicago, he was the secret of South Mozart Street.

It was Tim's birth that had propelled Aunt Kitty to America. There was no staying in Ireland after Kitty had become pregnant. She had no husband when Tim was born. His father, Tim Reidy, remained the creamery manager and neither acknowledged nor supported his son. Kitty Walsh left her baby with her brother Jack and sailed to America.

Kitty never asked Sara—freshly arrived from sixteen years of growing up in the same house as her son—about Tim. It led Nell and Sara to whisper and talk. They wondered if Kitty's husband, Tommy O'Brien, knew that Tim existed. They never found out. Sara wonders still.

Looking back now, it is hard not to wonder if Tim's absence made South Mozart Street what it was; if Billy and Jackie Ahern, the sons of a dead sister, came because Kitty needed to fill that absence; if Jack Walsh, Nell, and Sara crowded that house to bursting because Kitty, for all her resentment of them, owed Jack Walsh deeply for raising her son and keeping his silence. It is hard not to wonder if even Will Lynch, deserted by a Walsh woman, touched Kitty because she (a Walsh woman, herself abandoned) had been forced to desert her son. It is hard not to wonder.

Whatever drove her to offer shelter, Aunt Kitty became, for better or worse, the anchor of South Mozart Street. There had once been less need of the shelter she offered. She once had six sisters and two brothers in the States, all on the South and West Sides of Chicago. Teresa Holly says that in Chicago Aunt Kitty and her sisters would for a long time meet every Sunday when the weather was fair for picnics, but those were better times. Now three sisters—Lizzie, Nora, and Mary—had died; Nora had died after running off and leaving Will Lynch behind. Another sister, Bea, had lost a husband. One brother, Jack Walsh, had got himself detained at the border trying to enter the United States. When they got him out of Canada, he sporadically sent for children from Ireland who hardly knew him, let alone Kitty. She offered a haven from each disaster; she offered a haven to each arrival.

Death had come, sisters had died, but the family had not dissolved. The picnics were now just memories, but the family still came together at holidays. Sara arrived in November, and her first American holiday was Thanksgiving. She met more Walsh relatives than she had ever seen; she met her father's brother and surviving sisters and their families. Will Lynch roasted the turkey, but her memory of the holiday has less to do with turkey than with a stream of burly men entering the house and piling coats and guns on Aunt Kitty's bed. Most of the sisters had married policemen. And when the uncles came for Thanksgiving, they took off their coats and their guns and their billy clubs.

She remembers going into Kitty's bedroom and seeing the bed covered with billy clubs and guns.

That was Sara's impression of Chicago on Thanksgiving: guns and pumpkin pie. She had never tasted pumpkin pie. She thought it was the most awful stuff she had ever eaten in her life. "It was terrible," she says, "just terrible."

At Thanksgiving, with Kitty's brothers, sisters, nephews, nieces, and in-laws around the table, South Mozart Street was joyfully crowded, but when they left the house remained crowded. The density of the mass changed, and there was little celebration. Sara sensed that Aunt Kitty would have liked to cut loose all the relatives who made the bungalow as crowded as an Irish cottage. All the relations, that is, except Billy Ahern. He was to her what Nell was to Jack Walsh. But Kitty felt compelled to take them all in because they were family. She was obligated, and where else could they go?

Kitty's husband, Tommy, was no help. His drinking had cost him his job on the Chicago El the year Sara arrived, and now he devoted himself to drinking full time. He would hide the bottle from Kitty (and from Will Lynch, who had eyes of his own for it). With the foolish cunning of drunks, Tommy liked to hide it in the water tank of the toilet. It was typical of him in his drink to give people occasion to look at things they had no reason to look at and find things they weren't looking for. When the toilet wouldn't flush, Sara examined the tank and found Tommy's bottle jamming the works.

But Tommy was an amiable enough drunk, good-natured with the quick Irish wit. "He was easygoing," Sara says. "He had to put up with a house full of his wife's family, so he must have been easygoing."

Kitty offered shelter, but South Mozart Street drifted, for Kitty herself was wasting away. Tommy drank; Kitty took to her bed. Kitty was forever sick. She remained ill through the week, but she recovered some on Saturdays. On Saturday morning Tommy would take her grocery shopping to Markettown on Sixty-fourth and Kedzie in their old Chevrolet. And on Saturday night at nine o'clock, her friends would come over to play poker. They would play until the early hours of the morning. They played at the dining room table, which meant that Sara and Nell could not sleep until the game ended.

They would drink as they played, and by midnight, with enough drink in her, Kitty would start to sing. She had a good voice, and she always sang the same song: "Bury Me Not on the Lone Prairie." Every Saturday night at midnight on the South Side of Chicago in that Irish house, Kitty would sing: "Bury me not on the lone prairie where the coyotes howl and the wind blows free." In the summer, when the windows were open, her voice floated over the neighborhood. What Kitty knew about prairies and coyotes remained a mystery to the end, but then the song was really about dying, and Kitty did know something about that.

On Sunday, after Mass, Kitty took sick again. The housework fell to Will Lynch, Sara, and Nell. The cooking all went to Will Lynch because he really did cook pretty well for a drunk. Irish standards at the table were, in any case, forgiving.

During the week Dr. Carney would come, for he came every week. As time went on, Sara realized that in the midst of all this bed rest and poker and coyotes howling on the lone prairie Kitty really had become sick. Sara watched from the other room as Dr. Carney tapped her lungs. He drew enough green fluid to fill a glass jar.

Sara watched closely. She came home to the house on South Mozart Street, she watched, and she drew her own conclusions. It is a trait, I think, that comes from her childhood. She had to watch closely when so little could be directly questioned. She could hope to catch the whispers of adults, but she could not question them directly. Questions had their own gravity in Kerry and in Chicago. They could only move downward from the older to the younger, from the powerful to the subordinate. Questions could not rise.

As she had in Ireland, Sara moved among the shadows of events that had taken place long ago. The past is more than memory; fleeing it, forgetting it, or hiding it does not eliminate it. Kitty could leave Tim, maybe she could even forget Tim, but then her brother and nieces appeared, wearing the obligations that sprang from Tim like a bright glowing badge only she could see. And what could she do? Tommy O'Brien, who may have known nothing of that past and not cared to know, lived in its shadow just the same. And so did Sara.

Will Lynch was haunted by a past that also came to shadow Sara's first year in America. Will Lynch had been a carpenter. He still had his tools. My uncle Pat O'Hara has them now. Will Lynch was a carpenter who kept his tools but lost his wife.

By 1936 Will Lynch was only a drunk. He had a bed in an attic with a bare light bulb dangling over it in his sister-in-law's house. He drank. He hid his bottle under the bed. He and Tommy, at home all day when not in the taverns, drank up their pensions with Kitty abed in the other room. Sara cannot remember ever seeing either of them sober. Unlike Tommy, Will Lynch was not always an amiable drunk. He was sometimes vulgar, my mother says.

But most of the time, Will was the kindest man in the house. He was a big man, almost clumsy, but warmhearted. The loss of Nora always seemed to be with him, but it is never clear if he missed her or just felt the humiliation of losing her to another man. He would sit with his elbows on the kitchen table and bury his face in his hands, completely oblivious to what was going on around him.

Will spent most of his time in the kitchen. He learned to cook, which among the Irish usually means he learned to make soda bread and boil potatoes. Sara remembers him in the kitchen, a large man grown small in everyone's eyes, sad and drunk and alone with his bread and his memories.

Nora was dead by 1936, but everyone says my mother came to look like her. Will would wait for Sara in the kitchen that first year, when she went to Marinello Beauty School. He would give her tea and soup or potatoes and cabbage when she returned. If he hadn't saved food for her, there would have been nothing for her to eat. He would give her the news of the day. Maybe he saw Nora in her. Maybe he was being kind in ways he had never been to his wife. Maybe Sara was the only one in the house who had not witnessed his humiliation firsthand, and that was reason enough.

Will and Nell, more than the others in that house, provided Sara with the clues she needed to make her way in America.

23

They were definitely Americans, and I was the greenhorn. They were all American girls.   —Sara

South Mozart Street gave Sara a sense of her own oddity and difference, but she had no idea of how little she belonged, how little she understood about America, until her father took her to the Marinello Beauty School. Marinello's gave her a sense of her task. She knew how totally she must reinvent herself to live in the United States.

Two weeks after his daughter's arrival, Jack Walsh took her to register at Marinello Beauty School across from Marshall Field on State Street in the Loop. On the way, he instructed her about the streetcars. She was to take the streetcar to Sixty-third and Western, get off, cross the street kitty-corner, and then take the State Street car. She was frightened for her first month on the cars, but gradually the ride became just a simple commute. She learned a lot on the streetcars from the South Side listening to how men and women talked and seeing how they acted.

At Marinello's, Sara was initially less of a student than a challenge. She served as the "before" shot for the kind of ultimate makeover now featured in glamour magazines. Reduced in her own eyes to an ignorant, dumb, painfully shy, and frightened girl, she could only hope for a transformation. She became an object of ridicule at Marinello's, and she became a guinea pig.

Her first month there was a form of torture. The class took turns rolling her straight hair into curls. They also practiced with the hot marcel iron; they were clumsy and careless and left her neck and ears covered with burns. She was, Sara now says, becoming acquainted with the process of making oneself glamorous.

The students, these American girls, as she calls them still, succeeded in making her look like a poodle. They gave her a permanent, a very kinky one. But looking like a poodle was okay, she thought, for all the others looked like poodles, too.

But looking the same was not the equivalent of being the same. "I remember," she says, "all these people, and they were all so different from me. I would say things, and they would laugh at me. I think they were laughing at me not with me. And I had to learn a lot. I didn't dress as well as they did. I didn't have makeup like they had. And they were definitely Americans, and I was the greenhorn. They were all American girls."

Pushed, humiliated, and taunted at both South Mozart Street and Marinello Beauty School, Sara patiently remade herself: shopping with Nell, borrowing her clothes, learning, as she tried to make other women more beautiful, to make herself more beautiful. She changed to escape the daily doses of humiliation and ridicule. She began to look different, more American. She began to speak differently, modifying her speech, losing the brogue. And when gradual change was not enough, she removed the most common causes of her humiliation.

Her name—Sara—was spelled with an *h* in Ireland: Sarah. I never knew this. I have always known it to end in an *a* and have presumed it always ended in an *a*. My brother Stephen noticed the *h* on her old green card. He asked why she had changed the spelling. In Ireland, she explained, the *h* is pronounced *hayche* not *aitch*, as in the States. Every time my mother had to spell her name, she slipped into the Irish pronunciation of the *h*. She did not know the English pronunciation. They laughed at her every time she said it. They demanded she say it for others. They taunted her with her own name. And so she amputated the *h*. She began spelling her name Sara, without the *h*, and she does so to this day. The *h* is a small thing, but it marked a direction, a trajectory into America and away from Ireland. From necessity, she left little parts of herself behind as she moved forward.

And while all this went on, the only small solace Sara remembers was in food, in treats and sweets. The foods were American. "I remember," she says, "there was a Walgreen drugstore across the street. And when I got out of school, if I had a dollar, I would go across and get a hot fudge sundae. It was the best thing I ever tasted. And I remember that I even advanced. There was a DuMetz coffee shop downstairs, and I used to go in and get pecan pie, which I loved, and a cup of tea with it."

When the course was done, Sara took the state board exam for hairdressers and beauticians. At Marinello's, in preparation for this exam, they had studied the scalp with its blood vessels and nerves and what made hair grow. She was a nervous wreck, but she passed the test. It was her first American success. She is proud of it still.

She had a license to do hair and skin work in the state of Illinois. She got a job as a hairdresser. An Irish girl, who less than a year before had found her straight, auburn hair a source of ridicule, now styled the hair of others. She hated it.

She quit when she found a job, on State Street in the Loop, doing facials and selling cosmetics. Facials were better. No one expected instant transformations. She was good at the work, she remembers. The women were much easier to please. They would leave her dimes as tips.

A man and his wife owned the business. The man was supposed to be a chemist, but Sara came to have her doubts. He manufactured his own facial creams. Sara would give the women facials and sell them cream. She worked in the same building where she had gone to school. She still didn't like the work, but she did it.

Life found new patterns. In Ireland as a child she had been the only girl who had to take the milk to the creamery. She had hated the work, but she had done it. She had gone to school, which she hated, but she had gone. She had worked for the Heaphys and the O'Sullivans, tedious and menial jobs. She had hated those jobs, but she had done them. She didn't like being a beautician, but what possible indication did she have that she should find satisfaction in the work that allowed her to live? She hated it, but she did it, and she turned the checks over to her father. Whatever its flaws, being a beautician was better than working for Lil Heaphy.

In self-defense and from necessity rather than from desire, Sara learned the patterns of working-class and lower-middle-class Irish American life on Chicago's South Side. She still longed for Ireland, but she became accustomed to the rhythms of her new life.

24

*By 1930, St. Rita of Cascia parish numbered more than 6,000 persons,
with 1,400 children enrolled in the school.*
                        —Harry Koenig, *A History of the Parishes of Chicago*

There are no histories of Chicago in which 6420 South
Mozart Street, or even places like it, matters very
much. There are none that even recognize South Mozart Street existed, although a few describe places like it. But
for Sara, Chicago always existed in relation to South Mozart
Street. And all of America existed in relation to Chicago. South
Mozart Street, where she started and ended her day, was the
center of America.

Fittingly enough for an American house, 6420 South Mozart
Street was relatively new and surrounded by houses just like
it. The city had issued a building permit for the house on
South Mozart Street on July 8, 1915. Its original owner was D.
D. Hepburn. Its architect was listed as E. N. Braucher. Everyone who lived in the house except Sara was older than the
house itself. The house in Ahanagran, as much as it resembled
other Irish cottages, had come into existence at its own moment and in its own place. It was handmade and solitary, even
as it was of a kind. But 6420 South Mozart Street was part of
a vast fleet of houses, all created at once and all virtually iden-
tical.

South Mozart Street was in the heart of Chicago's bungalow

belt. Just before World War I, developers began to reach out to the undeveloped prairies. By the 1920s a building boom was under way. Nearly twenty thousand bungalows were built in the far margins of Chicago. The long, narrow houses faced the streets like docked ships.

The house on South Mozart Street was part of the first wedge of construction south of Sixty-third. In the mid-1920s the maps still showed largely undeveloped land south of Marquette Park, which, in turn, was just blocks from 6420 South Mozart. Well into the 1930s, a short walk along South Mozart Street led to Marquette Park, a vast open space, no longer open prairie but not quite an empty city lot.

Tommy O'Brien called his house on South Mozart Street, with its luxuriant growth of his wife Kitty's relatives, the Kerry Patch. The building was far different from any cottage in Kerry, but to listen to my mother, South Mozart Street drifted in a sea of Irish. Everyone, she says, was Irish.

I listen to my mother. She has the authority of experience. Within the house at 6420 South Mozart, I have no footing, no way to challenge her memories unless they contradict one another or clash with what I independently know. Mostly, I have a deep curiosity. I am swayed by her stories. I want to hear more. When her memories leave the house on South Mozart Street, when she ventures into the sea of Irish, I grow skeptical.

Reconstructing my mother's neighborhood, I find that the population around her was tinted only the palest of green. The house on South Mozart Street was part of census tract 842, a narrow strip of land only a few blocks wide that ran between Western and Kedzie just south of Sixty-third. The 1934 *Community Fact Book* put the population at 7,089 people, with a slight majority either foreign born (943) or having at least one foreign-born parent (2,751). Census tract 842 was, in turn, part of Chicago Lawn. There were about 47,000 people in Chicago Lawn in 1930. More than 10,000 were foreign born; about 3,000 of those were Irish born. There were more Germans than Irish and nearly as many Lithuanians as Irish in Chicago Lawn. This was not a place where everyone was Irish.

Yet my mother knows what she experienced. She deals in lived places, in remembered places, not in the more complete yet anonymous space of the census takers. She doesn't care about what passed her by; she cares about what stuck with her. The discrepancies between Sara's memory and the numbers in the census are not so much a problem as a solution. The question to ask is what happened to those Germans and Lithuanians to make them fade and disappear in Sara's memories. They most certainly were there. They stood beside her in the bakeries and stores. They were part of the crowds on the street and streetcars. They were the overheard voices in foreign tongues. They even lived next door, she remembers, but they were not the people that Sara talked to, cared about, or met in any private places. They were only possibilities and not likely ones at that. They leave only faint traces. They are the names on bakeries on Sixty-third Street: Jilek's Bakery, Koelbl's Bakery, Kiltz's Bakery, and Hardtke's Bakery. Otherwise, Sara has erased them from the neighborhood.

But it is not only my mother's accounts that provoke my skepticism. I am equally skeptical of what I know of Chicago Lawn itself. I begin to doubt such a place ever existed in the 1920s, when Lewis Wirth and Ernest W. Burgess, sociologists at the University of Chicago, and their students named and numbered every neighborhood in the city, or in the 1930s, when my mother lived there. Where self-identified neighborhoods did not exist, Wirth and Burgess made them up and gave them names. They named the area around Marquette Park Chicago Lawn. It is community area number 66. But nobody my mother knew, then or now, called it Chicago Lawn. My mother does not recall even hearing the name Chicago Lawn. People now call the area Marquette Park; but in the 1930s, if anyone had asked where she was from, she would have given her parish name: St. Rita's.

Chicago Lawn, so fully and carefully enumerated in the Chi-

cago fact books, appears to be real, but it is a creation of aca-
demics and bureaucrats. They measured an essentially arbitrary
area, and in bequeathing historians their measurements and sta-
tistics they created the illusion of an actual place. If historians
are not careful, such places that never existed can take on historical lives of their own. I can go back and get very precise
measurements of ethnicity, housing, race, and income for Chicago Lawn, even though, as far as the lived experiences of its
residents went, there was no Chicago Lawn.

In trying to understand South Mozart Street, the platform
from which Sara Walsh launched her American life, I have a
bifurcated vision, which I must try to resolve into a single field
of view. As much as I can, I must see what she saw as she saw
it. As much as I can, I must try to imagine what she chose not
to see or what was hidden from her. But to get at what was
hidden, I have only real numbers about an invented place that
contained the actual spaces in which she lived and moved. I have
only my own reconstructions of other meanings of South Mozart
Street.

When Sara Walsh came to Chicago, South Mozart Street was
simply the place where her aunt and uncle lived, where her father and sister lived. She had no other American places, no
other American conditions to compare it to. But to Tommy
and Kitty O'Brien and their neighbors, South Mozart Street
represented achievement, the most valued and yet the most
tenuous achievement of their lives. They not only lived on
South Mozart Street, they owned houses there. South Mozart
Street was a place where immigrants and the children of immigrants displayed their hard-won respectability. It was an area of
stable, lower-middle-class, and upper-working-class families.
Compared to other parts of Chicago, the rent charged for
houses in the neighborhood of South Mozart Street was above
average, from $37 to $44 a month. These were not poor people, but the Depression had hurt them badly. For those who
owned their homes, houses lost nearly 40 percent of their
value between 1930 and 1934, falling on average from $9,100

to $5,600. Although the majority of the houses on Sara's block were rented in the 1930s, residents still struggled to own them. In cities like Chicago (as the historians came to realize), owning your own home was not so much the American dream as the Catholic immigrant's dream.

The struggle of families to root, to gain some security and predictability, went on all around Sara, but she, as a teenage girl, could not recognize it. There swirled around South Mozart Street a population that was much more transitory than anything she had ever known. In 1934 roughly a quarter of the people living on the blocks around South Mozart Street had been in the area less than a year. These families sought homes, and, if they managed to acquire property, they were likely to stay. On Sara's block and in census tract 842 as a whole, just under half managed to own their homes. But on the blocks immediately around her, the majority of residents were homeowners. Most of the people on the blocks south of Sixty-third Street and west of California Avenue had lived there for ten to twenty years by 1940.

By American standards this was a rooted place. But Sara came from North Kerry where, although families shed children like trees shed leaves, the families stayed rooted in place for generations. Ten or twenty years was nothing. She was born in a house where her father was born and her grandmother was born before him. In Chicago she lived in a house barely older than she was.

All of this I can puzzle out from the census and fact books, but it is hard to recover more. Ernest W. Burgess and his sociology students at the University of Chicago were busy cataloguing the city in the 1920s and 1930s. They made Chicago probably the most studied large city in America. Without fully realizing what they did, however, they became urban pathologists. They sought to cure the body politic, and so they sought disease, or what they regarded as disease. They looked for delinquency and liquor and dance halls. Reading their material now—from published monographs to old student papers on delicate onionskin—is like watching doctors identify tumors and recommend their excision.

Chicago Lawn did not meet their standards of pathology. Once sociologists had created this area, marked its boundaries, and measured its social parameters, they ignored Chicago Lawn and the people who lived there. The residents were immigrants and children of immigrants, but they were not exotic or disorderly or resentful enough to excite much sociological interest. Sociologists weren't concerned with what they called Chicago Lawn. They were on their way to the Back-of-the-Yards, or the Black Belt.

South Mozart Street seemed exotic only to my mother and the thousands like her who had begun their lives in other places, yet at the same time South Mozart Street was a deeply and astonishingly familiar place. The names alone would make the South Side familiar. The names alone would punctuate and underline the connections between disparate places, for the people Sara knew in Chicago bore the same names as the people she had known in Kerry. The names are haunting. It was as if County Kerry had scattered itself across Chicago, and in a way it had. Just after the potato-famine decade, in 1852, when Chicago was young, the British took a census of the Parish of Aghavallen in the Barony of Iraghticonner, in which lay the townland of Ahanagran and its neighbors. Many of the names they recorded were of people whose relations were already dead or gone. The names belonged to people living in the aftermath of a horror. In fleeing that horror and the problems that followed, they would transfer their names to Chicago.

The people die; the names live on. The people Sara knew in Chicago and Ireland shared these names. Mulvihills had been her godparents, and it was a Mulvihill who married Aunt Bea in Chicago. The 1852 Irish census has a Michael Lynch, Patrick Lynch, and Timothy Lynch, whose lives in those post-famine years were probably sorrier than Will Lynch's life with his regrets and his drink on South Mozart Street. There is an Edmund Walsh in the census. He has a house and garden, and his worth mounts all the way to £1. In Ballyline West there is a Daniel Ahern next to yet another

Mulvihill, poor as cottars, and a John Walsh, who rented more than a hundred acres. These people may be blood ancestors of the people Sara knew in Chicago. They might just share names. But the names are the thing.

These are still the names in Ballylongford, and they are the names in Chicago. These were the names of neighbors and in-laws, of friends and enemies. The Irish crofters became cops, the sons of tenant farmers worked the trolleys, but still the same names recur in the stories. Surrounded now with Lithuanian names and German names and Italian names and American names and names from other parts of Ireland, these Kerry names create the web of family and friendship and relation that Sara traveled along.

Sara was Irish. Virtually everyone she knew was Irish or had parents born in Ireland. But this Irishness, seemingly the most obvious thing about them and the key to their lives together, was actually quite puzzling. The life they lived in America was not remotely close to an Irish life. The Irish in Ireland knew this and always referred to them as Yanks. They lived American lives, but they still distinguished themselves from other Americans by being Irish.

Everyone was Irish, Sara says, except, she remembers, there were Italians. "The Italians were different from us," she tells me. When I ask how they were different, my mother says: "They celebrated Thanksgiving differently."

Sara had never seen a Thanksgiving, or, for that matter, an Italian, until 1936. America gave her both, and no wonder she associated them. And it makes perfect American sense to mark the difference between Irish and Italians in how they celebrated American holidays. In America people do the same things but differently. Sara became Irish American by recognizing herself as different both from Italians and from the girls in the Loop she referred to simply as American girls.

I have no idea what an Irish Thanksgiving is except that the Irish grasped immediately and instinctively that the holiday must include root vegetables. I never saw a rutabaga or parsnip in my entire childhood except at Thanksgiving. These vegetables came to the table, I guess, less in commemoration of the Pilgrims' arrival in America than in commemoration of my mother's arrival in America. She chose to serve the foods she saw that first November and every November thereafter. There they were each Thanksgiving of my childhood, mashed in a bowl and, after a token, almost sacramental serving, ignored by everyone except my brother David, whose childhood tastes ranged toward bananas dipped in mustard. An Italian Thanksgiving, I guess, was marked by a dearth of rutabagas.

In Ireland, Sara had assumed her Irishness. She had resisted what seemed a contrived and forced nationalism: the Irish language and the learning of the schools. These seemed alien to the Ireland she knew: Ahanagran and Ballylongford. But in Chicago, Irishness was cultivated, even as its very cultivation marked the cultivators as more and more American. This was, and is, the great paradox of American ethnicity. Celebrating where you come from is but another way of underlining who you are now: an American, a Yank.

The creation of Ireland, both figuratively and literally, has long been an Irish American project. Irish nationalism has played well in America. It offered, for one thing, a chance to right the injustice of the immigrants' departure by punishing Britain, the ancient enemy, for the pain the immigrants had personally felt. In the promise of a return to a free Ireland, it paradoxically offered a real American identity. Irish emigrants joined as Americans to free Ireland. Irish Americans organized themselves into clubs that quickly came to serve American purposes and proclaimed American ideals and values. The more they emphasized their Irishness, the more American they became. Ethnicity has always been the preferred route to Americanism.

By the 1930s, of course, Ireland, except for Ulster, was free, and the Irish American clubs and organizations in Chicago had turned their attention to preserving Irish traditions. This was usually a summertime activity. It involved a lot of picnics. The Gaelic Feis Association organized the Feis of Tara, held late every July at Shrewbridge Field at Seventy-fourth and Aberdeen. It featured Irish music, songs, and dances. In mid-August there was Irish Day, begun in the mid-1930s and held annually during my mother's years in Chicago. August 15 was an Irish religious holiday, Lady's Day—the Feast of the Blessed Mother—that in 1930s Chicago became an ethnic festival in Riverview Park. There was an Irish queen, a contest for the healthiest baby, music, and dancing. There were Irish sporting events pitting South Side Irish against North Side Irish. And in 1937 there was a tug-of-war between an Irish team and a German team. In 1938 the organizers expected thirty thousand people to attend.

The girls who became Irish queens were girls like Nell who had become American beauties. Physically, symbolically, Irishness found its expression in those who could be proudly offered as examples of American success.

This amalgam of created traditions and everyday American events, of an Irish past and an American present, was typical. The Ancient Order of Hibernians, who inducted their new members at the monthly St. Rita's Knights of Columbus meeting, held their annual picnic on August 1. They mixed a baseball game with Irish step dancing and American dancing with four-handed reels.

The whole point of Irish Day, the Gaelic Feis, and the Ancient Order of Hibernians was not that their members were Irish but that they were a certain kind of American, an Irish American. Jack Walsh, who deep in his heart remained convinced that he was but a sojourner who had left the country with the intention of returning, never became a member of the Ancient Order of Hibernians and never roused himself to see Irish sporting events.

Sara's American uncles and aunts could be as sentimentally Irish as anyone in Chicago when the occasion demanded, but, unlike her father, they owned no Irish farms and did not steer by Ireland. They knew that the real Irish American traditions now lay in the Catholic Church and the Democratic Party. They capitalized on their Irish Americanness by specializing in American organizations where Irishness was established currency: the police, the Democratic Party, and the courts.

Irish American politicians had to be dutiful in their sentimental allegiance to Ireland, but such sentiment went as much toward American as Irish purposes. Irish Americans were generous in their aid to Ireland; they had given millions to the cause of independence. But in doing so, it would have been remarkable if they had not quarreled with the Irish they aided. Eamon De Valera, hero of the Easter Rising and later president of the Irish Republic, was born in Brooklyn and raised in Limerick. He tried to steer American money to Irish purposes, but he confronted men and women with intentions different from his own. His American supporters were often Irish born, but they raised their children in America and saw themselves living American lives. These Irish Americans supported the rebels, but they tied a free Ireland to their own standing in America. They wanted to be influential Americans whose concerns the American government heeded. Even at the height of the revolution, in 1919–1920, De Valera quarreled bitterly with the American leaders of Friends of Irish Freedom, which helped bankroll the rebellion, over control of the funds gathered to free Ireland.

Irish American politics neatly inverted the Irish politics my mother knew as a child in revolutionary Ireland. Her American uncles, themselves policemen, had given money so that policemen in Ireland might be ambushed and shot. Irish American politics were about securing a place in an established order, but her relatives gave money to men and women interested in overthrowing an established order. Irish American politics were a serious business, but people did not die for them. In Sara's Ireland people did die for their politics.

Sara did not at first understand the politics that engrossed her uncles and aunts; the Church was more familiar. Every Sunday she and Nell would sleep late and go to the last Mass at St. Rita of Cascia. St. Rita of Cascia was the mother parish of the Southwest Side. It had begun as an Augustinian mission before the bungalows had lined the streets, before the streets had even existed. When the Augustinian fathers founded the mission, there had been only seven Catholic families in the area. The movement of families out of the stinking area that housed pack- inghouse and stockyard workers—the neighborhood called Back- of-the-Yards—changed all that. St. Rita's grew rapidly; it yielded new parishes.

The parishes St. Rita's spawned grew up around it. Some were territorial, like St. Justin Martyr and St. Adrian, which took in areas once served by St. Rita's. Some were so-called national parishes composed of a single ethnic group. By 1927 the Lith- uanians had their own parish, the Nativity of the Blessed Virgin Mary, at Sixty-ninth and Washtenaw. Here the sermons were preached in Lithuanian. More than half the Catholics in the city were still in national parishes in 1936, when Sara came to the city.

Growth on the Southwest Side was so great that St. Rita's continued to expand even as these new parishes hived off from it. In the 1930s St. Rita's had six thousand parishioners, mostly Italian, German, Irish, and native-born American. The parish had a large church where Sixty-third intersected Fairfield. It had its own school run by the Sisters of St. Dominic.

Irish-born and Irish American clergy might dominate the hi- erarchy, but this was an American Catholic church. It was organ- ized, efficient, expanding. St. Rita's provided services for its members. The parish owned valuable real estate; it built the most striking buildings in the neighborhood. The Augustinians broke ground on a college, monastery, and chapel in 1905. The Augustinians had to temper some of their ambitions—the col- lege would become St. Rita's High School—but the parish con- tinued to grow. The church went up in 1916, along with a grammar school. The parish quickly outgrew both. There was a new church in 1923. A convent followed in 1926, a new school in 1927. The old school became a gymnasium. All this masonry and mortar proclaimed the American respectability its parishion- ers valued. Just before Sara arrived, Father James Green, the church's pastor since its founding, died. His death was worthy of front-page notice in *The Southwest News*. Mayor Edward J. Kelly and "friends from every walk of life" came to his funeral.

Father Patrick Kehoe succeeded him. The Church with its Irish priests and city hall with its Irish politicians were the anchors of Irish American life, even as, in the 1930s, Irish Americans became a smaller and smaller percentage of both Catholics and voters in Chicago.

Although the parish leadership was Irish, St. Rita herself was not. Cascia was in Italy, and St. Rita brought to Chicago the other face of this American church: the mystical and magical part. St. Rita performed miracles. She performed them every year Sara lived in Chicago. There had been, of course, miracles at the Irish holy wells, but the saints there were of the place itself. In America even the saints were immigrants.

St. Rita of Cascia was dead, of course. She had died in the fifteenth century, but she had quite literally come to Chicago. This was the Catholic Church of relics: of bones and other body parts. The Augustinian priests not only named the parish for her, they put one of her bones in a gold reliquary they displayed on her feast day.

The Southwest News would sometimes print the life of St. Rita. The newspaper printed it in April 1937, the first spring Sara spent in the city, in honor of the novena to St. Rita, which began May 13 and closed with the distribution of blessed roses on her feast day, May 22. The story of St. Rita, I presume, was taken from *The Lives of the Saints. The Southwest News* account has a *Lives of the Saints* ring to it: "St. Rita was born in Italy in the year 1381 in the province of Umbria in the town of Rocca Porena of a holy aged couple."

St. Rita lived a hard life. At the age of twelve Rita sought her "mystic espousement" by joining a religious order and dedicating her life to the service of God. But her parents commanded her to marry Paolo Ferdinando "a man of morose habits and sullen disposition."

This was not a good marriage, but St. Rita bore it. "For eighteen years like a giant figure from out of a storm, there arose from St. Rita's lone grief of married life, a calm resolve that the heavy yoke that bowed her head should not be borne in vain."

God eventually came to her rescue. He touched Ferdinando's heart and made him see the iniquity of his ways. Ferdinando poured out "his tears in repentance. Shortly afterward he was killed by an assassin." This is the way of Catholic stories. God shapes you up, then he has you killed. It is a mystery. And then, for good measure, "within a year's time, her two young sons were taken from her in death."

Thirty-five years old and a widow, Rita tried three times to enter the convent of Augustinian nuns at Cascia. They refused her, but she "at last was admitted through miraculous means." She died on May 22, 1457.

There was a lot of Chicago in her story. Married to a man of "morose habits and sullen disposition," the "lone grief of married life," the sudden loss of loved ones: there is much in this that women praying in the pews in the 1930s could recognize. St. Rita gets her wish by patience and "miraculous means." This is what St. Rita brought to Chicago: patience and miraculous means.

In 1936 alone St. Rita granted more than four hundred petitions made to her during her novena. By 1938 "blessings and miracles wrought directly through her intercession [had] been so numerous" that her "shrine on the south side" brought in people from across the city. They came not only for the spring novena but for the annual Christmas novena. They came for "miraculous cures and extraordinary favors." At the very least, they got a specially blessed rose and a pocket statue of the saint of Cascia.

By 1938 the parish was running five devotions daily, each with special novena prayers, a rosary, a litany, a sermon, a Benediction of the Blessed Sacrament, and a veneration of the relic. On May 17 they had a solemn procession, carrying the gold reliquary with the bone from her body. People came and prayed. The sick were cured, wishes were granted, miracles occurred, all within blocks of South Mozart Street.

But when I ask my mother about St. Rita's, the miracles, and the hard life of the saint, she seems surprised. She went to St.

Rita's for Mass. She went for the novenas, but she has no idea who St. Rita was. "But you went to her novenas," I say. "Why did you go if you didn't know about St. Rita?"

"We were Irish girls," she tells me impatiently. "That's what Irish girls did. We went to novenas."

25

She would circle that hall twenty times, flying around, flying around the edge.
    —Pat O'Hara, talking about Sara's dancing in the 1930s

During her time in Chicago Sara realized quite early that barring some unexpected and dramatic change her working life would lead nowhere. She gave it the attention necessary to secure the wages she turned over to her father, no more and no less. She looked elsewhere for reasons to get up in the morning. She sought other routes into the future. But the available routes were limited.

She was in her late teens. She was not what she had been when she got off the *Laconia*. She, like Nell, had become beautiful. I remember realizing that my mother was a beautiful woman. It happened twice actually. I recognized her beauty once retrospectively. It came as I looked through family photographs and saw her on a beach in Carmel, California. I recognized her, but it was as if I was seeing her for the first time. She was young and happy. She looked radiant. I also remember sitting in our living room in the San Fernando Valley, where we eventually lived after moving to California in the late 1950s. It was the early 1960s and I was a teenager, which meant she was in her forties. Everything was going badly and was about to get worse. I looked at her sitting in her chair and realized at that moment that she was still beautiful. I said something, or maybe my father did or one of my brothers. And my mother didn't blush or deny how she appeared. There was some part of her—never all of her—that recognized her beauty.

She learned to cultivate her beauty. That was what her job was about. Nell tried to teach Sara that her leisure should also be devoted to the cultivation of beauty. Sara shopped with Nell at Sixty-third and Halsted Streets. All the clerks in the stores knew Nell. She was there almost every weekend. The streetcar, elevated, and railroad lines that converged there helped make the intersection second only to the Loop as a retail area in Chicago. On Saturday night, after Nell was paid at Kiltz's Bakery, she and Sara took the streetcar down Sixty-third to Halsted. "Nell was a fashion plate, believe it or not," my mother tells me.

Nell could buy clothes, Sara could not, because Nell had money my mother did not have. Virtually all Sara's wages went to her father to pay her room and board. Nell earned more and kept more, and, besides, Kiltz's Bakery was just a few blocks away from South Mozart Street so she had no carfare. Streetcars cost only seven cents a trip, but fourteen cents a day added up in those years.

Compared to Ballylongford, Sixty-third and Halsted was an astonishing place. There was the Englewood El roaring overhead and streetcar tracks in the middle of the street, but automobiles dominated. There were cars parked solid along the curb and sometimes double-parked. Most of the buildings were unpretentious early-twentieth-century three- and four-story brick commercial buildings, although there was the huge block-long, five-story mass of the Byrne Building on Halsted and Garfield. But by and large, the district was, as the *Chicago Daily News* put it, "a millionaire in the clothes of a tramp." But even these humble buildings had awnings shading the sidewalk, and each store had electric signs protruding into the street beyond the awnings. The streetlights were elegant, almost delicate. There were four round globes on each with a fifth, almost like a flower, rising above.

During its prime in the late 1920s, Halsted was a mix of chain stores and specialty stores. There was, of course, a Kresge's and Walgreens, but there were also milliners, haberdashers, and cloak makers—terms that have become archaic. The Depression took its toll during the 1930s. When Nell had begun to shop there in 1930, specialty stores had crowded one another from Sixty-first to Sixty-fifth. Black's Millinery stood next to Morris Siecan's, whose huge sign proclaimed CLOAKS. But there was still life in the district in the mid-1930s. Sears, Roebuck & Co. bought the Becker-Ryan Building and adjacent properties on Sixty-third and Halsted to build a new $1.5 million store. All the goods Ballylongford had ever seen in its entire history could have fit in a small corner of that store. Sara, like most Americans, could not touch that abundance in 1936, but it was still there, simultaneously displayed to her and denied her. The stores were an education in wanting things. Nell instructed her in what she should want.

Sara wanted to look beautiful, to dress beautifully; she wanted to have fun. She went to the Irish dances every Sunday with Nell. Sara had learned these dances in Kerry, taking lessons along with her cousin Danny Holly. She loved to dance, and she danced with abandon. "She would," my uncle Pat says, "circle that hall twenty times, flying around, flying around the edge." The dances were held in halls on the South and West Sides.

Pat O'Hara was from Bohola in County Mayo and a few years older than Nell. He first had gone to England and then come to the United States just before the Depression began. He had worked briefly for the railroad and then quit when a position opened up at Crane's, a steelmaker that had a reputation as a good employer. He is quiet and soft-spoken but always quick with a joke. And like Sara, Pat watches. He has an astonishing memory. He remembers, and he remembers in detail.

Pat is in his eighties now and still speaks with a heavy brogue. He remembers the night he met Nell and Sara. It was at Cannon's at Fifty-second and Halsted. And it was on a Sunday. All the Irish dances were on Sundays. In the summer they were at Mill's Stadium, which had an outdoor pavilion. In the winter, spring, and fall, they went to Cannon's or to the hall at Sixty-fourth and Halsted or to the one at Forty-seventh and Lake Park or to West Side halls like Flynn's.

But that night was at Cannon's, because Pat remembers that Matt Walsh (who was no relation of Sara's) was there. Matt Walsh had a date with Eileen Madden. Eileen Madden was a very big woman, so large that years later my mother would think, seeing John Madden, the football coach and broadcaster, on television, that maybe Eileen was related to John Madden. When Pat went to get his coat to leave, he saw Matt Walsh with Eileen Madden, my mother, and Nell. Matt Walsh was taking all three home. "How do you do," said Pat. "You've got three, and I've got none."

This was nearly summer, for the next weekend they met again at Mill's Stadium. Sara was there with Nell. Sixty years later, my mother jokes with Pat that Nell was the prettier one. "You notice he didn't pick me," Sara says.

"Either one at the time, I didn't mind," says Pat.

Sara laughs.

"There was another guy there called Coleman," Pat says, "that had one of them. I didn't know which one, you know, so I found out."

Coleman was interested in Sara. They were together for a while. Sara does not talk about him. He gave her a watch at some point. And after a quarrel, she, in a fury, threw it into a sink. Nell retrieved it and gave it back to Coleman.

And so Pat met Nell. He gave Nell and Sara a ride home. "I was watching out for my sister," Sara now tells Pat. Not many of the men Sara and Nell knew had cars.

The next Monday, Pat was fixing his car. When he tells the story, he is a little startled that he was home on a Monday. Details matter to Pat, and he can't remember why he was home. He needed a part for the car. He went to an auto parts store at Sixty-third and California Avenue. He was living with his sister at Fifty-second and Sangamon then. He had to pass a considerable number of auto parts stores to get to Sixty-third and California. But the store at Sixty-third and California happened to be close to Kiltz's Bakery, where Nell worked.

After he got the part, he walked to the bakery. "There was herself inside, all dressed up in white," he says. He went to the door, and Nell, who was decorating cakes, saw him. She came to the door to talk. That was the beginning. A year and a half later, Pat became Nell's husband. He also became the best friend Sara had in Chicago.

But Pat and Coleman, whose watch my mother threw in the sink, open up other questions. You do not hear many stories about sex in Irish American families. Once, in a talk I gave while writing this book, I described what I was trying to do. A man in the audience, a biographer himself, asked whether I was going to discuss sex. My mother, I told him, is Irish Catholic. Irish Catholics don't talk about sex. Certainly, my mother's stories, her presentation of herself, lead only to the borders of sex: to dancing and beauty and boyfriends.

But in 1920s and 1930s Chicago, dancing and, more particularly, dance halls were synonymous with sex, at least in the eyes of social reformers. My mother makes it very clear she never went to dance halls; that is not where the Irish dances took place.

Ernest Burgess and his students at the University of Chicago were, however, obsessed with dance halls in the same way that some people today are obsessed with crack houses or topless clubs. These were places where lives went wrong; these were sites of sin; these seemed places that infected the whole city.

Pat O'Hara says he went to the halls occasionally. There is a graduate student paper in the University of Chicago archives about one of these dance halls—Gaelic Park—that he visited. The paper, written in the 1920s, is unsigned. The graduate student was fascinated and appalled by Gaelic Park. Sara doesn't remember ever hearing of Gaelic Park. It was on the fringes of her world, but men she knew passed through it. It is the background into which people like the Mulvihill boys and Billy Ahern and sometimes Pat moved. It is the lens through which sociologists saw the life of young men and women on the Southwest Side.

The graduate student enters my mother's story both for what he saw and for his way of seeing. He brought to his view of the lives of young immigrants and children of immigrants a restrained moral outrage and a transparent attraction that tried to pose as understanding. The graduate student studied people. And in this case, the people he studied may have been either my relatives or people my mother knew. He reveals to me, a person who studies people, the indignity of being studied.

My suspicion is that the graduate student was the child of Dutch Calvinists. He was from Michigan. He says he was "born and reared in an orthodox minister's home where dancing was looked upon with great disapproval." But at the University of Chicago he learned to dance. He took girls to dances. He found in dance "a sense of abandonment, which in itself gives pleasure." He creates himself as a young man who has escaped his puritanical past. He has come to feel that "dancing—when endulged in with the right attitudes—is a pleasurable experience."

The people at Gaelic Park definitely did not have the right attitudes. The graduate student tried to be fair. Their behavior might be "—perhaps—a perfectly normal manifestation of the folkways and mores of the cultural groups to which they belong." He went even further. His interpretations might, he thought, have been colored by his own desire "to achieve what may be possible through behavior such as observed in the study." He, in other words, desired what he saw as the unrestrained sexuality of these dances, but "concerning one's own accomplishment of the wishes one feels a strange restraint and feeling of inadequacy." The graduate student brought a lot of baggage to Gaelic Park.

Gaelic Park was an open-air pavilion a few miles north of Sixty-third; it was at the corner of California and West Forty-seventh Street in the Back-of-the-Yards. It was an area many of the people on South Mozart Street had come from. Gaelic Park was part of a past that the older people around South Mozart

Street were trying to put behind them. But sometimes their children would go back. My uncle Pat sometimes went to Gaelic Park in the 1930s before he met Nell. By then it had, he remembers, three pavilions. Once he tried to sneak in through a loose board in the fence that surrounded it, but as he came in there was a cop standing in front of him. He backed right back out. Pat had no sense of Gaelic Park being a dangerous place or even a disreputable place. Maybe it had changed since the late 1920s, when the graduate student visited it.

Gaelic Park had sprung up at about the same time that the bungalow belt began to spread across the West and South Sides. An Irish Athletic Club, which is to say a street gang grown prosperous and pretentious, built it. It could have been Ragen's Colts or, perhaps, the Shielders, itself an alliance of separate gangs. Both were political gangs tied in with the ward politics of the Irish South Side.

Thomas Philpott has recorded part of the history of these political gangs. Ward bosses cultivated juvenile gangs, whose major ambition was to get funds to obtain rooms of their own and become an athletic club. In the clubhouse they could smoke, drink, gamble, and loaf. They could hold stag parties; they could have collective sex with a willing girl ("gang shag" or "mattress parties") or rape an unwilling one ("gang bangs"). Frank Ragen, a Cook County commissioner, sponsored Ragen's Colts. He set up a storefront for them on Halsted, the Ragen Athletic Club. They distributed his flyers and put up his signs; they occasionally attacked those passing out flyers for Ragen's opponents and pulled down his opponents' signs. They voted, as the saying goes in Chicago, early and often. The Colts' alumni numbered mobsters and "aldermen, police captains, county treasurers, sheriffs, and so on."

During the race riots of 1919, Ragen's Colts, the Shielders, and other gangs enjoyed virtual immunity from the law. They acted as vigilantes against blacks pushing the boundaries of the Black Belt. They murdered, burned, and looted. The inhabitants of the Black Belt did not distinguish their assailants. They called them collectively the Mickies. In the 1920s the gangs became part of a coalition against the Ku Klux Klan and its anti-immigrant crusade and demands for a hundred percent Americanism. Ragen's Colts initiated an anti-Klan campaign by hanging a hooded Klansman in effigy. The Colts, as racist and anti-Semitic as the most ardent Klansmen, simply hated those who added anti-Catholicism to the mix.

The gang that built Gaelic Park held "athletic contests" there on Saturdays and Sundays and eventually constructed a dancing pavilion. But gang power was unstable, and one night a rival gang seized the pavilion and burned it down, or so the story goes. Eventually a court reporter, an Irishman, leased the land and subleased it to a Mr. McNamara and a Mr. McIntosh, who began to hold dances there once more. Mr. McIntosh and Mr. McNamara were, they said, interested only in the Irish dances held on Sunday afternoons and evenings. In the 1920s they subleased the park, in turn, to athletic clubs and promoters, who staged their own dances.

The graduate student moved through these jazz dances at Gaelic Park in a fog of desire. He was enamored with a girl called Chicky: a "slight but very graceful woman of good carriage and poise." She wears "a short black dress of conventional pattern." The graduate student watched the younger boys chase girls for a kiss. He watched couples in close embrace "loving up" on the dance floor between dances, their hips moving in and out. The men lifted the girls by their thighs and held them closer. They kissed passionately. Couples strolled out onto the grounds. It appears that the graduate student checked on them. He has a footnote: "Later evidence shows very little sexual intercourse on the grounds." He suspected it took place later. The boys who would talk to him assured him that it did.

Most of the people at the jazz dances were from Back-of-the-Yards and Bridgeport, but they might have come from all over the South Side. The girls were mostly under eighteen and Polish or Lithuanian. They worked in the stockyards. The majority of the boys were over seventeen, with most over twenty. They were largely Irish. The girls tended to be regulars at Gaelic Park. The boys were more transient. This was only one stop on a dance-hall circuit.

The graduate student recognized the clientele at a glance. The boys were the type "you invariably associate with the corner cigar store and neighborhood pool room." They wore "the indelible mark of Erin upon their countenances. Most of the remainder are obviously of slavic ancestry." They were vulgar, profane, and cliquish. They gathered in small groups, smoking and talking. They did not welcome the graduate student.

The graduate student was initially interested in classifying the girls by their availability. The Polish and Lithuanian girls were easy; the Irish were not. But then he qualified this. The Irish girls affiliated with two of the athletic clubs that sponsor dances—the Hamburgs and the Wallaces—were very fast but selective. He judged all this by the conversation of the boys, which he duly recorded: "Her belly gets the heebie geebies." "You can get it off her easily." "She fucks like a rabbit."

The graduate student reached the expected conclusions about Gaelic Park: "There could be no worse place for a young impressionable boy or girl to come than such a place as this." It was a place full of "fallen" girls who gave themselves up to the "life." It was a place where men valued girls only for their bodies.

But then on reflection and with further visits, he pulled back. Much of the talk of sex was just talk. The girls did the best they could. They just wanted to dance and have a good time. They couldn't afford a trip to the Trianon or Midway Gardens. He was astonished that boys and girls did not talk as they danced. They did not ask each other's name. To the boys, he said, the girls were just "cunts." The graduate student shifted between sympathy for the girls and sharing the boys' disdain. He could not get the girls to talk to him.

Boys and men moved between Gaelic Park and the Irish dances. Sara and Nell had a narrower world. Gaelic Park was over the border. The sexuality, the uncomfortable desire the graduate student saw at Gaelic Park were real enough; but in Chicago Lawn at least, when sex led to pregnancy, it also seems to have led to marriage. Less than one percent of the births in the area between 1928 and 1933 were "illegitimate."

If the graduate student had met Pat at Gaelic Park, he would have thought Pat a young Irish workingman of the kind that quit school at the first opportunity. Pat would not have said a word to him. But Pat would have taken in the graduate student, his clothes, his manner, what he said and whom he said it to. Pat would have watched, remembered in detail, and made his own judgments.

Neither the graduate student nor any of Burgess's students followed young workingmen like Pat back to the Southwest Side. Young working-class men merged into a single image that held none of the distinctions Sara and Nell saw among the Mulvihill boys, who were "just no good," on one extreme, Billy Ahern in the middle, and Pat on the other extreme. The glare of Gaelic Park erased such distinctions. But Pat's qualities appeared clearly enough on the Southwest Side. He was not like other men Sara and Nell knew.

26

When we lived on South Mozart Street, you could tell that when Nell walked into the room he was happy. When I walked into the room, it didn't mean a damn thing.

—Sara, speaking about her father, Jack Walsh

Sara's beauty gave her the confidence to become independent, but she actually had little choice in the matter. She had no one to rely on. She had not been able to rely on her father since she was four. Jack Walsh's greater attachment to Nell in Chicago was simply a fact of life. "When we lived on South Mozart Street," Sara says, "you could tell that when Nell walked into the room he was happy. When I walked into the room it didn't mean a damn thing." She laughs, realizing what she has said. "But I was never jealous of it. I was never jealous of it." After Nell became engaged to Pat, she came to enjoy Sara's company. But as time went on Sara did not need Nell as much. She was no longer a complete greenhorn.

She learned quickly that the house on South Mozart Street could hardly hold itself together, let alone support her. The problems were all entangled. There was the Depression, and the crowding it caused, and the constant worry about money. There was sickness. And exacerbating it all was drink.

When Will Lynch and Tommy O'Brien drank together, they would leave the house and go down to Sixty-third Street. There were bars—pubs, Sara still calls them—on nearly every block.

One night when Sara had been in Chicago for less than a year, Will was not in the kitchen when she returned from work. Tommy was gone, too. Kitty was in the kitchen, and she was angry. She sent Sara down to the tavern at Sixty-third and South Mozart to find them. "You go in there, and you tell Tommy O'Brien and Will Lynch to come right home," she said.

Sara had never been in a tavern before. The room was dark and smoky and full of men. There were no women. Many of the men were drunk, and when Sara, young and becoming a beauty, walked in, all the men started to whistle and yell and scream. Half a century later she remembers her humiliation. When she tells the story, the tenses change. She is in the bar again, full of anger, helplessness, and disdain. "There they are as drunk as they could be at the bar, completely drunk, and they both put their arms around me and made all kinds of stupid talk." Tommy and Will wouldn't leave with her.

She pleaded with them, but there was only jeering and refusal. She went home in tears to face Kitty's anger for "failing the job." The police brought them home sometime in the morning. Sara's going to fetch them was not common, but it happened. The police's bringing the two of them home happened all the time. Some cop was forever pulling Tommy and Will out of a neighborhood bar. The cops were Irish; Tommy and Will were Irish and the relatives of cops. The cops took them home.

It was a job to keep men from their drink or to get them, when surrounded by other men, to listen to the request of a woman. Will, at the bar, refused the request to come home with a young woman, Sara, who looked like Nora, the wife who had left him. Will, at the bar, refused even to challenge the things the men around him said about Sara; and to her, Will, saying those things himself, becomes a more manly and less sympathetic figure than Will at the kitchen table welcoming her with bread and tea. He probably never gave a second thought to that night in the bar. Sara had come into a place where she didn't belong. Maybe in Nora's leaving him, even for a man no better, there was a revenge exacted for other bars, other requests denied, other slurs unanswered. But then again, maybe not.

That they couldn't support her was one thing, but that they themselves were dissolving before her very eyes was another. Kitty's poker games and her imperiousness, her ostentatious suffering, all masked the fact that she was dying. Dr. Carney came every week, tapped Kitty's lungs, and drew green fluid into a glass jar.

It was Billy Ahern who usually occupied Kitty's thoughts on her long days abed. Billy and Jackie, the sons of her dead sister, Lizzie, still had a father, but he could not or would not care for them. The boys were opposites. Billy Ahern was loud and wild and never could hold a job. Kitty worried about him; he was her favorite. Billy had a knack for trouble, not trouble once in a while, as Sara says, but trouble every day.

The exact nature of the trouble remains elusive. Kitty would yell at Billy from her bed, and Billy would yell back from the kitchen. But he would soon drift into the bedroom, and the talk would grow quiet. She really did love him like a son, and Sara was something of a stranger that first year. They did not share accounts of trouble with her.

It was usually that way with trouble. The adults whispered about it or made cryptic and guarded references. But it wasn't talked about openly, at least in front of Sara. That there was trouble she knew, but in the early years she knew only the storm warnings. She rarely glimpsed the storms themselves.

I cannot think about Billy Ahern without thinking about Studs Lonigan. When works of fiction are strong, they create their own gravity. They draw actual lives into their orbit until we sometimes understand real people in terms of their resemblance to fictional characters. Nobody at South Mozart Street read anything much beyond the *Chicago Daily News* and the *The Kerryman*, which came once a week in the mail from Ireland. Billy Ahern certainly never read *Studs Lonigan*, but *Studs Lonigan*, James Farrell's trilogy about the Irish South Side, covers the drinking, fighting, and probably whoring (which my mother wouldn't talk about, even if she knew) that made up Billy's trouble.

Billy Ahern hung around with the Kirbys at a place called the Shack on Sixty-third Street. They did a lot of drinking and gave Aunt Kitty, Tommy O'Brien, and Jack Walsh much grief. Billy Ahern patrolled the extreme boundaries of the South Side life that surrounded Sara. This territory was closed to women, at least to girls like Sara, but they all knew the men who inhabited it.

Billy and Jackie Ahern were brothers, but they seem to have sworn that having been condemned to share blood and genes they would share nothing else. For Jackie the web of relations that tied him to South Mozart Street was a curse. He quietly raged against being born amid mechanics, streetcar conductors, and drunks.

Jackie, like his brother, was second generation, born in America, and he worked in an office, not among the streetcars, as Jack Walsh did or Tommy O'Brien had. He was not a man dissolving before your eyes like Will Lynch. He was a man who pinched himself tight and held everything but his scorn inside. He dressed (for my mother always noted these things) "very nice and was very neat." Knowing full well that he would always be of these people who sheltered him and whose very existence seemed to shame him, he tried to isolate himself as if from a contamination. He seldom spoke to anyone in the house. He ate alone at the kitchen table or else took his food into the bedroom and shut the door. He made it clear that he would rather be living someplace else. And even though he was in the house, it was as if he didn't live there. Jackie wanted nothing to do with the cops, conductors, carpenters, mechanics, beauticians, and bakery workers who were his relatives and who lived in this house.

Jackie was the planet farthest from the sun, but the gravity binding most of them to the house was weak. Sara and Nell were there because Jack Walsh was there. There were, I am sure, reasons why Jack Walsh was on South Mozart Street instead of with his sisters Nell Butler or Bea Mulvihill, with whom he had lived before, but those reasons have not survived. Will was there simply from necessity and charity. Tommy, Kitty, and Billy Ahern were the core of the place. They leaned on one another.

They were the only ones whom it would take more than a slight change of direction or a better opportunity to dislodge.

Sara watched them all, those who could barely care for themselves, like Billy Ahern and Will Lynch, and those who just didn't care for anyone but themselves, like Jackie Ahern. She gauged them all, measuring them for the aid, comfort, and love that they might give beyond the obligations due to family. Those obligations they all but Jackie were grimly determined to meet. She would get a bed and a roof and a share of the house's ` labor. Sara would get a father's concern. She would get, thanks to Will Lynch, food and conversation. Beyond that, she and Nell would grow, to their mutual surprise, attached to each other. It was not a bad bargain for the time and place, but neither did it make independence look frightening or unnecessary.

27

I came into a house in America that was kind of a nightmare.
                    —Sara, on the house at 6420 South Mozart Street

Even now, after more than half a century, Sara is astonished at how quickly things fell apart and how thin the floor was that separated them all from tumbling down into disorder and death. They died so quickly that today Sara sometimes has trouble keeping the chronology straight. For all practical purposes, they seem to have died together.

When she remembers those days, she says, "I came into a house in America that was kind of a nightmare." Drinking was part of the nightmare. So was sickness. Together they threatened the foundation of South Mozart Street. People died.

After a while, death became a coda to nearly every story. "We spent all our time going to funerals," Sara says. "What they all died of, I don't know." Sickness gradually wore away Kitty; drink took its toll on Tommy and Will.

"It was always something," Sara remembers. She doesn't mean to trivialize their dying by mixing it with the drinking and the doctor's visits. It is more a sign of how it wore on her, a teenager. Her life remained to be lived, but there was always something in the failing lives of those around her that seemed to block the way. Always something.

She dealt with drunks and called the doctor for Kitty. Of the older people, only her father seemed partially immune. He neither drank nor died. Bleeding ulcers put him in the hospital in the late 1930s, but he recovered. He worked and watched the White Sox while others died around him.

Will went first. One Sunday morning in 1938 Will did not come down from the attic for his tea. "We found him," Sara says, "dead in bed in his lonely attic room with the dangling light bulb still burning from the night before."

The undertakers who buried Will were friends of Jack Walsh from the West Side. They dated from earlier days in Chicago, when he had lived with his sister, Nell Butler. William Butler was a police sergeant then. It was before he became a captain. One of the undertakers was named O'Keefe, the other has drifted from memory.

The undertakers buried Will. A humbling death had followed a humbling life. In Irish American wakes the casket remains open, allowing mourners a last view of the dead.

There is an initial shock in seeing someone only recently alive and vital so waxy and still, but the shock fades. A corpse can only hold the full attention of children or those seeing one for the first time. Sara had seen dead people before, but she had never touched a corpse. She remembers the touch to this day. The corpse was cold, and only she, not Will, could feel the chill. If she could have peeled back the clothes, peeled back the skin, there would have only been ice, she thought. She cried uncontrollably. They had to lead her away from the casket. The cold would not leave her.

But wakes are not usually times of absolute sorrow. Conversations drift. Acquaintances are renewed. Will, laid out in a suit, wasn't Will waiting with some soup or soda bread and the day's news. He was a corpse. By avoiding physical contact, she would get used to corpses. She would maintain her composure.

By the time Will died, Kitty was almost constantly sick. She was in and out of the hospital. Dr. Carney continued to come every week to tap her lungs. When there was too much fluid in Kitty's lungs or when Kitty grew weak, she went back to the hospital.

Kitty was in the hospital when her husband, Tommy, died. Sara and Tommy O'Brien were alone in the house. Sara was getting ready to go to work in the Loop when she heard Tommy fall and scream. By the time she reached him, he was unconscious and bleeding from the mouth and nose. Sara could get no response. She called the fire department, and an ambulance took him to Cook County Hospital. They let Sara ride in the ambulance with him. Nell, Billy Ahern, and Jack Walsh joined her at the hospital. It was late afternoon when the doctors told them that Tommy was dead.

Kitty came home a widow to a house emptying of people and filling with trouble. Death broke the strands binding those who remained. Jackie Ahern moved out shortly after Tommy's death. The deaths seem in some way to have given Jackie his release. Or maybe he had just accumulated enough money to leave a place that was such a constant affront to his image of himself. When he left, he broke contact. He stayed in Chicago, but the few miles he put between himself and his relatives created more distance than the ocean that lay between Chicago and Ireland.

Billy stayed; he hoped the house would be his. Kitty wanted to leave the house to Billy Ahern when she passed. There was no doubt about that. Billy had replaced Tim as her son. Billy Ahern drank and hung around the Shack and found his trouble, but the house, at least, would be his.

The house, however, was slipping from Kitty's grasp. The house at 6420 South Mozart Street was the sole tangible result of Kitty's and Tommy's lives in America. But with Kitty sick and Tommy drinking, they had diverted the money they received from the others to pay the medical bills. They fell behind on the mortgage and taxes. Kitty was about to lose the house.

Losing the house would have been too much for Kitty. Forced to abandon her own child, she had always taken in others. She had taken in her sister Bea when the Italian shot and killed Bea's husband, Ed. They had lived on South Laflin Street then; only later had they bought the house on South Mozart Street. She had taken in Jackie and Billy Ahern when their mother, her sister

Lizzie, died. She had taken in Will Lynch, deserted by her sister Nora. She had taken in my grandfather and his children. Kitty, for all her faults, had been the shield against the dangers America presented to her family. Now, in her last sickness, she would lose the shelter she had offered others. That such losses were common on the South Side in the 1930s made them no less bitter.

And so an accommodation was reached that remained a source of recrimination for years and of defensiveness to this day. Billy Ahern is long dead and unable to plead his case, but Sara, justifying her father, speaks of the transaction defensively. She tells me that after Kitty's death Jack Walsh paid the back taxes and saved the house. But she was a teenager and did not fully understand these things. She talked to Pat about it. Pat, by then, was engaged to Nell and as close to Jack Walsh as anyone but Nell could get.

Jack Walsh was the only one earning a workingman's wage, and it was greater and more secure than it had been when his daughter Sara arrived. He had behind him a union that had turned the corner after 1936. By 1937 it offered him a paid vacation, a pension plan, and wage increases won in arbitration. It was building up a credit union and promised death and disability benefits. He could, in addition, draw on the money earned by his two daughters, who did not question his right to their wages as long as they lived with him. He commanded greater resources than ever before. He had come here to save an Irish farm, but if he saved only that farm, he would find himself evicted from his sister's American home. He made an offer. He would make the mortgage payments and pay the back taxes and all of Kitty's doctor bills and give Kitty a place to live. She would live as she had always lived, but she would turn over the house to him.

To do the deal, they called on the Butlers. The Butlers remain Sara's models for American success. Nell Butler was her aunt, one of her father's sisters. She had married a Chicago cop, who rose first to sergeant and then to captain. She worked for John Clark, a West Side alderman. Aunt Nell Butler lived and breathed Chicago politics. Her son Joe Butler became a lawyer for the city and later a Chicago judge.

In a family of cops and trainmen, the Butlers represented imaginable success. And because the Butlers were family, they provided a mark of respectability and a source of favors for working-class cousins, nieces, nephews, brothers, and sisters of the South and West Sides. My mother makes it clear to me that they were important people. The Butlers could fix things—small things, it is true, but still, life was easier knowing them. They pulled strings. And there was the currency of having a brother-in-law or an uncle who was a police captain, a sister or an aunt who worked for John Clark, and, later, a nephew or cousin who was a judge. Being able to say you knew these people mattered.

They got young Joe Butler, who was only a lawyer then, to draw up the papers. Billy Ahern supposedly pleaded with Kitty to sign over the house, for if she didn't, he said, they all would be out in the street. They only had another month. Kitty refused to sign. But the next week they called Joe back. Kitty had changed her mind. She signed. "Everybody was happy," Pat says.

Kitty turned over the house to her brother Jack. He promised to shelter her and pay her bills for the rest of her life. But Kitty only lasted a couple of months after signing over the house. Billy was furious. "It was my house," Billy said, "and Uncle Jack has robbed me." Pat says my grandfather took a gamble and won. The house that had bound them together divided them in the end.

I do not know if Kitty realized the bitterness and anger that would follow her death. When the sickness turned into a death-watch, Nell, Billy Ahern, and Sara took turns sitting with her at night. This went on for a month. Billy had ample time to talk. On a Sunday afternoon, Dr. Carney told them the end was very near. Everyone who remained in the house was at her bedside when she died. It was a peaceful death, Sara remembers. Billy left the house after that.

How these deaths and quarrels affected my mother is not clear to me, although it is she who tells me about them. There was already in her that combination of compassion and detachment that marked her path through the world. She had, to be sure, the Irish weakness for sentiment, but she segregated her sentiment. It did not permeate everything she saw or did. Sometimes when she speaks, there is not a trace of sentiment. Kitty was always dying, she tells me at one point. Sara was young and impatient with dying.

There is a story she tells about the handsome undertaker's assistant she began to notice in this series of wakes and funerals. The young undertaker's assistant, alive, dark haired, and handsome, grew more and more interesting in comparison to Will, Tommy, and Kitty, each, in turn, dead, pale, and somber in their open caskets.

Sara went with the family to the wakes, and Dorothy Boland, a friend she had met while working at the beauty shop, came with them. Sara wasn't the only one to notice the young undertaker's assistant. Dorothy Boland saw him, too. He gave no sign of noticing either of them during the wakes. And they did not speak to him.

It was Sara who mentioned a wish to see the undertaker's assistant again to Dorothy. Dorothy suggested how. Following Kitty's funeral, they got a paper and scanned the list of wakes and funerals. They were looking for a wake, any wake, conducted by the young undertaker's funeral parlor. They found one on the West Side. On the evening of the wake they took a streetcar to attend it.

They went to the wake not even knowing if the deceased was Catholic, but the casket was open, which was a good sign. They went up to it, knelt down, and prayed. The woman was very old. They scanned the room for the undertaker.

They did not see him. A man as old as the woman in the casket approached them when they stood up. "Did you know my Mame?" he asked.

There was a pause. "She was our girlfriend," Dorothy said.

Dorothy was eighteen; Mame must have been in her seventies. Maybe his grief allayed suspicion. What else, after all, would explain these young women at his wife's funeral? He seemed touched and pleased that a woman he had loved could still attract friends who were so young.

But when Sara thought of Dorothy and Mame as girlfriends, she started to choke. It probably seemed like grief.

Mame's family came over. Everyone was introduced to my mother and Dorothy. "These were Mame's girlfriends," the old man told them. "They came to the wake."

Sara and Dorothy never did meet the undertaker's assistant. He was not at the wake. They took the streetcar back to the South Side. They never went to the funeral; they never saw the undertaker again. "Did you know my Mame?" Sara says now. She shakes her head and laughs. It was very long ago, when she was young.

What was dying during those days was the tight little circle of relatives that was her first America. Her father and Nell she had known in Ireland, but Kitty, Tommy, Will, and Billy and Jackie Ahern she had known only as Americans. But in a family so large, death did not necessarily open the door to strangers. As Will died and Tommy died and Jackie left, there were other relatives to move into South Mozart Street, if only briefly.

Sara was eighteen when the deaths started in 1938, and more willful than when she came to America. In Ireland, even as death and emigration winnowed the people around her, even as revolution came, the world had seemed changeless. Choices, insofar as they existed, were made by parents, employers, and priests. But now she was becoming both an American and an adult. She quit jobs and took others on her own decision. Even if the money still went to her father, she was not about to be the slave of relatives. Harriet Connors, Sara's cousin, moved in sometime during this flurry of death and division. She was Aunt Mary's daughter. She had arthritis. She was "very masculine," my mother says, "and bossy." One night after Sara returned from work she ordered—"she didn't ask me, she ordered"—Sara to run her bath. She did. She filled the tub with cold water.

She called Harriet sweetly: "Come on, Harriet, get in." Harriet got a foot in and began to curse. Sara was no longer a greenhorn. She was no longer the one to be commanded and laughed at.

Harriet Connors and other cousins moved into and out of Sara's world, but Pat O'Hara moved unobtrusively to the center of it and stayed there. Pat became engaged to Nell, and, before Kitty went into her last decline, Pat took over the task of driving her to the Markettown at Sixty-fourth and Kedzie every Saturday. Pat became friends with Jack Walsh. They stand together in the picture taken that day of the Notre Dame football game.

Sara liked Pat because he was funny, because he was good to Nell, and because he presented possibilities beyond the range of Irish American men she knew. He was neither a drunk like Tommy and Will, nor stolid and uncommunicative like Jackie Ahern and her own father, nor wild and irresponsible like Billy Ahern and Aunt Bea Mulvihill's sons. She also liked him because he had a car and she and Nell now got rides to the dances on Sunday nights. One Sunday, Pat drove them out beyond the city's suburbs. They saw green fields and cows, the first Sara had seen since leaving Ireland. And then the homesickness and the thoughts of her mother were too much, and she cried there on the Illinois prairie thinking of Ireland.

Sara also liked Pat because he was an immigrant like herself. Not only would he understand tears provoked by cows in a pasture, but his American relatives were as mixed a bag as her own. "We have never had a cross word," Sara says of Pat. "I always think of Pat when I think of something my mother said to me before I left Ireland. She said, 'Laniv [Irish for child], if when you are dying you can count on one hand five true friends, you will have been very lucky indeed.' Pat O'Hara tops that list for me."

In Sara's telling, it is her mother who imparted life's lessons; in Sara's telling, it is women who seem to dominate all these Irish American families. These women were as flawed as the men, but they supply the power of these households. It was as

true in Pat's family as in her own. Pat's aunt Peg, his uncle Tom
O'Hara's second wife, was a terror. She was the bane of Pat's
life.

When my mother talks to Pat, she says, "Tell me the stories
about Peg."

Peg was mean: she was stingy and cruel. She was good to her
sons, Buddy and Jimmy, but she beat her daughter, Meletta,
something awful. For her the Depression served to cover her
intrinsic meanness; the Depression allowed her to make meanness seem a virtue. She could deploy it as if she only meant to
protect her immediate family.

Tom, a policeman, kept his job during the Depression. And
Pat boarded with them for a while early on, sleeping in a room
with two-year-old Buddy and paying ten dollars a week for food.
Peg was better-off than most, but she could not bear to pay bills.
It was not lack of money that prevented her from paying. Tom
gave her the money. She didn't pay because she resented paying
any bill, just or not, or meeting any obligation.

Peg held her dollars as if they were prisoners and creditors
were laying siege to carry them away. In Pat's telling, it is as if
that house were a fortress and utility companies a blockading
army trying to cut its lines and break its communications. Tom
was a diplomat trying to create a fragile peace that Peg would
disrupt.

Tom never saw a utility company man without suspecting
trouble. "What's the matter?" or "How is my wife doing with
the bill?" he would ask. The answer was never reassuring.

Peg didn't confine her meanness to strangers. Pat was the old-
country nephew come to live with American relatives. He had
lived with Peg and Tom on South Richmond Street for a year
and a half after he came to this country in 1929. The ten dollars
a week he paid supposedly entitled him to three meals a day.

Peg did make him lunches. Her sandwiches were two slices
of bread with a graham cracker stuck in between to separate the
bread and make it look like a sandwich.

There was rarely breakfast or dinner. Tom worked an evening
shift at the airport and left for work at 4:00 in the afternoon.

When Pat came home at 6:00, Peg had already eaten, leaving nothing for him. Peg hid the food. Pat never could find it. In Peg's logic maybe Pat's hunger meant more food for her children. More likely, the Depression gave full vent to a nastiness always ready to be tapped.

Peg was mad for money; the Depression, if anything, increased her hunger, for it seemed money might disappear before she could satisfy her appetite for it. The Depression drove her into business in the midst of bad times. If greed and thrift alone could yield success, Peg would have owned Chicago. She and Tom opened a four-lane bowling alley. It failed. She opened a beauty shop after going to Seeland's beauty shop for lessons. Tom would pick her up each afternoon.

Peg started the business in a small storefront on Kedzie. Tom fixed up the shop, making plywood partitions for individual booths. The shop stayed on Kedzie a year. It attracted few customers. Peg moved the operation into her bedroom. She had one customer who lived in the apartment across the way. The customer was known as the girl with blue hair.

From the bedroom, the beauty shop was moved into the basement. Peg preyed on relatives. She once gave Nell a perm, scorching her hair. Pat called Peg about it. "What did you do?" he demanded. Peg came over to South Mozart Street in a white coat as if she were a lab technician. She examined Nell's hair, looking for some hidden fault. She took a strand of Nell's hair. "I'm going to have it analyzed," she said, as if there were a lab, as if Peg would pay if there had been a lab.

Peg kept her business in the basement until the market for burned blue hair dropped beyond recovery. Then, as Pat says, "she retired."

Peg was perfectly suited for exploiting the tensions between obligation and resentment that ran through those immigrant families in hard times. She acted on the resentments that Kitty usually kept suppressed. But Pat could read what my mother read: the whispers, the gestures, the slight pauses, the jokes that were meant to seem harmless.

In many stories told by old people (and those not so old),

details pile up like snow until they bury a point they were meant to reveal and freeze listeners into dazed inattention. Pat's details have work to do, and they always serve their task.

There is a story Pat tells. It happened after Kitty died. And although no one died, it is a story, like most of those from these years, with at least a touch of death in it. Nell, at least, when she saw the guns, thought about dying.

One night three weeks before they were married, Nell was working at Kiltz's Bakery. She was closing that night, and Pat was waiting for her in the back room. He was reading the paper.

As Nell was about to close, a guy came in, a little guy, a nice-looking guy. Pat heard the door open. He heard Nell say "You want a slice?"

The customer said yes.

And just as he was saying that, this second guy came up behind Pat and tapped him lightly on the back of the head with a gun.

"Get up," he said. "Keep your face to the wall."

As Pat got up, Nell saw the gun. She broke for the door. "If the door opened out," Pat says, "she was gone."

"Tell her to quit," the guy with the gun told Pat, "or we'll stop her."

Pat told her not to run.

She stopped.

The two men put Pat and Nell on the floor. They tied them up with long, white towels.

They asked Pat if he had any money.

He said no.

"We'll find out," one of them said. They took his wallet. He had twenty-one dollars.

"You lied to me, you son of a bitch."

They took two hundred more dollars from the till, and then they left. Pat untied himself. He freed Nell and called the police. They waited twenty minutes for the police to come.

"Where are they, where are they?" asked the cops.

"I'd look on the outside," Pat said.

"Smart guy, huh?"

"I mean it," said Pat. "I called you twenty minutes ago."

A plainclothesman, a sergeant, came in.

"Where were you?" Pat asked. "This call took twenty minutes."

"We were up at Seventy-fourth and Ashland," the sergeant said, as if this explained it. "What did they look like?"

"One of them looked like a policeman," Pat said. His uncle Tom O'Hara was a cop. Pat saw a lot of policemen. He noticed how they looked, walked, and talked.

"Smart again?" the first cop said. He didn't like the answer.

Two weeks later Pat and Nell got a call asking them to come and see if they could identify one of the suspects. There was a lineup of ten men.

"Can you see him?"

"Yeah," Pat said.

"Go on out, put your hand on him."

Nell nearly got hysterical. "Please, please, don't do it. Please, please, he'll kill us."

But Pat was so mad, nothing would stop him. He looked for something heavy to put in his hand. He was going to hit the guy and wanted the blow to count. The gunman's hands were tied behind him. "It was a good chance," Pat says. "I couldn't miss."

But the police didn't give him the chance.

The next week, they caught the second guy in a holdup at a market. He was an ex-policeman.

I am curious about the crime, and it turns out it was not the first crime by a policeman in the neighborhood. In 1934, before Sarah arrived, Bernadine Dunning took Detective Sergeant Lewis Kolb's gun from his holster and shot him. They were sitting in his car at Seventy-fourth and Irving Avenue at the time. He had, she claimed, "forced his attentions upon her." The jury deliberated less than two hours before acquitting her. Kolb's pregnant wife was at the trial. "Under the circumstances," she told reporters afterward, "there is nothing for me to say."

That same year a patrolman named Lowler was drunk at a gas station at Sixty-seventh and Western. When another customer, Frank Mlnsa, drove in, Lowler demanded a ride home, even though he didn't know Mlnsa. Mlnsa refused. Lowler drew his service pistol and started firing. One of the bullets struck Mlnsa below the left eye and killed him. Mlnsa, too, it turned out, was a cop.

But, of course, most criminals were not cops, and crime was far rarer in that neighborhood in the 1930s than it is today. Still, it was there. Soon after Sarah arrived, a "moron"—as the paper described him—kidnapped, raped, and robbed Mrs. Frances Hughes near Sixty-third and Kedzie. Sara remembers the incident, because at about that time, early March 1937, a man started to follow her after she got off a streetcar on Sixty-third. He stopped when he saw too many other people on the street.

The random violence was there, but it never touched them. It was the sickness and drink, their own failings, and not the crimes of others, that had the impact. The dying created an opening. Sara moved through it.

28

Bea was a great character. She called a spade a spade, which did not endear her to a lot of people.

— Sara, on her aunt Bea Mulvihill

As South Mozart Street fell apart, Sara moved toward a new life. That life was, however, still around a corner. She would not see it until, gaining security in the America beyond South Mozart Street, she dared turn that corner. Until then, that new life was invisible to her, even as she drew nearer to it.

She thought of herself, when she considered her situation at all, as navigating a course somewhere between her father and Nell. Jack Walsh still steered by Ahanagran. He always would. Although he was passionate about certain American things—the White Sox and his American daughter, Nell—his Irish farm remained his beacon. Nell, on the other hand, despite her immersion in the Irish American world, had no desire to go back to the cows and their dung and the damp and heavy labor. Her world was the Southwest Side of Chicago. Sara zigzagged between the courses set by her father and sister: imagining herself back in Ireland but living more and more fully in the Irish American neighborhood of the Southwest Side.

Nell's marriage to Pat rooted her permanently in the South Side. The area around St. Rita's prospered in the 1940s and 1950s and then turned poor again in the 1970s and the decades that followed. Over the years they and everything around them would change. By the 1960s and 1970s the Lithuanians and Irish and Italians were disappearing. African Americans and Mexican immigrants would replace them. Nell and Pat would stay long after most other whites had fled. Nell would raise a family there, plant rhubarb in her backyard, and harvest it every summer. Nell would die there.

No one, of course, knew any of this when they gathered at St. Rita's for the marriage on September 7, 1940. Stories contain their own endings; telling them grants a logic and stability to things that once were, or at least seemed, contingent and indeterminate.

What was predictable about the marriage was that Nell shopped and Sara accompanied her. The trip to pick out the bridesmaids' dresses for Sara and Rita Leahy, a cousin, took six hours. A friend of Pat's had driven them to Sixty-third and Halsted; they found him sound asleep in the car and snoring loudly when they returned. It took several more trips to find matching shoes.

It was predictable that the marriage would be Catholic. The Chicago family came, and, for the day at least, old quarrels were patched over. Billy Ahern was there in a double-breasted suit. In one picture he stands with Rita Leahy. In the pictures, Sara and Rita and Nell are in white with veils and carry flowers. The men have pinstripe suits and pompadours, their hair rising like waves on their heads. Sara stands in a picture with Nell and Pat and Jack Clark, Pat's best man and best friend.

After the marriage, Nell and Pat moved into the house on South Mozart Street that Jack Walsh now owned and where he continued to live. Sara moved out shortly afterward. The once crowded house had no more people than its bedrooms could contain.

Sara's first steps beyond South Mozart Street in 1941 did not take her far. They took her only to Aunt Bea's. Bea Mulvihill, her Irish husband murdered, doted on her sons and had worked hard for them. She had scrubbed floors during the 1920s. She

had used that money, her husband's death benefits, and, I suspect, a widow's pension from the county to buy the house on
Talman Avenue.

Aunt Bea lived for her sons, Bill and Jerry: the two altar boys
who served at the mass of their murdered father. Bea was, Sara
says, "a great character. She called a spade a spade, which did
not endear her to a lot of people." She had survived tremendous
blows. Life had toughened her, but she was defenseless against
her sons. It would take her own children to bring her down.

By 1941, when Sara came to live with Aunt Bea, she had lost
her house on Talman Avenue and lived in a basement apartment
at Sixty-second and Talman. Bill, the story goes, had co-signed
a note for friends. The friends reneged, and the holders of the
note came after Bill. Bea had mortgaged the house to bail him
out, and then, when she could not meet the mortgage payments,
she lost it.

Bea had moved into a "garden apartment"—which in Chicago
means a basement—on Sixty-second and Talman Avenue. Jerry
was still living with her when Sara moved in.

"She made bread," Sara remembers. "Oh, did she make
bread." As they ate bread and drank tea, Bea told Sara about
her life, her sufferings, and her hard work: "about how her husband was shot and killed, and how she used to scrub floors for
those two kids." She was a woman who had worked hard and
lost what she had gained. For Sara, Bea was above all the aunt
who worked; in Sara's stories she is set beside Kitty, the aunt
she never remembers "doing a lick of work. Kitty was always
sick or playing poker."

Bea lived life as melodrama, but she got only the supporting
roles. "She did everything for those two boys," Sara says. "She
spoiled them rotten. They both turned out to be alcoholics."
Jerry and Bill borrowed money, they gambled, they failed to pay
their debts. They had loan sharks after them. She relents sometimes, not wanting to speak ill of the dead, and says that Bill
was not so bad.

During the time Sara lived with Aunt Bea, Bill had met a

woman with some money. He convinced the woman, Louise, to back him in a tavern. She apparently convinced him to marry her in return.

From a drunk's point of view, buying a tavern probably makes a certain sense; it is harder to re-create the investor's logic. But then, from Louise's perspective, investing in the tavern was the smart move. Marrying Bill Mulvihill was what was dumb. Their life together would not be easy.

Sara worked at the grand opening of the tavern, when everything was as hopeful as the Christmas tree lot before the woman fell in the pit. There was still, however, the chronic problem of limited resources. Bill came to his mother and said, "I sure could use a waitress, but I don't have any money to pay one." Bea, as Bill knew she would, asked Sara.

"Would you do it, Sara?"

Sara said, "I've never done it, but I guess I can." For Aunt Bea, she would have done anything.

She went to the tavern, an Irish bar, on Sixty-third Street. She worked only those opening Friday and Saturday nights.

"It was the experience of my life serving these drunks beer," Sara remembers. "They would pinch me. I was embarrassed to death. Bill would keep saying to me, 'It's all right. They can't hurt you. I'll take you home. You don't have to worry about it.' So I kept on serving the beer."

Buying a bar for a drunk had predictable results: Bill lost the tavern in no time. "Those two," Sara says, meaning Jerry and Bill, "were just no good." She saw Jerry before he died. Pat took her to see him in the early 1980s. He was by then an addle-brained old drunk living in a derelict's room on the South Side. His brain was burned out, even the memories scorched away. He didn't remember Sara. Even as far as he had fallen, however, the old ties from Talman Avenue still had some strength. The McCarthys never forgot him. Old Dr. McCarthy and young Dr. McCarthy, his boyhood friend, would care for him until the end.

Maybe it was the disappointment at how Bill and Jerry turned out, maybe it was her resentment at their failure or her anger at the murder of her husband that left Bea looking for someone to blame. Maybe it was her own years of hard work that had culminated only in the loss of her house. Maybe it was all of these things and probably more.

God knows, the Depression and the poverty she faced were not her fault, unless her love for her sons was a fault. There were plenty of people worthy of blame in 1930s America for the disasters she and millions like her faced, but Aunt Bea was not a good chooser. She was wild for Father Coughlin, and Father Coughlin knew about blame.

Father Charles Edward Coughlin was everywhere in the mid-1930s. His radio program was the most popular in the nation; his resonant voice reached from ten to forty million people every Sunday afternoon at 3:00. Father Coughlin began his career attacking the Ku Klux Klan; during the Depression, he turned to attacking Prohibition and Communism. He lamented the decline of the American family, became an enthusiastic backer of the New Deal, and assaulted conservatives "bent upon preserving the politics of greed, of oppression, and of Christlessness." But in 1936, the year Sara came to America, Father Coughlin broke with Roosevelt, who had always disliked and distrusted him, and grew ever more conservative. He would end his career a rank anti-Semite, peddling his theories of international Jewish bankers, who, in collaboration with the Bank of England, manipulated the money supply and caused the Depression. By 1936 he had his own political party, the Union Party, and his own presidential candidate, William Lemke.

Everyone listened to Father Coughlin on the Southwest Side of Chicago. He had a rich, inviting voice and a rolling brogue. He spoke the language of the street. "Radio broadcasting," Coughlin explained, "must be human, intensely human. It must be simple." Sara thought Aunt Bea called a spade a spade, and Aunt Bea, I think, certainly thought the same of Father Coughlin.

Father Coughlin eventually went too far for the Irish of Chicago's Southwest Side. Few other than Aunt Bea would choose

Lemke over Roosevelt and the Democratic Party in 1936. Aunt Nell Butler certainly wouldn't touch Lemke. The Chicago machine feared Coughlin's threat to Roosevelt enough to try to prevent him from holding rallies in Chicago during the 1936 campaign. It failed, and he came to Soldier Field in September and drew a hundred thousand people. But in the end the Chicago machine proved more than Coughlin's match. It had powerful allies. Cardinal Mundelein of the Chicago Diocese called the priests together to condemn Coughlin's actions. The Chicago machine beat Lemke handily at the polls.

Bea seems to have been among the hard core of Coughlin's followers who stuck with him even after he slid toward fascism, racism, and disgrace. Father Coughlin provided explanations to Aunt Bea and others for the hardness of their lives and the unfairness of the world. He explained her trouble in paying the mortgage and maybe the troubles her boys faced. Coughlin identified all the dangers to her life as outside her local community. These dangers were beyond anything she could change, but they were also connected with ancient enemies that her Church and birthplace had created for her: the Jews, whom they blamed for killing Christ, and Great Britain, the country that oppressed Ireland. These were understandable. Coughlin linked Jews with both Communism and high finance, and, as he did so, his voice made the radio a pulpit that resonated with Ireland. You could not miss his brogue in the rich cadences of what were barely secularized sermons. He offered her an explanation of why, after she had worked so hard, she faced such misery.

Sara came to America just after Lemke's defeat. To her, Coughlin was just the radio priest. He was Aunt Bea's enthusiasm. She accorded him the distant respect due priests. She paid him little mind. My mother does not like Father Coughlin intruding into her stories. She doesn't like me making Coughlin a presence to be reckoned with on the Southwest Side of Chicago. She paid no attention to him, she insists, and she doesn't like my defining Aunt Bea in terms of her devotion to the radio priest.

She is sensitive about anti-Semitism. Sara says she remembers no Jews on the Southwest Side. She says she knew no Jews and heard no talk of them. She says she can't remember anti-Semitism. Sara adored Aunt Bea and Aunt Bea adored Father Coughlin and Father Coughlin was an anti-Semite who touched a deep river of anti-Semitism that flowed through the Southwest Side. But as deep as the river was, its currents from a distance seem confusing and contradictory. There were, Sara remembers, two programs that Aunt Bea would never miss on Sunday. One was Father Coughlin's. The other was Jack Benny's. Jack Benny, of course, was Jewish.

Anti-Semitism might have remained what it seems to have been to Sara, an unexamined, almost reflexive cultural response. "He jewed me out of this," "the miserable Jew," "the filthy kike"—words heard on the street, the reflexive spawn of anger and resentment. It might have been but background noise had her life not turned beyond the Southwest Side.

The time with Bea and the two nights she spent in Bill's bar were among the last steps Sara would take along a path that could only have carried her deeper into the world of the Southwest Side Irish. She would remain there for several more years, but her trajectory had changed. It changed because the country changed, and the country changed because it was going to war.

 **29**

There were 42,425 arrivals and departures of scheduled airplanes and a total of 76,052 arrivals and departures of nonscheduled airplanes, including the military, making a grand total of 118,477 arrivals and departures of all airplanes, an increase of 34.1% over that of last year.
—Chicago Municipal Airport, described in the Sixty-eighth Annual Report of the Department of Public Works for the Year Ending December 31, 1943

Public and private worlds are never fully separate. Private joys and public tragedies not only intermingle, they are sometimes indistinguishable. World War II transformed Sara Walsh's world, and it changed her life.

The very things about which she had no choice created the contexts in which she made choices. The war, the end of the Depression, the opening of jobs previously closed to women, and the rise of the airline industry were beyond her control, but they widened her world. They created new opportunities, and she seized them.

Sara Walsh took a job at the Chicago Municipal Airport. Open up that flat statement and a world of changes spins out. Accepting that job and all that followed involved far more than Sara Walsh's deciding to take her life in her hands and advance into the world.

Across half a century the airport job perhaps appears commonplace. It, like everything else in my mother's life, moved along lines of kinship, family, and friends. Pat's uncle, Tom O'Hara, had taken a job as an airport cop at Chicago Municipal. When he learned the airport was hiring women, he told Pat, and Pat told Sara.

Men in Sara's family had long shared the wage-yielding prizes that got snared in the family web. Jobs as cops and trainmen and carpenters had all been secured because of the webs woven among relations, friends, priests, and politicians. This is how Sara's relatives had built their life in Chicago. Looked at in this way, this job seems but another prize.

Looked at in a different way, however, the job becomes extraordinary. Jobs at the airport terminal had been closed to women before 1940, but the old rules had been temporarily set aside. The world was at war. The United States, not yet at war, was rearming, and the Depression was slowly ending. For nearly a dozen years workingmen had been as much a part of the economic surplus as the crops rotting in fields or the sheep slaughtered to save the cost of feeding them. The economy had no use for the labor these men could provide. But now the war was absorbing the glut of workingmen that had grown during the Depression. Fighting and making the things necessary to fight demanded human labor. In the United States in 1940, that meant, first of all, white male labor. The factories, mills, and farms, and the armed forces, all quickly exhausted the available supply of white workingmen; the country faced a deficit. The men at the airport information desk had quit for better jobs or had been drafted. Employers turned to other pools of labor: African Americans, other racial minorities, and women. The airport management decided to move women into jobs once exclusively male. And word filtered through family channels.

Sara performed work previously done by men, did it well, and was proud of it, but changes, such as those her new job represented, made men that Sara knew nervous. Although Jack Walsh at least temporarily benefited from his daughter's new income, semiskilled and skilled workmen like him worried about how far such changes might extend. In 1942, with the war under way, his union's newspaper, *The Union Leader*, editorialized against the "highly dubious experiment of female operation" on streetcars and buses.

Sara Walsh was the second woman hired by the airlines at what was then the Chicago Municipal Airport at Sixty-third and Cicero. It was not yet Midway Airport. The Battle of Midway, for which the airport was eventually renamed, would not take place until June 1942.

In 1941 airports were still exotic. The city, with the assistance of the Works Progress Administration and the Public Works Administration, had expanded and improved the Chicago Municipal Airport in the years before the war. Workers ripped out the railroad tracks that bisected the mile-square airport and extended the runways. When in 1939 one of the Chicago daily papers polled readers on the seven wonders of Chicago, the airport ranked only behind the Art Institute, the Buckingham Fountain, and the Chicago Stock Yards.

A man named Roberts controlled the hiring at the information desk where Sara first worked. He liked a certain type of girl, Sara says. He particularly liked auburn hair. Sara had auburn hair, and she was slim and attractive. The first woman Mr. Roberts hired looked much like my mother. Her name was Valerie Foley, and she, too, was from Ireland. "She was absolutely gorgeous," my mother says. She had "very big bosoms." Sara makes herself beautiful by association. She would never directly say such a thing about herself.

Although Chicago Municipal Airport was the country's busiest airport, with links to major cities all across the United States, the knowledge of American geography that Sara brought to her job at the information counter was pretty much limited to Chicago. The very first night on the job a man came up to Sara and said he wanted to go to Washington. The only Washington she knew was Washington, D.C. So she directed him there, telling him what time the planes departed for Washington, D.C. He seemed pleased.

He came back very angry. "Oh, was that man angry," Sara

remembers. He didn't want to go to Washington, D.C. He wanted to go to the state of Washington.

He complained to Mr. Roberts, who told her that she had to give the right information or lose her job. She told him that she hadn't studied the map but that if he gave her a chance she would. She tells me now that she knows the map of the United States better than most people who went to school here.

She learned American geography and how to work the phone system; she moved from the information counter to the ticket counter. The airlines had formed a consortium called the Chicago Airline Ticket Office (CATO) to handle all their ticketing. There were eight airlines operating out of Midway in 1941. She must have issued tickets for all of them: American, Braniff, Chicago and Southern, Pennsylvania-Central, Eastern, Northwest, TWA, and United. She remembers them all except Pennsylvania-Central.

Sara still talks very precisely of the equipment and the airline regulations now more than half a century old. The airlines flew DC-3s, twenty-one passengers and a crew of three. The stewardess had to be a registered nurse. At the ticket counter, Sara tallied each passenger's weight and the weight of his or her luggage. She remembers how a man, traveling with his wife, came to the counter alone. She checked his luggage and his wife's, got his weight and then, assuming from the luggage that they were traveling together, asked if he was checking in for both of them. The man gave a different meaning to "both"; he looked amazed. "How did you know she was pregnant?" he asked. Things like this stick in her memory.

Sara loved working for the airlines. It was the first work she had enjoyed. The work was varied and the people were, in that most universal and neutral form of American praise, "nice." "The pilots were real nice," she remembers. They'd come in and talk to the ticket agents.

The Chicago Municipal Airport had been the busiest airport in the world since 1932. Eight hundred thousand people flew into or out of the airport in 1941. In 1942 the government took over 25 percent of the airlines' equipment for the war effort, and passenger traffic declined for the first time in the airport's history, but it rebounded in 1943. People who flew eventually came through Chicago. Eleanor Roosevelt used to fly through Chicago frequently. She was "very plain and very nice." She'd sit in the coffee shop because she didn't want to be out in the terminal when it was crowded. Once, Sara remembers, a cockroach tried to climb onto the First Lady's plate.

Charles Lindbergh came through. He was flying on TWA. Sara had to take him to the passenger agent's office so he could get some privacy. "When the flight was ready, I had to come in and get him. I remember he was real tall." Howard Hughes came through as a passenger on his own airline, TWA. He asked Sara if she knew what the initials stood for.

"Transcontinental and Western Air," she answered. (It was not yet Trans World Airlines.)

He seemed pleased.

"We had a lot of movie stars," Sara remembers. "Martha Raye. She came in drunk. They wouldn't take her on the plane. It was a really interesting job. I learned a lot working for the airlines."

"I learned to be an American, really," my mother tells me.

"What do you mean?" I ask.

"I got to know the American ways. I got to know the American food. And I got to like coffee. A lot of things I learned."

She had learned to mask her brogue, announcing the flights in a clear American voice that Pat says would carry all the way back to South Mozart Street.

She was moving in wider circles. She met people her own age, people neither Catholic nor Irish, and she enjoyed their company. She would sometimes go with coworkers to a bar called Danny's when their shifts ended. And there is a picture of her taken about this time where she is leaning against the fence at what appears to be a racetrack. She still loves racetracks. In the picture she is wearing a long skirt and carries a big black purse.

All of these changes came at the price of appalling carnage. Like all Americans her age, she remembers the American entry into the war with the kind of detail usually reserved for the birth of a child or the death of a spouse. The Japanese bombed Pearl Harbor on a Sunday, December 7, 1941. Sara had slept late. When Bea woke her for Mass, she knew something was wrong. The radio was on in the kitchen, and on Sundays Bea turned the radio on only in the afternoon to listen to Father Coughlin and Jack Benny. She knew from Bea's face that something was wrong. At first she thought someone had died.

Someone, of course, had died. The Japanese had bombed Pearl Harbor. Bea said that the Japanese had killed all the sailors and sunk all the battleships. "We are going to war," Aunt Bea said.

When the President addressed the nation, the radio carried his speech. Fifty years later, Sara can still hear his voice, still hear the phrase: "A day that will live in infamy." By then Aunt Bea was crying and saying, "My two sons will have to go to war." Between the news broadcasts, the radio kept playing Frank Sinatra. He was singing "Sunday, Monday, and Always." The President speaking, Aunt Bea crying, Frank Sinatra singing: the day fused these things together so that now, for Sara, to remember one is to remember them all.

Sara was late for Mass. She remembers that she had a new hat that Sunday, one she had bought the night before at Sixty-third and Halsted. The hat came down over her right eye. Ever after, she thought of that hat as her Pearl Harbor hat. At the church the priest prayed for the dead servicemen and asked for prayers for the Japanese that God might forgive them. She doubts they got many prayers.

That night she and Nell returned to Sixty-third and Halsted. Everyone, she remembers, was wearing the same look that Aunt Bea had that morning. There were crowds of people on the street, but people were quiet. They seemed both somber and angry. That was the night, she thinks, in which everything changed. After that, the country was not the same. Men left; jobs became plentiful; women could do work no one would have imagined them doing.

When the United States went to war, Sara was not an American citizen. And since the Chicago Municipal Airport was a hub for American pilots going overseas, she became a security risk. The airlines told her that she needed citizenship papers before they could issue her the identification papers necessary for work at the airport. So on July 29, 1942, she went and filed her declaration of intention to become a citizen.

She had moved from Aunt Bea's by then and was living at 6115 South Rockwell. She now lived on the outer edges of family but still within the network of the Southwest Side. The apartment was in a basement, two doors down from Pat's uncle Tom O'Hara. She was twenty-two years old. She swore that she was not an anarchist or a saboteur. She looked straight into the camera, a young American woman, and they took her picture. The declaration of intention was enough to get her a security clearance.

After that the story becomes confused. At various times my mother has told me that she thought she was a citizen because her father had become a citizen or that she thought her declaration of intention made her a citizen. She acted like a citizen. She voted. But citizenship was only a preferred, not necessarily a required, prerequisite for voting in Chicago. The Chicago machine voted the dead when necessary; Sara was a living, breathing Democrat, intimately acquainted with citizens, if not a citizen herself. They were not going to challenge her right to vote. And having voted in Chicago, she continued to vote afterward.

As a child, I always assumed my mother was a citizen. Only while writing this book did I learn that she did not become a citizen until I was an adult. After she received her wartime security clearance, the issue did not arise again until 1969, when she prepared to go back to Ireland for the first time since her departure in 1936. She needed a passport. She had, it turns out, never completed the final papers. She got new copies of her birth and baptismal certificates from Ireland. She was living in the San Fernando Valley then, and in 1970 my father drove her to the federal building in Los Angeles. The Immigration and Naturalization Service asked her a few questions and then sent her home. She received her citizenship papers in the mail. She is embarrassed by this long lapse between her immigration and her citizenship, but the story is not that unusual.

Certainly, she felt and reacted like a citizen during the war. The war itself was horrible. Billy Ahern joined the Army and so did Jerry Mulvihill. Even if loved ones didn't die, there was the fear of death and the separation. There was rationing and the everyday hardships at home, but there was also something more.

The war was nearly sacramental. It blessed those civilian activities it touched; everyone sought to anoint themselves with it. What had been mundane activities became holy in the service of the war. On June 26, 1942, Studs Terkel, then at station WAIT Chicago and already a Chicago personality, interviewed Don Sterling, a streetcar repairman like Jack Walsh. It was part of a series of Friday evening interviews with trade union members.

Studs led Don through a series of questions, and Don in his answers praised the union, the Amalgamated Association of Street, Electric, Railway, and Motor Coach Employees of America. "That's some title," said Studs.

"That's some union," said Don.

The union, by bringing "Joe Citizen" to work, was doing its bit "to lick the Axis." The interview went through bad jokes and war bonds, civil defense committees, and the children of union men in the service. It culminated in Don's ringing defense of the union and his attack on Westbrook Pegler, the right-wing columnist then demeaning unions.

The largest bastions of privilege would hold, but during the war the rich, for the first time in American history, lost a portion of their wealth as those below them gained. There seemed a sense that working people had weathered the worst. The future, once the war was won, would be theirs. Don listed the union's achievements: a special fund for members in distress, pensions, sick benefits, disability insurance, credit unions, and higher wages. Such things were triumphs for Jack Walsh and his family.

The war was a moment in American history when collective

effort was praised, when what people did together seemed to matter more than what they did alone, and when common interest and a common cause could claim to rise above private interest. Jack Walsh's daily work seemed to have a purpose beyond the daily wage, and the conditions of that work no longer seemed totally beyond his control.

The way public events altered private lives became most apparent in hindsight: World War II created a point of departure for Sara and Nell. Since Sara's arrival, their lives had been shared experiences lived within the same house and around the same people. During the war, imperceptibly at first, they disentangled, separated, and became different. Sara's life was drawing away from Chicago; Nell became a receding figure rooted in the Southwest Side.

But that is not entirely true, for, while Nell remained nearly stationary on the Southwest Side, the place itself changed around her. Nell was married, and Pat got a deferment for his work at Crane's. By 1941 Nell was in the midst of her second pregnancy. Yet it was not marriage and pregnancy in themselves that made the difference.

The night of December 7, 1941, when Sara and Nell went to Sixty-third and Halsted, was the last of Sara's stories that feature her and Nell together. By then Nell had already changed. The somberness of the crowd probably matched her mood.

The change, according to Sara, came with Nell's first child. Sara remembers that the pregnancy seemed normal. The child was a boy, whom they named John, after his grandfather. He died shortly after birth. Nell was devastated. Sara was no longer living on South Mozart Street, but she came back to be with Nell. Nell could not, Sara says, control her emotions.

What Sara remembers is the funeral, or rather the lack of one. Jack Walsh and Pat put the baby's body in a small white casket. The casket contained the older man's namesake and the younger man's son. They did not hire an undertaker. They put the coffin in Pat's Chevrolet and drove across the city to bury the child in a cemetery on the Northwest Side. Jack Walsh knew the North Side, for he had lived there with the Butlers, but such a burial was still an exile of a sort. The Northwest Side was not a place any of them usually went. Sara offers no explanation of this. It was what they did.

After that, Sara remembers, Nell was not the same. The shopping and the clothes, which had defined her in the stories, ceased to matter. She took to wearing plain housedresses. She became pregnant again; that child lived, and more children came, grew, and prospered. But Nell the beauty queen, Nell the shopper, Nell the arch critic of her sister's greenhorn ways became a figure of the past.

Sara remained in contact with Pat and Nell over the next several years, but she was going in a different direction. She left the basement apartment near Tom O'Hara's and moved in with coworkers from the airport. She wanted to be with young people. That they were what she still calls American girls did not bother her. They were, she means, non-Irish, usually non-Catholic, and of no immediately obvious ethnicity. They moved into a relatively new apartment building on what she calls the East Side. I have never heard the term "East Side" used in reference to Chicago before. She means that the building was near Lake Michigan.

Her job and the airport, rather than South Mozart Street, became the center of her life. Every day at the airport she saw evidence of lives uprooted, reordered, and rearranged. It did not frighten her. It attracted her. The airport was far more interesting than giving women facials. There were possibilities at the airport that the rest of the Southwest Side did not offer.

The war changed the country in ways that people would have resisted in peacetime but that in wartime seemed unavoidable and even welcome. Old categories broke down. The Army and war work mixed people who otherwise would have remained separate. Sara did not resist these changes; she yielded to them.

As Sara watched the pilots and passengers move through Midway, she was swept into the swirl of people lifted up from all over America, moved across the country in trains, planes, buses, and trucks, and mixed together in ways once unusual and now common. It was how she met my father, a meeting that would have been unimaginable in peacetime.

PART IV

30

For the first time, I felt like I was an American girl.
  —Sara's memory of her first meeting with Harry White

One of the benefits Sara received while working for the airlines was a free trip every six months. As a nonpaying passenger, however, she was bumped whenever an airline had enough paying passengers to fill the plane. Even paying passengers were bumped whenever the military needed seats to ferry pilots to their destinations. She was last in line. She spent a lot of time sitting in terminals. But "youth was with us," she says, and waiting in the airport was not so bad.

Her destinations suggest her growing confidence and independence. The first time she traveled she went to Newark for the weekend because Pat had an uncle there. She stayed with him and his wife; their daughter Kay and her husband lived nearby. Kay's husband was a jeweler; he gave Sara a brooch as a memento of the trip. She has it still. This was movement along the customary lines of family; it did not take her beyond her South Side Irish connections.

But after that, her trips and destinations changed. The trips sometimes lasted more than a weekend, and Sara chose to go where she was unknown, where there would be no one familiar to greet her when she arrived. This is how she, along with Dorothy Boland, who also had a job with the airlines, flew south to New Orleans, San Antonio, and Dallas in 1942. For her whole

life she had lived in places she knew, or came to know, deeply
and intimately. Now every six months she could be a stranger
beyond the customary constraints of family, friends, and neighbors. Dorothy was her only connection to the Southwest Side.

On the way to New Orleans they were bumped in Atlanta and
had a very long wait before getting seats on another flight. They
had saved money for a cab ride to the hotel in New Orleans.
They arrived exhausted and slept for at least twelve hours.

After that they wandered through the French Quarter fascinated by the enclosed gardens. It was a place unlike any they
had ever seen. At night, after dinner, they walked through
crowds of rowdy and drunk GIs. Eventually, the military police
would come, sorting through the soldiers like men looking for
the ripest fruit; they threw the rowdiest and drunkest into their
trucks and drove them off. It was wartime, Sara says, and you
could not forget it, no matter where you went or what you did.

On the third day in New Orleans, Sara was sitting with Dorothy in a restaurant having a late breakfast when a waitress
brought a note saying a soldier would like to buy them a drink
and wanted to know what they would like. They chose two
drinks, which the waitress brought promptly. With them she
brought another note asking if the soldier could join them. They
said yes, and Sara remembers him arriving at their table rather
quickly.

He was an officer, handsome, a first lieutenant in the Signal
Corps. His name was Harry White, and he was on a short leave
from Fort Sam Houston, Texas. He would become my father.

I have a picture of him taken at about this time. He gave it
to his sister, who was a teenager. She gave it to me. It says,
"With love, Harry." He is in his Signal Corps uniform with
crossed semaphores. He has a broad forehead and dark black
hair combed straight back.

The picture is in my office now, and I am always taken aback
by it. It is not how I remember my father. He looks remarkably
cheerful. Even though I, obviously, can have no memories of
him then, my memories of him later lead me to concentrate on
what is not there more than on what is. When I look at the

picture, I see what is absent. There is no sign of the anger, the sudden and terrifying eruptions, that I associate with him. I realize that I am looking at a person I never knew.

I feel odd when I look at his picture so intently. At the time of the photograph he was twenty-four, the age my son is now. I am now only a few years younger than he was when he died an early death in 1972.

My mother, although she, too, has to struggle against memories of a later time, can possess and understand this picture in ways I cannot. This is the man she knew, not the man her children knew. Knowing this, she is irritated at my attempts to understand him in the light of the person he became later.

They went to dinner that night. He told them he was undergoing tests at Kelly Field in order to become a pilot.

He asked them where they were from. And when he heard her accent, her speech still faintly tinted with a brogue when she was tired or relaxed, he asked her if she was born in Chicago. "No," she said, "I was born in Ireland."

When they left the restaurant, he walked through the French Quarter with them. He explained the history of the area and its French connection. He answered their questions. He was, she says, very interesting and easy to talk to.

He invited them to dinner the next night at a lovely restaurant. They lingered over their meal, and after that, they went to a nightclub where all Sara remembers is the noise. It was, like all of New Orleans, full of soldiers, and someone was singing at a piano, but the roar of the soldiers drowned out her voice.

He walked them back to their hotel and asked if he could see them the next day. They agreed, and when they went up to their room, they argued about which of them he was interested in, each picking the other.

The next day was their last day in New Orleans. He took them on a bus to Lake Pontchartrain. Although she lived near Lake Michigan, Sara remembers thinking how big this lake was. That night he took them to dinner again, and then they went dancing.

When he walked them back to their hotel, he asked Sara if

he could write or call her. She was shocked; she was sure he was interested in Dorothy. She gave him her address and phone number. He kissed Dorothy on the cheek and Sara on the lips. That was, Sara remembers, how it started.

She felt as if she were walking on clouds. For the first time, she felt like an American girl. She hoped to see him in San Antonio, but he had remained in New Orleans. San Antonio gave her a terrible sunburn but no romance.

To make her feel like an American girl was an achievement he would have savored. His parents' great ambition was to make him an American boy. Like Sara's father and Sara herself, Harry's father was an immigrant.

Sara and Harry met on American ground that only the war could have made possible. World War II was the matchmaker for that meeting in the restaurant in New Orleans. It is hard to imagine other circumstances that could have thrown them together.

He was Jewish from Boston. She was Roman Catholic from Chicago. Sara plays this down, but Harry, my father, never did. Sara says she didn't know anything about Jews, and his being Jewish was inconsequential. Harry knew little enough about County Kerry, but he knew Boston and its Irish Catholics. He knew Irish Catholics as friends and associates of his father and his family, but he knew, too, that Father Coughlin had a rabid following among the Irish who distributed pamphlets outside Catholic churches during Holy Week claiming that Jews had "ruined" Dorchester, Roxbury, and Chelsea. Harry and his parents lived in Dorchester.

There was her Irishness and his Jewishness, but there were other differences. He had graduated cum laude from Harvard. She had finished fourth grade at the Ballylongford National School. But neither could recognize such differences when he approached her table that first morning. What she found out and cared about in those idyllic two days was that he was polite, handsome, and easy to talk to.

Sara at first finds it hard to talk of how they regarded each other in those early days, then weeks, then months. These things, she tells me, bring back too many memories, some good and some sad. To ask her to remember is to bring back more than memories of the war years. The Harry White she knew then, the Harry White she fell in love with, can never again stand out as clearly as he did the moment he walked through the restaurant in the French Quarter toward her table. He is surrounded in memory now with other versions of himself. This memory of him in the restaurant—if she does not concentrate on it intently—yields to other memories of a long and tumultuous marriage.

The chronology that I as a historian want is not the way that this past survives in my mother's mind. In memory all the events of her romance with my father—the great romance of her life—and their marriage mix together like coins dropped for years into a jar. Reconstructing the order of their arrival, their chronology, is hard. A chronology of her feelings is virtually impossible.

I want the impossible. I want her to remember the past as if she did not know what followed after their beginning. I want her to put things back where they were that moment in 1942, when she did not yet know all that would follow. I want her to pretend with me that chronology is more real than the mixed and tangled remnants of her past that she now keeps in her mind.

Initially, she refuses. She does not refuse directly. She just does not tell me what I want to know. That is not how my mother does things.

So then I write what I know, what I have heard from others, including my father, and, when she reads the first drafts of this book, she reacts with indignation, anger, and hurt. She thinks that I treat him badly. She wants to protect his memory, her memory. She wants her silence to be final. Here, more than anyplace else, she wants her memory uncontested. She does not want me talking to others, gathering other stories, looking into the remnants of my father's past. When she is silent, she wants those things about which she refuses to speak to remain as quiet as the tomb. That is the ultimate power of stories. They take on themselves the decision about what will be remembered and what will be told. The part of the past she claims most fiercely is the part she wants forgotten.

Against her memory, my history rummages and pries and guesses. It draws on other memories of my father—my own, my uncle's, my aunt's. And since I, cruelly, she thinks, insist on invading this past, she eventually speaks about things she would rather let lie. It is the cruelest work in the book, not because what it reveals about the early years of their romance and marriage is bad but because the happiness they achieved did not last, and to remember one is to acknowledge the other. First death took him, and now I make public a version of him that sticks like a shadow to the memory that she has worked so hard to preserve for herself. She insists on her memory. To her, it seems I wish to deprive her of him again.

31

5-14-37. A dark and typical NA non-resident. . . . A good student but that is his only claim to an award.

                    —From Harry White's student file at Harvard

arry White, too, told stories about his past. The central story, the story that served as a prism through which to view all the other stories, was the story of the trial, conviction, imprisonment, and pardon of Samuel White. Samuel White was my *zeyde*. As a child, I thought that *zeyde*—Yiddish for grandfather—was my grandfather's proper name, just as I thought *bubbe*—Yiddish for grandmother—was my grandmother's name. I adored Zeyde as fully and completely as a child can admire an adult. I admired him in a way that I will never be able to admire an adult again. I remembered everything I was told about him. I believed everything Zeyde told me. He died before I could ever change my feelings, and it is hard, even now, for me to imagine that I ever could have become disillusioned.

I once watched Zeyde invent Thousand Island dressing. We were in the kitchen in Wantagh, New York. I was his audience. I was his audience for everything. When he didn't want me as his audience, when he was calling bookies from the rear room of his liquor store in Roxbury, he knew how to dismiss me gently. "Dickie," he would say, "do me a favor. Get some soda and potato chips for you and your brothers."

But this evening, I was his audience, watching raptly as he mixed together catsup and mayonnaise as if such a thing had never been attempted before, as if such a thing had never been considered before. He looked doubtful; this was, I recognized, an untried experiment. He gave me a taste. I tasted it with the wonder that Columbus's crew must have felt while eating the fruits of the New World for the first time. I was amazed that he could discover this combination lying, unimagined until then, in my own refrigerator. I ran to tell my father what Zeyde had done. Not for the first or last time my father thought he was raising an idiot.

What I was told about Zeyde I remembered. My father did not tell me the whole story all at once. The basic plot was always the same, but I have reconstituted the story from the various versions I heard as a child.

Zeyde, my father told me, had once been rich. He had been a very successful lawyer in Boston in the 1920s, and he had dabbled in politics. He had been tight with the political machine of James Michael Curley, the mayor of Boston.

In the 1920s, my father told me, Zeyde had been involved in a street-paving contract that was, like many street-paving contracts under Curley, crooked. Samuel White and his collaborators had been caught and indicted. Accused along with Samuel White were two Irishmen. It was clear that somebody was going to have to take the blame. The judge was Irish, my father said, and he picked the Jew to take the fall. Zeyde was sent to the federal penitentiary in Atlanta. He lost his wealth and his law practice, and his family sank into poverty. The Depression came, and, my father told me, Bubbe had to stand in line for food. Eventually, Herbert Hoover pardoned Zeyde, but he had been disbarred. He had to wait another year before he could practice law again.

Harry White was nine, soon to turn ten, when his father went to prison in 1929. He vowed to kill that Irish judge when he grew up.

This story was my father's book of Genesis. This was the story that explained his childhood, his college years, and, later, even his marriage. It explained the divide he had crossed to marry my mother.

The Irish were what divided them: the Irish codefendants who walked, the Irish politicians who betrayed his father, the Irish judge who sentenced Zeyde. The Irish, in his story, betrayed the Jews, just as the Jews, in Father Coughlin's stories, betrayed the Irish. The Irish in the story threw the family into poverty. Around this central story of betrayal, he grouped other, smaller stories of the Irish street toughs he had to fight.

In this story Zeyde's conviction divided my mother and father into partisans of opposing camps, even though in everyday life my mother admired Zeyde only slightly less than I did. After Zeyde's release, the Whites were poor, but they slowly climbed back to a measure of prosperity. My uncle, my father's younger brother, provided me with details he remembered from his youth. Zeyde resumed his law practice, watched it fail, and eventually got work with the Works Progress Administration. Later, when the war broke out, he became a welder in the shipyards. He invested his savings in two liquor stores, one in Roxbury, the other in Nantasket. He still owned them when I was a child.

Prison did not break Zeyde, but it tempered his ambitions. He kept his political connections; he got small favors, but he never tried anything big again. He had sympathy for people whose lives had slipped out of control; he never condescended to them; he granted them no nobility just because they had suffered. He knew how much of a role simple chance can play in life.

This was not Bubbe's attitude. Bubbe knew whom to blame, and she had, I guess, good reason to blame Zeyde, given the trajectory of their lives. There was a determination in Bubbe that brooked no opposition. She knew how things were to be done. She knew that my brother should drink his orange juice before, not after, he ate his cereal. She knew that I should never read indoors on a sunny day.

Her determination was something my brothers and I struggled to subvert when I was a child, but it is precisely that determination that had seen her through those Depression years with her husband in prison. She would trust her own judgment and her own resources. Her engagement ring became her final recourse in times of trouble. Her son Harry remembered that was what she hocked last and redeemed first. When I married, she sent me that ring for my wife.

She always suspected human flaws, and she always, of course, found and denounced them, but she was also tremendously loyal and attracted loyalty in return. When she was only a child, she formed with friends a club they called the Pansies. It was a reading club. They met every month to discuss books. They met as children. They met as young women, when Zeyde was a successful lawyer. They met when Zeyde was in prison and Bubbe was on relief. They met through the Depression, and through two world wars and the Korean War and the Vietnam War. They were still meeting when Bubbe died.

My uncle told me a story to illustrate the difference between Bubbe and Zeyde. Once Bubbe, who disapproved of liquor and never drank, was helping Zeyde at the liquor store in Roxbury. In the morning when they opened the store, there were already winos lined up for their muscatel and fortified wines. One of them, particularly dirty and disheveled, had no money. This man was constantly around the store; he was a nuisance. To Bubbe's disgust, he stayed behind that morning wheedling Zeyde for a bottle. She wanted Zeyde to get rid of him, but the man stayed and begged. He promised to come back and pay later. Zeyde waited until everyone else was gone. He gave the man the bottle. The wino took it in disbelief and left.

"What are you doing?" Bubbe demanded in astonishment. "Do you think he'll ever pay you? Do you think you'll ever see him again?"

"No," said Zeyde, "I'll never see him again."

"So what are you doing?"

"Look," said Zeyde, "you wanted to get rid of him, right?"

"Yes," said Bubbe.

"So," said Zeyde, "you'll never see him again."

When still a child, with his father in prison and his family crashing into poverty, Harry had to shoulder an enormous burden. He had become his mother's main reliance. It was a burden thrust on him, and, if he resented it, he still did not throw it down. Even as a teenager, he seemed, at least from the outside, the core of the family as Zeyde struggled to regain his lost fortune and steady his marriage. When Harry was old enough, he worked during the school year; as a senior in high school, he worked at the Boston Public Library and contributed to his own support. The family needed the help.

But the real burden was not so much what he did without or what he needed to contribute, it was, instead, the future. Harry became the brilliant child who after his father's fall carried the family's hopes. How much hope Bubbe and Zeyde invested in him I do not know. It must have been substantial.

As a teenager, Harry talked only rarely and elliptically about his father's imprisonment. And except for Harry's guarded references, you never would have known from Zeyde's actions the severity of his fall. Zeyde went about his business as best he could. He practiced law, with an office on Devonshire Street in Boston. He specialized in real estate, but as the real estate market collapsed, he struggled. In 1936, when Harry applied to college, Zeyde owned no real estate, had no savings, and had borrowed the limit his life insurance allowed. Eventually, he gave up his practice entirely. By 1939 he was working for the Works Progress Administration. He did not accumulate much.

Harry had, as far as I know, only two refuges from the burdens of his family. The first was the Trachtenbergs' house. Mort Trachtenberg was his closest friend. He lived a few blocks from Harry in Dorchester. Mort's parents adored Harry. Mort's mother, in her last years, more than one hundred years old, still talked about Harry. He would play chess at their house. "No quarter ever given and gloating encouraged," Mort tells me.

Boston Latin was his other refuge, and, more than this, it provided a constant validation of his worth. Boston Latin served as a prep school for young boys, mostly Jewish and Irish, whose families would not have been able to afford prep school even if there had been a prep school interested in them. He entered from Christopher Gibson School in the fall of 1930, a month after his father returned home from prison. His family was struggling to get off relief, but Boston Latin was a different world, an escape from his family's shattered fortunes. Here, it seemed, only his abilities mattered. His classmates remember competing to get in and competing to stay in.

I have things he once owned, yearbooks and things he won or bought during these years, the early 1930s. They are little bits of history, memorializing some achievement, some momentary desire. Some of them he gave me; some Bubbe gave me; some my mother gave me. Some I borrowed from my sister. They are little things, books and prizes.

There is, for example, the book *A Thousand Years of Jewish History*, written by the Reverend Maurice H. Harris. Harry received it in May 1931, when he was eleven, almost twelve, and at the Mishkam Tefila School preparing for his bar mitzvah. Mishkam Tefila, the tabernacle of prayer, was a large temple in Dorchester. He studied hard. S. Zucrow and Arthur O. Green autographed the book they gave him as a reward "for excellence in work."

The most telling thing I have is his yearbook from Boston Latin. He went there for six years, graduating in 1936. His attachment to that school seemed almost crazed to me when I was younger and thought it just evidence of his perpetual competition with his own children: our record could never equal his record there. And it couldn't. He needed that school much more than we ever needed ours.

He thrived there. Every year there were the prizes: Classical Prize, 1932–33–34–35; Modern Prize, 1930–31–32–33–34–35; Class of 1885 Prize, 1932–33, Approbation Prize, 1935–1936.

He was there on a spring day in 1936 when the students gathered for yearbook pictures. Divided into groups, the students sat and stood in front of the camera in schoolrooms or, more often, on the school steps. There he was sitting in the first row with the Yearbook Committee, Arthur Cantor (later the Broadway producer), chairman. And there he was with the staff of *The Register*, the student paper. Arthur Cantor, editor in chief, thanked him for his book columns, which "have been pleasing in their frankness and style," and added that he has "acted as stabilizing influence upon the Staff during the difficulties that arose at times." He was with the Literary Club as their president. In November he had delivered a talk on the Pulitzer Prize drama awards of the past years and had made his predictions for the current season. He was with the Physics Club as their secretary and the Math Club. And he had served as class registrar and on the Farewell Dance Committee.

The responsibilities of all this apparently had caused him to drop out of the Debating Club after four years, as well as the Latin Club, the Chess and Checker Club, and the Chess Team, all of which he had participated in at one time or another.

I imagine that Boston Latin must have occupied most of his waking hours, but late many afternoons he also went to Hebrew Teachers College, at the time a center of émigrés and Eastern European Jewish learning. There he would have studied Hebrew, rabbinic texts, and the Bible. A colleague of mine, Hillel Kieval, who attended Hebrew Teachers College a generation later, said that it always had had a contingent from Boston Latin. The students in the Prozdor, the high school division, would come for two hours several days a week. Boston Latin and Hebrew Teachers College offered extraordinary intellectual opportunities for a young student in love with writing and ideas. They were also, I can't help but think, welcome respites from family catastrophe.

The pictures show that he was small and wiry; they can't show that he was a superb swimmer and a devoted Boston Braves fan. He read voraciously. In July 1935, he bought, or had bought for him, two books: cheap, used editions of Alfred Lord Tennyson's *The Princess: A Medley and Other Poems* and *Sheridan's Plays*. He inscribed his name and the date, July 1, 1935, on the flyleaf of each book.

All through his school years he was locked in rivalry with Izzy Rosenberg, who, in the end, beat him out to become both class president and valedictorian. A cartoon in the yearbook identifies them as the "Harvard professors."

He and Izzy Rosenberg graduated in 1936. They and eighty-seven of their classmates intended to go on to Harvard.

I am able to track down some of his classmates at Boston Latin. "It was sixty years ago," one tells me ruefully, as if he cannot imagine it. The memories of his classmates are vague and generic. He was "very smart" and "lots of fun," one classmate commented. I already knew he was very smart. He never tired of telling me so, and I have medals he won at Boston Latin even beyond the awards listed in the yearbook—the Washington and Franklin Medal for Excellence in the Study of United States History and the Gift of Franklin Medal.

Harvard allowed me to see his student files. Harry's original application is there. Question 19 is "Why do you wish to come to Harvard?" He writes of Harvard's tradition, of the "exceptional facilities that will prepare me for the law or medicine or teaching as I may decide." Second only to this, he concludes, "are the friendships and social contacts I hope to make at Harvard. I'll be a Harvard man, a brother under the skin to thousands before me and thousands to come after."

His letters of recommendation are all from Dorchester, from a neighborhood largely of immigrant Jews like Samuel White and their children. All the letters were very brief, and all were from his father's friends. Abraham Trachtenberg wrote a one-sentence recommendation: "A very brilliant boy with an alert mind, a fine sense of humor, of good character and high intelligence." Hyman Rudofsky praised his "sense of duty to both his parents and his fellow man." Louis Brown says he was "a fine type of American young man."

He was admitted in July, but, for some reason, in August Harvard asked his father for more information. Zeyde wrote in the kind of language that I think he imagined Harvard expected to hear: "Replying to your letter of August 19th, in which you ask certain information about my oldest son Harry Eli who has been admitted to your worthy institution. I beg to advise that he is a boy of gentle manners, a natural and thorough student, one who enjoys the finer things in life such as operas, good music, and the reading of worthwhile literature."

The letter is stilted and touching. It is about a young gentleman who respects his elders. "The game of tennis seems to be a great enjoyment to him." Harry was honest. His father cannot "recall a time when he has told me an untruth." He has attended Boston Latin and "the private Hebrew Schools where he obtained a knowledge of Jewish life, history and tribulations." He has also taken piano lessons, but unfortunately he has shown no aptitude.

Harry went to Harvard as a scholarship student. Harvard gave him the Henry D. and Jonathan M. Parmenter Scholarship, but it covered only $200 of the roughly $1,000 that tuition and living on campus cost. To make up the difference, he worked and lived at home, at 90 Corbert Street in Dorchester, the first and second years.

There is a certain serendipity to research that no longer surprises me. I have boxes of books stored in the basement of Smith Hall at the University of Washington, where I teach. The dusty and sometimes mildewed books aggravate my wife's asthma. To find my father's books, I need to rummage through the boxes stored in a room that is intended to be an office for professors emeriti.

Tom Pressly was working while I rummaged. I was his teaching assistant years ago, and to him I owe a great deal of whatever I know about teaching history. I explained what I was doing. I have long known he was at Harvard when my father was there, but now it turns out that they were in the same class, although they never knew each other. He has kept the yearbooks that have continued to appear through the years and a list of surviving members of the class. It was through Tom that I was able to look for people who remember my father.

Tom Pressly was also a scholarship student at Harvard. He came from the small town of Troy, Tennessee. His mother was nervous about the temptations that the North, Boston, and the Ivy League would present to a boy from Troy. Surveying an imposing array of dangers, she gave him a single warning: "Watch out for the Unitarians."

For Tom Pressly, being a scholarship student meant waiting on tables in the residence houses. That, Tom tells me, was hard, psychologically hard. It marked you and set you apart, but it could be survived. James Conant was changing Harvard during those years, and being a scholarship student had partially ceased to be a term of opprobrium. Tom was preoccupied with grades and making the dean's list, for his scholarship depended on it. He thinks of Harvard now as a world of merit, where everything rode on academic rankings.

And, in part, Harvard was a world of merit, but it was something more and less than that. Harry's freshman year at Harvard was a brilliant success. He had As in English, chemistry, history, and mathematics. Harvard ranked its students in six groups then. Group 1 represented highest distinction and numbered about two percent of his class of 950 students. He was in group 1. He made the dean's list but not the very select group of only seven students that included Izzy Rosenberg. Harry won the Detur, a major prize, and was presented with two handsome volumes of Plato's *Dialogues* bound in red and black. I still have them.

Harry's tutors recommended an increase in scholarship aid to allow him to cease working and move on campus. They praised his potential, ranked him with the best students they taught, and proclaimed a great future for him.

Then he confronted the limits of merit. On his scholarship form beneath the line where it tells the applicant not to write, there is a short note.

5-14-37. A dark and typical NA non-resident. Has financed current year through earnings, money from home and $200 scholarship. Will need same set up next year. A good student but that is his only claim to an award.

Dark and typical NA nonresidents like Harry were not part of the Harvard brotherhood he had imagined a year earlier. I didn't know what NA meant. Tom Pressly, however, had the address of the man who had served as assistant dean for freshman. He didn't recall NA as being commonly used, but from the context he guessed "that it might mean 'non-Aryan,' if your father was Jewish." Harry was dark, non-Aryan, and only his record as a student qualified him for an award. That was not enough.

He never read this file, but at some level he suspected what it contained. He came to know the limits of merit, and he guessed why he could not move beyond those limits. When advisors in the placement office asked why he had not used the Harvard placement services to help find the jobs he needed to continue in school, he replied that "this office did nothing for Jewish boys." Someone noted on his record that he didn't look particularly Jewish and with his name could probably pass. I can't find his later application to Winthrop House, but at that time the tutors interviewing for the house put asterisks by the names of Jewish applicants.

For the rest of his time at Harvard, Harry worked from twenty to forty hours a week as a Gray Line clerk and guide and relief office clerk. His grades predictably declined, but there was more than overwork involved. When he met disdain, he returned it. One instructor remarked that he was "rather careless in appearance." In 1938 his instructor in chemistry noted, "This man's weakness lies in his personality which in my opinion is somewhat non-cooperative." He did well on tests but neglected assignments.

As a sophomore biochemistry major confident in his German, Harry failed to attend a class on scientific German for weeks at a time. When he did show up late in the term, the professor stopped the class.

"Gentlemen," he said, "we have a guest in our midst. Mr. Harry White has deigned to honor us with his presence."

Harry White then got up and left the class. He came back only to take the final. He got a C in German.

During his junior and senior years, his record was erratic, mostly As, an occasional B, but then an E in biology and a D in chemistry after three As in previous years. In biology he fell behind in his lab work, but his final seems to have been decisive. The examination was of a new type. The class was surprised. Harry wrote his answers in verse denouncing the new exam format. In his last chemistry class he did poorly because, as he told Mort, he felt the instructor was "a man of no consequence." He spent his time, his instructors in the sciences complained, auditing English and history classes. His two poor grades in biology and chemistry delayed his promotion to the senior class. Harvard even called his father in for a talk. Zeyde was surprised at his grades. Often, he told Harvard, Harry could get good grades with hardly any studying at all. This did not help his son's case.

Harry's resentment and his heavy workload did not totally isolate him during these years at Harvard. When Tom Pressly counted the number of students in Harry's class at Harvard from Boston Latin, he came up with fifty-five. It is far fewer than the eighty-nine who intended to go, but still substantial. Harry knew others like himself.

In his junior and senior years he lived in Winthrop House. Among the others living there were John F. Kennedy and J. P. Morgan II. Kennedy had allegedly come to college with a servant, but he still was Irish American and could not become a member of the best student clubs. Harvard exacted even from a Kennedy a certain humiliation. It exacted more from Harry White, but it simultaneously opened to him a world of privilege. The opening was admittedly partial. From my father's stories I always had the sense that people like Kennedy and Morgan were known to him the way partygoers in the next room might be known. The party could be heard and seen, but no one invited him to join it, as they might have if Zeyde had not lost his money and gone to prison. Partially, his exclusion was because he was Jewish, but it was also because his father's fall had denied him the privileges that class secured even for Jews. Kennedy and Morgan and the people at the party had the confidence of their class; my father had only his confidence in himself. To Tom Pressly and, initially, to my father, Harvard with its inexorable rankings seemed a meritocracy. But for Kennedys and Morgans merit came with birth and wealth; their grades at Harvard would hardly enhance or mar their standing in the world. Their grades were mediocre to poor; their privilege was great.

Harry White was always immensely proud of having gone to Harvard. He had learned a fundamental Harvard lesson: being at Harvard was what mattered. In the long run what you did there mattered much less. Where you came from mattered. He now came from Harvard.

He was, in any case, hardly helpless in the face of Harvard. In Harry's senior year Mort Trachtenberg, who had gone to Bowdoin, came to Harvard for a year of graduate school. He and Harry had grown up during the Depression. They had little in the way of illusions. They tended, Mort remembers, "to look at things rather cynically" and were "pleasantly surprised when things didn't fall apart."

"That year," Mort says, "they had a lot of fun." Harry was a playboy, his sister says, but with his work schedule, his classes, auditing other classes, and voracious reading, it is hard to believe he had much time to be a playboy.

In his junior year he tried to change his major from biochemistry, but he was unable to do so. In his senior year he listed his intended occupation as lawyer. Mort says it was a whim. He never had any serious interest in the law, but he had already been told that medical schools would think twice before admitting him. Neither he nor Mort had the slightest idea what they wanted to do after college. Both were convinced that war was coming and that any immediate decision would inevitably be futile. In the end Harry graduated cum laude. He won no more prizes.

There are hints in all this, I think, of his life to come. He pushed at the edges, but he never really tried to break through. He had a fear of falling. His father had fallen. He was cynical about the world, but his cynicism was not debilitating. Knowing the world was unfair, he thought he could use knowledge to find a way through. He rebelled enough to be noticed but never enough to precipitate trouble that might cause him to forfeit the rewards Harvard promised him. When he talked to me, he always mentioned what he almost did or what he wanted to do. In 1937 or 1938 he considered joining the Abraham Lincoln Brigade to fight against Franco and the fascists in Spain, but he never did. He wanted, he told me, to be an academic, but there were quotas that limited the number of Jews a university would hire, and he wouldn't take the chance, particularly after the war, when he had a family to support.

He wanted to be respectable, but more than that, he wanted to be responsible, although he would define responsibility largely in terms of securing the financial success that would support a family. Together, respectability and responsibility warred with his instincts and his anger at what had happened to his father and the limits he confronted. Zeyde's legacy made him both rebellious and cautious: he remembered all too well the consequences when a father could not support his children.

He took only one big chance: he married Sara, my mother, who came far from his familiar worlds. Everyone who knew him was stunned, Mort says.

In the form he filled out for the Harvard Placement Office, he reverted to caution. He said he wanted a position as a "clerk or office assistant, with long term possibilities and promotion if possible with a technical concern." "I have always displayed," he wrote, "a natural aptitude for figures, and a marked adaptability and versatility."

Financial irresponsibility would never be one of his failings. He supported his children. "Say what you will," my mother would tell me, even after the bad times, "your father was a good provider."

He never found his job as clerk with a technical concern. In 1940 he and Mort and others huddled around a radio and listened as numbers that determined the order of the military draft were pulled. They drew Harry's number early.

32

Intermarriage? Back then, you stuck your head in the oven.

—My aunt on intermarriage in the 1940s

With a low draft number staring him in the face, Harry White enlisted in the Army after he graduated from Harvard in 1940. Early enlistment promised him choices of where he would go and what he would do. Enlistment, in fact, gave him few choices until he had waged his own private war with the Army. These are stories my father never told me. He did not tell stories of his failures.

In the Army's view Harry White's choices had all been made before he enlisted. He had majored in biochemistry, so they put him in the Medical Corps. They stationed him at Camp Edwards, a hospital on Cape Cod.

At Camp Edwards "they decided," his brother said, "based upon his record and so forth and so on that they wanted to make a lab technician out of him. So they sent him to Walter Reed Hospital. And he did so well at Walter Reed Hospital that they asked him to stay on and teach. But his superiors at Camp Edwards had sent him to be a lab technician, and they needed a lab technician." The people at Camp Edwards demanded that he be sent back.

He went back to Camp Edwards very reluctantly. It seemed he would spend his entire enlistment as a lab technician. He did not want to be a lab technician, and so he refused to work. They assigned him, or so the family story goes, to clean latrines until he changed his mind. He cleaned latrines for weeks.

But new possibilities arose. In the fall of 1940 the Army started officer candidates schools. Which school an enlisted man went to depended on where he was stationed. If you were at Camp Edwards, you apparently went to Signal Corps officer candidates school. He applied and was accepted. He escaped Camp Edwards and the latrines, and by 1942 he was at Fort Sam Houston. He was on leave from Fort Sam Houston when he met Sara Walsh.

For a long time my mother did not tell me stories of their romance or their marriage. They met in 1942. They would be married in the fall of 1943. Gradually and reluctantly she tells me. She does not want to talk about the tensions the marriage produced in his family and hers.

But to me the difficulties they confronted seem only more evidence of the romance between them then because this was not and never could be a marriage of convenience. It was wartime; they did not see each other again for months after their meeting in New Orleans. When Sara returned to Chicago, the letters began to arrive. They came often. She read each of them several times over, but she did not save them. He wrote and told her that he had failed his eye exam and was back in Fort Monmouth, New Jersey. There was hardly a letter in which he did not ask her to come and see him there.

The romance grew with each lover from necessity partially inventing the other, each fulfilling needs the other lover may never have imagined. She did not tell her family about him. My father never even mentioned her to Mort Trachtenberg, his best friend.

After several months she went to South Mozart Street where Pat, Nell, and Jack Walsh were still living. Only Nell and Jack were home. She did not tell them anything about Harry White except his name and rank. She just said that she was going to New Jersey to visit a Lieutenant White whom she had met in New Orleans. Jack Walsh got up and left the room. This was,

Sara says, what he did whenever he did not agree with a subject under discussion. On the Southwest Side of Chicago in the 1940s young women did not go to distant cities to visit a man.

Harry was waiting for her in Asbury Park, the closest town to Fort Monmouth. They were, Sara says, happy to see each other again. He took her to the officers club for dinner that night. He asked her to marry him. It was only the second time they had seen each other.

He told her that he was Jewish. She was, she says, not very clear about what this meant. Protestant meant something to her, but she wasn't sure if Jewish meant a religion or a nationality. She knew Father Coughlin did not like Jews. On South Mozart Street she had heard the word "kike" along with "wop," "dago," "nigger," and the whole vast assortment of American slurs, but they never had much meaning to her then. At sixteen she had come over too late to be much concerned with the specific varieties of non-Irish in America and the particular prejudices against them; she knew mostly the distinction between American girls and herself.

She wanted to be married by a priest, and he agreed. He had been religious until his mid to late teens. More religious, indeed, than his parents. When he walked away from religion, he walked away from something he knew and had studied.

He had applied to religion the same relentless, probing skepticism he applied to everything else in the world. He had questions that could not be answered to his satisfaction. And so he walked away. It wasn't as if he ceased regarding himself as a Jew. When Harvard asked his religion for his graduation form, he wrote Jewish. He no longer believed; but he did not feel the need of any new belief to replace the faith he had lost.

He was an atheist. It was not a big decision. He became an atheist in the same way he later became a New Yorker or a Californian. He just moved on. What other people wanted to believe was up to them. If she wanted a priest, she could have a priest.

They were married in the fall of 1943. She had married a Jew, and he had married a Catholic. No one in either family seemed pleased about it. "Intermarriage?" my aunt says. "Back then, you stuck your head in the oven." Theirs were two lives heretofore largely defined by family, and at their wedding there were no family members present. Her father did not give her away. Her sister was not a bridesmaid. Her wealth of cousins and uncles and aunts were not in attendance.

There is one more story about the marriage. Harry came home on leave in the fall of 1943, and when he was about to go back to Fort Monmouth, he told his mother that he would be seeing Sara. She knew about Sara. She knew, of course, that Sara was a shiksa.

"Harry," she told him, "just don't marry her."

On October 10, Harry called home. It was his mother's birthday. "Mom," he said, "I'm married." Sara had flown to New Jersey, and they were married at Fort Monmouth. They had been married by a priest on October 5. Listening to this story years later, my aunt says of her brother, "He had sadistic tendencies."

Mort was stunned when Harry called him to say he had married, as Mort wrote me, "an Irish girl. (AN IRISH GIRL???) and was . . . as happy as a clam." For his part, Mort "was as dumbfounded as a clam." But now Mort thinks it was the war; everything was changing. And besides, he tells me, I could understand after I met your mother.

They made a date to meet in a week in the bar at the old Hotel Pennsylvania in New York. Mort arrived with the girl he was going with at the time. Harry and Sara never showed up. Mort and his girl waited, got drunk, and the occasion passed.

Neither family knew much about the person their child had married. It would be months before Sara went back to Chicago. She stopped off on the way from California, where Harry had been stationed, to Pennsylvania, where he had been sent. It was then she told Nell and her father that Harry was Jewish. Jack Walsh got up and left the room. Nell made herself busy and changed the subject. Pat was not home. Sara went to see Aunt

Bea and told her. Aunt Bea got up, hugged her, and said, "God bless you child." It was the last time Sara would see Aunt Bea, who died soon after.

Sara tried to make contact with Harry's family, but things did not work out as well as she hoped. She sent Bubbe a Christmas card. That, she says, is when she found out the meaning of marrying a Jew. Bubbe was furious. Harry sat down and explained to her about Jews and Christmas. She had not known until then. The catechism, Sara says, had not been that explicit.

Later on, when she and Bubbe had become close, Sara regretted the pain she had caused by loving Bubbe's son so much. Maybe, she says, if she had known how much it would hurt his mother, she would not have married him. But then, instantly, she partially retracts that. I did it, she says, because I loved him and he me, and then the old defiance shines through.

Six years after Harry had graduated from Harvard, his class issued its fifth-anniversary yearbook. The war had delayed it for a year. When it came out in 1946, it didn't say much about Harry White. He was overseas. The yearbook said Harry was in military government and had married a Sara O'Hara. They did not even get her name right.

33

I protested my innocence as well as any intentional participation in the alleged conspiracy as loudly as I could, but to no avail.
—Samuel L. White, petition for pardon

After my mother and father met, their stories intersected and began to intertwine. I don't know what they told each other, what each learned from the other, or how much of what they heard became part of their memories. Eventually, my brothers and sister and I lived at the intersection of their now partially merged stories. First, when we lived on Long Island in the 1950s, and later, after we moved to California, we were the ones who heard them, ignored them, wondered about them, tried to reconcile the still visible differences, and sometimes forgot them.

It is only because I write about my mother's stories that I have come to revisit the stories my father told me in any serious way. In part his stories claimed to explain their marriage and what it represented. His stories as much as hers were an attempt to muster a past that would explain their unexpected present.

Because the centerpiece of Harry's stories is the story of my grandfather, his imprisonment, and his pardon, this is the story to which I must turn. In my father's stories my grandfather's relation with the Irish is the context for Harry's relation with my Irish mother. My grandfather, he told me, was sent to jail by an Irish judge. My grandfather, my father told me, was the only Democrat ever pardoned by Herbert Hoover.

Like all the family stories I investigate, my father's story is neither a fabrication nor much of a match with the sources I can recover. Harry was five when Samuel White supposedly committed his crime; he was nearly eleven when his father was released from prison. Harry was four years older than his brother. Another child, Leonard, had been born and died in between them. My brother Lenny bears the dead child's name. My father, being older, experienced Samuel White's trial and imprisonment more vividly, more memorably than his brother and sister.

My father told me and my brother Stephen the story of Zeyde's imprisonment, but it is a story the rest of the family would just as soon forget. My uncle and aunts willingly talk of Bubbe and Zeyde's life in the 1920s and 1930s and of how, before that, Zeyde went to Northeastern University and later Northeastern Law School and how he became a lawyer for some bootleggers. My uncle has told me about the restaurant Zeyde once owned in the 1920s, a restaurant from which I still have a large stockpot. He has told me that Zeyde lost his money before the Depression began. He and my aunt both remember Bubbe on relief.

There is no story of Zeyde in prison.

"Wasn't Zeyde disbarred?" I asked my uncle once. It was only for a year, he said sharply. This was clearly a subject he did not want to discuss.

I dropped the subject. I am not out to interrogate my uncle and aunts. They have been kind and generous to me, my brothers and sister, and my mother. This story has a different valence for them than it does for me. It is, my uncle later tells my brother Stephen, "ancient history."

But the story matters to me. I cannot tell my mother's story without it, for in an odd way it is at the center of my memory of my father's version of the marriage.

I resign myself to a search through the Boston newspapers from the late 1920s looking for some mention of the trial and the conviction, at least a date that I can pursue in court records.

This is tedious work, and newspapers are notoriously unreliable sources.

Then, one day, months later, thinking about Zeyde in the back of my mind, I remember my father's inevitable ending: "The only Democrat pardoned by Herbert Hoover." If he was pardoned, there must be records.

What is strange about this clue is that I can pursue it immediately. Archives and libraries have spilled guides to their contents onto the Internet. That same afternoon I find what the possibilities are at the Hoover Presidential Library and the National Archives. There is some pardon correspondence at the Hoover Library. I ask the librarians to look for correspondence from Samuel White. The only Samuel White they can find is a dismissed postmaster in Pennsylvania.

The National Archives, however, has Record Group 204, the records of the pardon attorney. These records contain pardon case files from 1853 to 1946. My search now becomes more old-fashioned. I have an old acquaintance, Willy Dobak, working in the National Archives. The files are in College Park, Maryland.

Willy checks, and from box 1413 he sends me the file of Samuel Louis White. Samuel Louis White may not have been the only Democrat pardoned by Herbert Hoover, but he was a Democrat, and he was pardoned by Herbert Hoover. The pardon file provides the information I need to find the trial records and the records of the appeal, but it is the pardon file that is most useful. In it Zeyde speaks most clearly. The file is very full. I can construct a story from the documents it contains.

The story I construct is partially a story my grandfather told, partially a story told about him. A small part comes from information my father and uncle gave me. The material in the pardon file and the court transcripts, like the material I can recover around my mother's stories, stands in complicated relation to the stories my father told.

This is the story I can construct. It comes largely from Samuel White's application for executive clemency and the comments people in the pardon attorney's office and the Department of

Labor made on the application. It comes also from the trial records.

The story begins in 1907 when Schmel Belei, "a mere child," arrived in New York City with his parents. He was a Russian Jew, born in Sheptovia, Russia, in 1894. (The present city of Shepetovka is now in the independent Ukraine.) He was twelve or thirteen years of age when he entered the country. Belei is Russian for white. Translate Schmel Belei, and you get Samuel White.

Samuel White learned English quickly for a child who was probably a teenager when he arrived. Only his writing, which is somewhat stilted and formal, betrays an underlying unease with the language. He graduated from Northeastern University in Boston. He married young. He was only twenty-one when he married Jennie Anne Cohen in 1915. She was American born and raised by her immigrant, strictly orthodox Russian Jewish family. In 1916 Samuel White took out his first citizenship papers. He was in law school at Northeastern at the time. In 1917 he was admitted to the Massachusetts bar. Like my mother, the woman who would become his daughter-in-law, he did not immediately get around to completing his citizenship application.

He was drafted during World War I, but Samuel White got a medical deferment. His first son, Harry Eli, was born in 1919. Samuel began a law practice and prospered. He defended bootleggers. He bought automobiles. He became active in politics and was, according to family stories, a campaign manager for John Dever, who later became governor of Massachusetts, in one of his early campaigns.

At some time in the 1920s he took a vacation in New York. He drove a nearly new Lexington automobile, and he may have gone to Niagara Falls; he crossed into Canada for either a few hours or for an overnight stay. He gave varying accounts of this vacation at different times.

On March 21, 1925, Joseph Goredsky came to see Samuel White. White had been Goredsky's attorney since 1923, and he later explained how Goredsky brought with him a "man named Bromfield who was a licensed dealer in used automobiles and trucks." Goredsky was selling some trucks to Bromfield, whom Samuel White had never seen before. White drew up a bill of sale, dated it March 21, 1925, and told Goredsky to give it to Bromfield upon receipt of the purchase price of $3,000. But, according to my grandfather, Goredsky did not complete the transaction that day. Bromfield wanted to make sure that Goredsky had "good title" to the trucks. They did not complete the deal until March 26, and it took Bromfield much longer to give Goredsky the full purchase price, because, the trial records show, Bromfield, afraid of losing the interest, took back the check and redeposited it in his account.

The delay would not have mattered much, it would hardly have been remembered, except that on March 23, 1925, J. Cushing, Goredsky's partner, purposefully forced the firm into bankruptcy. There was no need to do so. Cushing owed money to his relatives; he asked them to force the bankruptcy so he could stop Goredsky from selling the partnership's property. The bankruptcy prohibited Goredsky from disposing of their property, which would go to pay their creditors. The March 26 payment for trucks was thus illegal, and thus the March 21 bill of sale looked suspect. The long period before final payment created at least the appearance of wrongdoing.

Bromfield, Goredsky, Harry Gordon, who was Goredsky's brother, Samuel White, and a fifth man, Hyman Wyner, were indicted for violating the U.S. Bankruptcy Act. The U.S. attorney accused Samuel White of concocting the plan to conceal Goredsky's assets, of wrongly dating the bill of sale, and of receiving $600 from the proceeds in addition to $50 from Bromfield. Samuel White denied it all. The $600 was, he said, a payment for bills Goredsky had accrued since 1923. Bromfield's payment might look like a commission for arranging a bargain on the trucks, but, Samuel White insisted, it was merely a charge for his time since Bromfield insisted on negotiating over the trucks. "I protested my innocence as well as any intentional participation in the alleged conspiracy as loudly as I could," Samuel White said, "but to no avail."

He went to trial on August 14, 1928. It was a sweltering August in Boston, and Samuel White sat there and watched his future melt away. In the trial Bromfield testified that the bill of sale had, indeed, been drawn up on March 21 and not backdated later. But Bromfield was illiterate and when offered a chance to plea-bargain took it. He pleaded guilty; he received a fine and a suspended sentence.

Neither Bromfield's, Gordon's, nor Samuel White's testimony had much of a chance to sway the jury. Judge James Lowell, who presided, characterized them all as liars in his instructions to the jury. From their names the jurors appear to have been largely Yankees. All the defendants were Jews. The judge with the Brahmin name told them that these Jews were liars.

The jury handed down a verdict of guilty on August 17, and then for nearly two agonizing months Samuel White awaited sentencing. On October 2, 1928, Judge James Lowell sentenced him to two years in the federal penitentiary at Atlanta. Samuel White received the harshest sentence of all the defendants. Of the other three convicted conspirators, only Goredsky received a jail term. He served six months of an eighteen-month sentence in a local jail before being paroled.

Samuel White appealed, but on February 9, 1929, the federal appeals court upheld his conviction. He tried to take the case to the U.S. Supreme Court. On June 3, 1929, the justices denied his petition for certiorari, refusing to hear the case.

Roughly four years elapsed between the time Goredsky and Bromfield first walked into Samuel White's office and the day he shut down his law practice and went off to the penitentiary in Atlanta. During those four years, the restaurant he owned went broke. A bank in which he owned stock collapsed. A civil suit recovered the money paid for the trucks and Samuel White's legal fee. His legal practice suffered, and his remaining money went to finance his own case and appeals. His law practice ended on June 20, 1929, when he began his journey to the federal penitentiary. He had, he said, "for the purpose of bringing the truth to light expended every dollar that he or his family owned, and when the final blow did come his family brought up in luxury and plenty was reduced to want and poverty."

He served fourteen months of his sentence before being paroled. He performed what he called his "regular duties" as well as "his special work as teacher in the prison school conscienteously and with a full sense of duty to officials and prisoners alike." For those fourteen months, his family was "dependent on public aid for their daily maintenance and shelter."

The parole board heard his case in the spring or summer of 1930. It recommended parole beginning on July 1, 1930. Along with his parole notice, Samuel White received a second notice. The immigration authorities filed a detainer against him. Under section 155 of title 8 of the *United States Code* any alien who had committed a crime of moral turpitude carrying a sentence of more than one year within five years of their last entry into the United States had to be deported. The immigration bureau asked that Samuel White be held while deportation proceedings began against him.

Samuel White was an alien who had committed a crime of moral turpitude for which he served a sentence exceeding one year, but he had entered the country in 1907. Yet he knew that this letter was not a mistake.

He was a lawyer and must have realized that there would be no idle questions when immigration officials came to his cell in July 1929. But he was careless. He could only have been a worried man, his money gone, his family thrown on public aid, himself now a month in prison. He didn't think how much more could go wrong.

They asked if he had left the country since his immigration. He told them, yes, he remembered the vacation trip he took to New York. They had crossed into Canada, he couldn't remember how long—for a few hours, maybe overnight. He thought the vacation had been in August 1923; it may have been 1924. He couldn't remember. It didn't matter. Whether in 1923 or 1924, that trip meant that his crime had been committed within five years of his last entry into the United States; it meant he was eligible for deportation.

By November 1929, when the district director of the Immigration Service at Atlanta wrote him, he knew he was in trouble.

He realized his mistake. He tried to push back the date of those few hours in Canada so that they came five years before Joseph Goredsky walked into his office on March 21, 1925. The trip, he thought, had to be before 1920 because he had made it in a Lexington automobile that he purchased in 1919 and the "automobile was practically new when I made the trip." There was another hearing in January 1930. He categorically testified that the trip was in 1918 or 1919. There was no evidence available to substantiate the time of the trip.

In May 1930 the board of review held still another hearing. It recommended reopening the case to secure some record so as to determine when White had acquired his Lexington automobile and to obtain testimony from those who accompanied him on the trip.

Samuel White, by now routinely referred to in the record as "the alien," believed the car record would clear him. Massachusetts did not at the time keep automobile registration records as far back as 1919. His own counsel, after much work, found old personal property tax records in the basement of city hall in Boston. In 1919, 1920, and 1921 Samuel White was assessed as the owner of a 1918 Chevrolet. On April 1, 1922, he was assessed for the first time for a 1921 Lexington touring car. He was assessed for the same car in 1923.

"While these facts are, to say the least, not helpful to the alien," his attorney reported, "counsel believe it their professional duty to disclose what they found in these records." Counsel could not find Samuel White's companions.

It was then that the Department of Labor formally requested that he be detained in the penitentiary for deportation to the Soviet Union. Samuel White's attorney, however, successfully argued that there was no point in detaining him since the United States had broken diplomatic relations with the Soviet Union and could not deport him until they were restored. To keep him in prison after the parole board had ruled him eligible for parole would only serve to punish him because he was an alien. "No one will argue," his attorney said, "that there is any possibility of White leaving the country." His whole aim was to stay in Boston.

The Department of Labor eventually withdrew its detainer, but not until Samuel White spent six more weeks in prison. On August 13, 1930, Samuel White was released. He immediately began efforts to secure a presidential pardon. The statutes demanding deportation of criminal aliens did not apply to pardoned criminals. Only a pardon could free him and his family from the consequences of his few hours in Canada.

He was, as I remember him, a sweet, charming, and ingratiating man. Those qualities and the old contacts from his prosperous days in Boston were all the weapons he had available. He applied for executive clemency. He appealed to his "unquestioned reputation for honesty, right living, and law observance." He promised to resume it. He asked for pity on his family.

He got Judge James Lowell, the man who had sentenced him, to write recommending his pardon. He got Frederick Tarr, the United States attorney for Massachusetts, to write in support of Judge Lowell. But Tarr, whose office had prosecuted him, wrote that "White apparently planned and put into operation the method by which the trucks were to be concealed." He admitted that the fee of $600 was not unreasonable given that "Goresky" had not paid him for previous services, but then he wrote that "the evidence clearly showed that White was guilty of the offence." In the prosecutor's mind "apparently" still quickly elided into "clearly . . . guilty."

"White had," Tarr wrote, "a fairly good reputation for honesty and square dealing in his profession as a lawyer." "Fairly good" may have been "very good" for a man who defended bootleggers. Both Tarr and Lowell protested that deportation was totally out of proportion to the offense. "The immigration authorities threaten to deport him for a most frivolous and unjust reason," Lowell wrote.

He got other attorneys in Boston to support him. Daniel A. Shea sent a letter, as did Edward Meagher. He got John Mc-

Cormack, the congressman from Irish South Boston, later Speaker of the House, to make his interest in the case known. On December 23, 1930, Samuel White inquired about the status of his petition for clemency. He closed the letter, "Thanking you most sincerely for your courtesy, and with the Season's Greetings, I am Sir, Yours Most Respectfully, Samuel L. White." The pardon attorney's office was, however, unwilling to act until there was a formal order for his deportation. In December 1930, the Immigration Bureau granted him a rehearing. A Mr. Riley from the Bureau of Immigration remained in contact with Mr. James Finch of the pardon attorney's office. There were delays. Samuel White waited.

On April 20, 1931, Mr. Riley phoned Mr. Finch. The Bureau of Immigration had issued an order on April 16 "to deport the alien to Russia." Riley had so informed Congressman George Tinkham, a Republican, who had also expressed interest in the case. The deportation, Riley explained, was unlikely to have any effect until relations were resumed between the Soviet Union and the United States.

The cause for deportation was the presence of "Schmel Belei, alias Samuel Louis White or Samuel Belei" in the United States "in violation of the Act of February 5, 1917 in that, subsequent to May 1, 1907, he has been sentenced to imprisonment for a term of one year or more because of conviction in this country of a crime involving moral turpitude." Robe Carl White, the assistant secretary of labor, conveyed news of the deportation order to the attorney general. It was now up to the pardon attorney to act on his appeal for clemency.

Although Samuel White had no way of knowing it, James Finch of the pardon attorney's office was not sympathetic. This was in the wake of American immigration restriction and the Red Scare. James Finch didn't like Judge Lowell's denunciation of the Immigration Bureau's actions as frivolous and unjust. He had it struck from the quotations included in the pardon attorney's report. The law, he insisted, is "a salutary one & often enables us to deport undesirable aliens who might otherwise be allowed to stay." James Finch didn't particularly like Samuel White. "Except for his wife & children I would have no great sympathy of this man. He doesn't seem to have been interested in becoming a citizen. He must have deceived some one to get admited to the bar being an alien."

Still, even if grudgingly, Finch drafted the pardon letter. Samuel White could legally be deported, Finch argued, and the immigration authorities were free of any taint of injustice since they "had no discretion and were bound to order his deportation," but the deportation would nonetheless be "harsh and excessive punishment."

The attorney general acted a week after the deportation order was issued. He wrote President Hoover reiterating Finch's decision that the deportation "would be harsh and excessive punishment." He recommended pardon. The President granted the pardon. On April 25, in his usual large, bold hand, Samuel L. White signed for his pardon warrant. On May 1, 1931, the Department of Labor halted deportation proceedings.

How much of this story my father knew I will never know. He was, after all, only five when Joseph Goredsky walked into his father's office. It was a complicated case. He was only eleven when his father was released. His parents may very well have never told him that the danger was not over when his father was released. He may never have known what was happening while his father sweated through the ordeal of awaiting deportation. How much he absorbed, how much Zeyde later told him, I will never know.

All I do know is that by the time he told me this story, he had changed it, wittingly or unwittingly. The crime had become political and tied to the machine of James Michael Curley. Zeyde's codefendants had become Irish, and the judge had become Irish. Deportation, and the judge's intervention to prevent it, had dropped from the story entirely. Most of the Irish whom I can find in the pardon file intervened on behalf of Zeyde. John McCormack, Daniel A. Shea, and Edward Meagher all sought to help Samuel A. White. They did not seek to betray him.

There is one exception. The assistant U.S. attorney who pros-

ecuted Samuel White was named John J. Walsh. The name was
not only Irish, it was, of course, my mother's maiden name. The
prosecutor had the same name as her father. In a sense, then,
the man who sent Zeyde to prison was Irish; my father's story
transmuted him from the prosecutor to the judge. The Irish who
tried to aid him became codefendants. Like so many other stories, the details changed to make another point.

The history that matters most to me now, in understanding
my mother's and father's romance, lies in neither the story in
the pardon file nor the story my father told me. It is within the
space between these stories, the space where somehow one becomes the other. It is this transformation that I want to know,
and it is this transformation that I can only guess at and never
recover.

In his telling me a story of ethnic rivalry, of betrayal, of his
own revenge put aside, I thought then and I still think that my
father was telling me of how Jews are always betrayed by Gen-
tiles and of the hardships he, unlike me, had faced.

He was telling me, too, perhaps, of the deep tensions that he
thought simmered in America and within our own family, tensions that meant little to me. I noticed only that my mother was
secretive when she went to Mass when Bubbe was visiting. I
was a child, and to me having one parent who was Jewish and
another who was Irish Catholic was just another possibility in
the world. It was the way things were.

And my father was telling me, I later suspected, of the league
of irresponsibility that his father and his children, particularly
me, had formed against him. He never told me that my grandfather was not guilty. He left that responsibility on Zeyde's
shoulders. I knew as a child that he envied the unquestioning
adulation I had for Zeyde. I didn't know the source of his envy
then, but I guess now that he envied my adoration not because
he wanted me to adore him but because he had wanted to adore
his father in the same way and never could, at least not after the
trial and imprisonment. Later, when with some reason my father
distrusted my own and my brothers' good sense, he gave me

advice that could only call up memories of his own father. "Just don't get arrested," he said.

My father may have been telling me all these things when he told me about Zeyde's imprisonment and pardon, but what never occurred to me then was another possibility that I recognize now: he may also have been telling me a love story. He cast himself as Romeo among the Jews and my mother as Juliet among the Irish. It was not unlike my father to suggest several meanings at once.

34

It seemed like forever.   —Sara, on waiting for Harry to return

When Harry White married Sara Walsh, his passion for her overwhelmed, at least temporarily, his hatred of Germans and his desire to go overseas to fight them. When the Germans marched east, they marched across the bodies of his relatives. Those members of his mother's and father's families who had not fled were either dead or destined for the camps. Yet the war also brought him his wife. Their happiness seemed incompatible with the deaths of his European relatives.

The first years of their marriage were years of movement from city to city. Sometimes they were places Sara knew from her work with the airlines; more often they were places that she had hardly imagined. From Fort Monmouth they went to Los Angeles. She remembers waking up with him in a dingy hotel room on Christmas morning. They had trouble finding a place in the deserted streets to get coffee.

Harry went to Needles, California, for desert maneuvers. Sara lived in Alhambra with a Chicago friend, Myra Murphy, who was married to Peter Lisagor, a well-known reporter at the time. Myra, too, was a Gentile who had married a Jew. Myra's mother was a Christian Scientist, and she also lived with them. Sara remembers Myra's mother being in pain and refusing to call a doctor.

Harry was, according to his brother, excited by the desert maneuvers. He was, his brother says, assigned to the Ninety-fifth Infantry, and he was sure they were going overseas. And he was right, they were going overseas, but he wasn't going with them. Just before the division shipped out, he was reassigned.

Harry was, however, not discouraged. He took a troop train to Indian Town Gap, Pennsylvania. Sara stopped in Chicago and then joined him there. They lived in Harrisburg. They liked the town, and a friend had a car that they could take for long rides in the countryside. They were happy and oblivious to Chicago and Boston.

Indian Town Gap was a staging area, and Harry was certain he was going overseas, but instead he was sent to a camp near Blackstone, Virginia. They lived in a room they rented in Crewe. Every room in the town was rented to GIs and their wives.

By marrying Harry, Sara had crossed one social boundary, but all around in those Southern towns was a racial boundary even stronger than the boundaries between black and white that she had known on the South Side of Chicago. Sara remembers her landlady in Crewe telling the hired man to plow a field. He was black, and he followed the plow across a large field for hours in the hot sun. The landlady never offered the hired man either food or water. When Sara went into the Catholic church for Mass, she knelt in the last pew. A man tapped her on the shoulder and told her to move forward. The last pew, he said, was for niggers. Gradually, she says, she was learning what kike and nigger signified.

From Virginia they went to Fort Bragg, North Carolina. They lived three miles from the post above a bar that had two small apartments. They rented one; a hairdresser had the other. It was, Sara thought, a good business. All her customers had GI haircuts. How much work can you do on a GI haircut?

Her own life was good. She would meet Harry for lunch, play cards with other officers' wives. They would sit and talk about life and their future after the war ended. At night they would have dinner at the officers club, and on Saturdays they would go there to dance.

When Harry left Fort Bragg in 1944, he lost hope of fighting

Germans. The Army sent him to Princeton. His assignment was supposedly secret, but all the wives knew their husbands were studying Japanese. Even the Army would not teach him Japanese to send him to Germany.

Princeton was pleasant and idyllic. They made friends; but there remained the odd juxtaposition of their happiness and the war. Harry's brother was fighting in Europe where he would be badly wounded in the Battle of the Bulge. Mort Trachtenberg was an aerial gunner until they tested his eyes and grounded him. Then they shipped him out, and he spent the last year of the war in the European campaigns. Mort's roommate in New York, a man from Omaha whom Harry knew from the days he came into the city on leave and slept on Mort's floor, was fighting in the Pacific. He would die there.

From Princeton, the Army sent Harry across the country to the Presidio at Monterey, California. They lived in Carmel. This was the Army's main foreign-language school. Life now seemed to Sara completely like a storybook. They would both later speak of their time in Carmel as the most idyllic period of their marriage.

This was not the modern Carmel, undifferentiated, except by its setting, from Aspen, Jackson Hole, and other Western places whose appearance and tone serve as so much proof that money is wasted on the rich. It was an earlier Carmel, developed as an artists' colony, slightly derelict and worn during the war. There were cages of exotic birds on Seventeen Mile Drive. There were few cars. Harry and Sara walked everywhere: to the post office to get their mail, to the beach. Sara walked to church at the mission.

Harry would meet her after Mass, and they would eat breakfast at a small restaurant with no more than eight tables. From there, they would go to the beach and read the Sunday papers. They had friends in Carmel, including people they had known in Princeton.

And while they sat on the beach in Carmel, V-E (Victory in Europe) Day came when the Germans surrendered. And later that summer, V-J (Victory in Japan) Day came when the Japanese capitulated. The war ended as they took pictures of each other on the beach.

I remember as a child seeing pictures of my mother in Carmel. She was young and happy. My father, looking at these pictures, once told me that she had climbed trees there. "Can you imagine," he had asked me, "your mother climbing trees?"

He seemed still charmed at the thought of this young woman, his wife, climbing on a whim into the windswept pines at Carmel. The pictures and my father's remark stuck with me. I marked the incident not just for what it revealed about my mother—of impulses in her that I had never seen—but also for what it revealed about my father and their marriage. From the wonder in his voice when he told me this, it seemed that he had married her because she was young, exuberant, and often did the unexpected.

Yet marriage to my father and the five children that followed had relentlessly worn away the traces of these qualities. What remained she buried out of sight, safe from assault. I would not glimpse them firsthand until years later, long after my father was dead.

I glimpsed them in 1995 while writing this book. In Ahanagran one evening, I wanted her to show me the lower fields. I walked down the road with her and my wife, Beverly. We walked past my cousin John Joe's house to the gate. The gate was wrapped shut with wire, and I went to unwrap it. "Don't bother," my mother told me, "we'll climb over it." She was halfway up the six-foot fence, which was old and rickety, an unstable Irish construction of wood and wire. It swayed as she climbed, and I imagined what a fall would do to a seventy-five-year-old woman. She ignored me and was over.

And a year later, I brought her to Paris, where I was attending an academic conference, so she could recover from jet lag before we went to Dublin, where there was family research to do. Beverly and I took her to dinner on the summer solstice. Paris now gives the first day of summer over to music. There are concerts all over the city. We had been to a concert of medieval music in the courtyard at the Hôtel de Cluny. In the middle of it an argument broke out between the listeners in the courtyard and staff members who were talking too loudly in an adjoining room. We ate that night in a Lyonnais restaurant on the Rue des Fossés-Saint-Bernard that Beverly and I had first gone to fifteen years before. We ate late, but not as late as Parisians do. It was ten or eleven o'clock when we came out from dinner. There were crowds streaming down the street. There was Latin music a few blocks away along the Seine.

The owners of the restaurant were out in the street. What is going on? Beverly asked them in French. They shrugged. The solstice, they said. We followed the crowd out of curiosity. I just intended to go a few blocks. My mother was seventy-six.

There were calypso bands and marimba bands and steel-drum bands on trucks. There was a convoy of them. People danced and snaked in and among them. The city along the Quai de la Tournelle formed itself into a parade and surged down the Left Bank where the Quai de la Tournelle becomes the Quai de Montebello opposite Notre Dame and La Cité. And when I looked, my mother had joined them, following the bands for a mile in the Paris night, clutching Beverly's arm hard so as not to lose her.

But this is memory not history. It joins a moment I never witnessed on a Carmel beach, a story my father told me. It is not my mother's memory but my own. It surprises me. Just as with the heroes of the Time of Troubles, like seeks like across the years, memory jumping swiftly across time.

For Sara and Harry, Carmel became a repository of memories. Sara still loves Carmel not for what it is now but for the memories it prompts. After we moved to California from New York and lived in Los Angeles, we always stopped in Carmel whenever we were near the central coast. She still visits it nostalgically now.

Their stay in Carmel ended because the war ended. Only

then, only with the war over, did the Army send Harry White overseas. It was a long time before she heard from him. When the letter arrived, he told her he was in Korea with the American troops who had come to occupy South Korea after the surrender of the Japanese there. He was assigned to military government.

She moved back to Chicago. She got a job with Braniff Airlines and spent her spare time with girlfriends. She rarely visited South Mozart Street. Nell and Pat had children and were busy. Her father was shamed by her marrying a Jew. She waited for Harry to return. He was in Korea for a year. "It seemed like forever," she says.

35

Jennie's shiksa.
    —Talk overheard on the street when Sara first visited my
                bubbe, Jennie White, in Dorchester

While she waited for Harry to return, Sara was suspended between whatever her future life with Harry would be and her old life and family in Chicago. Separately, she and Harry had a place to return to. Together, neither Chicago nor Boston would welcome them.

When Harry returned, he came directly to Chicago. He was still in the Army, although he was no longer on active duty. He would serve in the reserves until 1953. Sara took him to South Mozart Street to tell her father that they were going East. The visit was very short. Jack and Nell were polite, but they offered them no food. This was the detail that mattered and the one she remembered: they did not offer any food.

From there they went to Boston. This visit was, I think, Zeyde's doing. I suspect they came at his invitation. He was disappointed in the marriage. He wanted Harry to marry a Jew, but he was a man who had learned to work within the possible. Bubbe would not accept the marriage. Harry's phone call on her birthday had hurt and infuriated her, and Sara inadvertently made it worse with the Christmas card.

Zeyde worked Bubbe, but she was adamant. She was rigid where Zeyde was flexible. Zeyde was very unhappy, but he could not budge her. Determination was her only weapon against the world.

Still, when Harry brought Sara home, they were both gracious and polite to her. They were angry with Harry not Sara. Only when Sara walked the neighborhood did she find evidence of the hostility their marriage created. She could hear people talk about her. They didn't talk to her.

"Jennie's shiksa," they said.

Harry was not a man of much forbearance. What he heard I don't know, but he was a man to bring things to a head.

In Carmel, before he went to Korea, Harry had bought Sara a gift. It was a small gold cross on a chain. He asked her to wear it to dinner at his parents' on what would be their last night there.

When Sara sat down at the table that evening, Bubbe glared at her, her eyes fixed on the crucifix.

"Take it off," Bubbe said.

"Excuse me?" said Sara.

"Take it off, take the cross off," Bubbe repeated.

It was a perfectly choreographed moment. It was a moment my father anticipated. It was the kind of moment he relished. The next move was his.

"She's not taking it off," Harry said. "I gave it to her."

And Sara, reduced to a prop in a family drama, watched nearly four years of anger and hurt erupt around her. Bubbe and Harry were on their feet, yelling and screaming. Zeyde, dismayed, sat silent at the table. Sara was the catalyst, irrelevant once the reaction had been produced. From the uproar she remembers not a word.

The story, like all stories, changed with the years. Different versions survive in different parts of the family. My aunt remembers the crucifix being put up in the bedroom. But Sara insists it was a small cross around her neck, and the gift of a cross to bait his parents seems to me quintessentially my father. Sara would think of it as an unfortunate accident.

Harry and Sara left the next day. They went to Maine for two weeks. They had a small cottage close to the ocean. They would buy fresh fish from the fishermen, walk on the beach and in the woods, and go to a small restaurant nearby.

The visit to Maine was a return to the first years of their marriage, but they couldn't live there any more than they could live in Carmel. Harry needed to earn a living. And they knew they couldn't live in Boston or Chicago.

New York attracted them. Harry had a distant cousin in New York, Sam Spector. He ran a company called Insuline, and he offered Harry an office job at forty-five dollars a week. Sara and Harry got an apartment in Flushing, Queens, over a dry-cleaning shop. She was pregnant, and the fumes were awful. They made her ill, and her only relief was to go out on the roof on a day windy enough to blow the fumes away.

Harry and his mother ceased speaking. It was a silence that, left to either of them, would have endured until death. "Harry," his brother says, "didn't care."

Sara was back in the city where, as a greenhorn, she had first set foot in America. She was back in the city that her mother had come to and loved. She was back in the city as an American wife. And in a city with all these connections to Ireland, she was as distant from Ahanagran as she would ever be.

It was Zeyde, in a role I now associate with his daughter-in-law Sara, who took up the frayed strands of family and began patiently to knit them back together.

Harry worried about his wife's illness as the pregnancy progressed. He did not want her alone as she approached term. He continued to talk to his father, and Zeyde arranged for his daughter to go to New York to help Sara as soon as she got out of school.

The baby was three weeks late, but my aunt was still in school when Sara gave birth in May 1947. Although his parents had long had a telephone, Harry did not call. Instead he sent a telegram. There was, my aunt remembers, a popular song called, "Open the Door, Richard, and Let Me In." His telegram said, "Richard finally opened the door."

I was that baby, and the birth of a grandchild was the beginning of patching the breach between them. Flowers for Sara came immediately, and within two days Bubbe and Zeyde followed. I was born into a world of adoring grandparents, and I never imagined that the world could be any different.

36

All I ask of you is, to remember me at Mass and Holy Communion.
—From the memorial card of Margaret Walsh, June 7, 1959

Lives are not stories. A day, a month, a year, or a lifetime has no plot. Our experiences are only the raw stuff of stories. The beginnings of our lives are arbitrary; usually their endings come too soon or too late for any neat narrative conclusions.

We turn our lives into stories, and, in doing so, we can stop them where we choose. Our stories do in a small way what memoirs and autobiographies do on a grander scale: they allow a self-fashioning that gives remembered lives a coherence that the day-to-day lives of actual experience lack. History, of course, also imposes coherence, but the historian works with less malleable stuff than memory. Memoirs are seamless; good histories disrupt.

For the most part, Sara's stories end in the late 1940s and early 1950s. She has lived a full life since then. She has become the strand along which the beads of a diverse, divided, and often difficult family are strung. It is hard to imagine my family cohering without her. But her stories, at least so far, do not cover the last half century of her life except for her returns to Ireland and the death of her parents and Harry's parents.

I am not sure that I know why she tells so few stories of these years. Sometimes I think too many of those years were painful, and stories would reopen wounds she has struggled to heal.

Sometimes I think the problem lies with me, the listener. Stories depend in part on the listener's ignorance, and as the years passed my memories and my mother's overlapped. I was always much more interested in hearing of places I had never seen and people I had never met than the immediate world of my childhood, which I could and did explore for myself.

But at other times, I think the stories end because in her eyes a resolution had been reached, something important had been decided for her by the late 1940s. What happened after that is another set of stories that she chooses not to tell. To write about her life after this would be to write a biography and not this dialogue between a crafted memory and a recovered history, this anti-memoir.

The concluding stories of the saga my mother has told are those of 1947. There is a smaller batch of stories that cover the early 1950s, but they act more as an epilogue. I was born in 1947, but, far more importantly, 1947 was the year Jack Walsh returned to Ireland. The tide of Irish history and her own family's emigrations had dropped Sara on to an American shore. The return of her father represented the tide's ebb.

In 1947 Jack Walsh left Chicago and passed through New York on his way to Ireland. He had retired; he was going home. He left with no regrets that he ever mentioned. He had come to save his farm, and he had saved it. It had been twenty-three years since he had left Ahanagran, his wife, and his family. The farm now drew him back. And for the first and last time, he visited his daughter Sara as a married woman. I can't guess what he thought about seeing Sara with a child in New York, and she doesn't tell me. I only know what he did. He stopped in Flushing, where she then lived. He stayed the night in Harry and Sara's apartment. He gave Sara $200 for the baby. It was a large amount of money in 1947. That is what she remembers.

Jack's leaving reduced her contact to her own family, both Irish and American, to letters, which no one saved. She never called her uncle Jack Hegarty and his wife, Maureen. They seemed above her, she says. Nell and her brother Bill, newly immigrated, remained in Chicago, but for years there would be little contact between them and Sara.

When her father disappeared back into Ireland, his absence bothered Sara less than the pull of Ahanagran, to which he was returning. He had always been absent; it was her own longing for Kerry and her mother that remained strong and always present. Later, when that American life seemed hard or unbearable, Ireland grew correspondingly softer, gentler, and more comforting in her memories. That farm, which never had room for her, never gave up its hold. But her own mother, if Sara had told her of her longing, would have urged her to stay. She knew too well the cost of return.

My mother's Irish origins, with their twinned sense of loss and possibilities, always seemed strongest to me on her birthday: December 26, St. Stephen's Day. St. Stephen's Day lies irrevocably in the shadow of Christmas, and my brothers, sister, and I often hurt my mother by losing her birthday in the larger holiday. In rural Ireland, St. Stephen's Day was the time when the wren boys carried their dead bird door-to-door begging pennies to bury it. Killing a wren on St. Stephen's Day both fascinated and scared me; it always made my own mother, born on such a day, seem a little exotic. To have traveled from such a birthday to a birthday nearly forgotten in the aftermath of the abundance of an American Christmas marked a passage and a distance greater than anything I knew. And yet the passage was incomplete. The ties with Kerry were never really broken.

She never tired of receiving news of Kerry. Jack Walsh resumed his Irish life, but he never could be only an Irish countryman again. America shadowed him everywhere. He looked like a Yank in his American clothes, and his talk was full of American words and references. He had saved that Irish farm, but the real price was a transmutation that set him forever apart. He could never again be fully an Irishman of Ahanagran.

But he could bring to Ahanagran the money that it could never produce, and he could turn that American money into Irish land. Everything else had followed from his determination to save his

Irish farm, but he would live only briefly on it. He was too old to work it, and Gerard and Tim had worked it for decades in his absence. The land was Gerard's now, and Gerard was married to Josie.

Mary, Nell's twin, was also married, with a fortune that her father's work in America provided. She and John Bambury lived on a farm of their own and would later live on a far better one in County Meath.

Margaret Walsh, Tim, and Johnny Walsh—Jack Walsh's youngest son and namesake—all moved to Guhard, a townland next to Ahanagran, on Jack Walsh's return. Jack Walsh bought the land and built a new house there for his youngest son, Johnny, and Johnny's future wife, Sheila. Sara always presumed that Jack Walsh's money alone, plus, perhaps, the fortune Sheila brought to the land, paid for the farm in Guhard. She only recently learned differently.

When Kitty died on South Mozart Street, she had, it turned out, another asset in addition to the house. She owned an insurance policy. The beneficiary of her life insurance was her Irish son, Tim Walsh. She never mentioned him, but in thinking of her own dying, she thought of him. Tim must have banked the money. And when Jack Walsh returned home, Tim's money went into the farm in Guhard. There was a larger part of South Mozart Street in that farm than Sara knew at the time. Tim would live out his life on land his mother had partially provided.

Margaret died in 1959. Sara tells me that she died on the eve of her first Irish vacation. Her husband, Jack, was going to take her to Ballybunnion a few miles away on the Atlantic. She died of a heart attack with the vacation before her.

I remember the day that my mother received word of Margaret's death. I had come into my parents' bedroom looking for my mother. She was seated on the bed crying, and she held the picture of Margaret in New York. I had never seen her cry like this. She was sobbing—a child's crying—and it astonished and scared me. I asked what was wrong. She told me that her mother had died and she would never see her again. She said it sharply, with a bitterness that made me think it was my fault that she had not seen and never would see her mother again. And, in a sense, I guess it was my fault. My birth, and the births of my brothers and sister, had made it impossible for her to return to Ireland even for a visit. We absorbed the family's money, and we absorbed her time. She asked me to leave, and I went out, closing the door behind me.

Someone in the family sent Sara one of the small cardboard memorial cards they print in Ireland. It had a picture of her mother, the date of her death, June 7, 1959, and her age, seventy-six. Under her name it said Guhard, Ballylongford, County Kerry.

Jack Walsh lived another four years. By the time Margaret died he was more than a decade gone from the United States, but he had one more dealing with the United States government. I know of it only because there is a final notice in his immigration file. He had taken the oath of allegiance to the United States on June 28, 1933. He had become an American citizen. But at the bottom of the page someone had scrawled the word "expatriated." The final document explains the scrawl. It is dated August 2, 1961. It is a letter from the Immigration and Naturalization Service to the clerk of the U.S. District Court in Chicago. It said John Walsh, certificate no. 3696554, had lost his United States citizenship. At the time the law said that naturalized aliens who resided for a prolonged period in their countries of origin would lose their citizenship. By 1961 Jack Walsh had been back in Ireland for fourteen years. Within two more years he would be dead.

My guess is that the loss of citizenship hardly mattered to him. American citizenship had served its purpose. National allegiances, even familial ties, always seemed attenuated and weak compared to his passion for that farm. That is what drove him.

Jack died in the spring of 1963. The memorial card says April 28 and lists him as living in Guhard, Ballylongford. He was eighty-three years old. There is a picture of him in which the old determination shows through, but, like his eyes, the determination is clouded, as if he were confused about what it was that he was determined to do. He was, everyone says, often confused in those last years.

Tim, the bridge between the generations, died next. For Sara, his death was not so hard because she had visited Ireland in 1970 and had seen him again. He died in the new house in Guhard that money from South Mozart Street had helped build. Tim had not come into the world easily nor, more literally, would he exit easily. Tim was a tall man, and when he died, my mother tells me, his casket was so long that they had to pass it out the window into the yard, for they could not maneuver it through the bedroom door. By then there were abundant Walshes, a whole new generation of them, to mourn him.

Once Jack Walsh had left, the Ireland stories became largely stories of death until Sara herself began returning regularly in the 1960s. The last American stories are different.

In 1947 Sara had a baby as well as a husband and lived above a dry-cleaning store in Flushing. She tells me the stories of the apartment in Flushing as if they belong only to me. And, perhaps, they do. My brothers and my sister may very well have stories of their own that revolve around their births. These are their stories. I don't ask about them.

In Flushing, she tells me, the stairs to their apartment were so steep that going up or down them was like climbing a ladder. From the apartment she watched the wind like a sailor, and when it blew the fumes from the dry-cleaning store below away from the building, she would carry me outside for air. It was in Flushing during the great New York blizzard of 1947 that my father had to trudge through the snow to find a special baby formula I needed.

And in Flushing, she tells me, Bubbe and Zeyde arrived within days of my birth. Samuel White, her father-in-law, and Jennie White, her mother-in-law, entered fully into her life just as John Walsh passed out of it.

Jennie White became as loyal and friendly to Sara as she had once been distant and judging. Years later, when Bubbe herself lay dying, Sara would go to Boston to help Bubbe's daughter and other daughter-in-law care for her. It was a reconciliation greater than Bubbe's son Harry had made.

Any of these threads could carry her stories along, but they don't, and the ultimate reason, I think, was that the late 1930s and the 1940s were the years my mother and father lived the most intensely. These years set the standards against which they would measure the rest of their lives. My mother viewed them as the years of her metamorphosis and her meeting with my father as the great love affair of her life. What happened afterward would always lie in the shadow of these years and be measured against them. Later experiences never equaled those in the past.

I cannot be sure about what my father thought, for he has been dead now for nearly a quarter century. But seeing him through the prism of my mother's stories, I think that for him, too, the 1930s and 1940s created the pure poles of his experience. He would never be able to love again the way he loved my mother then, and his pride and anger at his own children probably came in part from the sense that we had distracted her and weakened her absolute devotion to him.

For my father, I think, there was also something more. He would never hate so purely again either: neither the child's hate for the judge who imprisoned his father nor his young man's hate for the Nazis who obliterated the world from which his family had emerged. He could never exorcise either hatred. He turned the judge into an Irish American, and then he married an Irish American. He enlisted in the Army to fight Germans, and the army sent him to Korea. He had only his anger.

My mother and I differ about what I should say about him. She wants to freeze him in the 1940s. After that he became a successful man in jobs he did not always care about. He was an aerospace executive, and later he worked for MCA, the Music Corporation of America. By the 1960s he was making a considerable amount of money. I remember that he worked among people whom he mostly despised. He wanted us to admire him for what he did well, but he didn't admire his own success in business, nor did he think much of businessmen, although he would certainly have despised himself if he had failed. By the time I was a teenager, on the best nights he drank and read. I can't freeze him in a time when I never knew him, but, although my mother sometimes thinks otherwise, I did admire him. He died a Los Angeles death in 1972. He was driving on the Golden State Freeway when he suffered a heart attack. Despite the pain, he pulled off and got to a gas station. He called his own ambulance. The ambulance came and rushed him to the hospital, but he wouldn't let them carry him in. He insisted on walking. He walked into the emergency room of, as chance would have it, White Memorial Hospital, suffered a second massive heart attack, fell to the floor, and died. The doctors could not save him. He would have taken grim satisfaction in that. He had always hated doctors.

I admired him when I heard that story the first time, and thinking about it now, knowing what I know about him and my mother, I recognize in the man walking into that emergency room something of the man my mother saw walking across that restaurant in New Orleans so many years ago. The best of my father came out walking toward life and walking toward death. At least, I would like to think so. In any case, I can glimpse why my mother protects her carefully constructed memories against other memories and stories and my history. These stories are her treasures. What choice does she have but to guard them?

Epilogue

The past has its own gravity. For years now I have given an assignment to students in my American history survey class. They come to the class with an American innocence, thinking the past is always safely behind them, that the future is possibility without limit. My assignment is a simple one. They are to take their family—a person, a generation, people from several generations—and explain how their lives intersected with major developments or trends in American history. When the assignment works, they see the lives of their ancestors and relatives as part of larger currents. Their ancestors make choices, but they are constrained choices. I push them to see that their own lives also move in historical currents, that their choices are choices constrained by a past that it might benefit them to know. The past has its own gravity, and it will hold them.

The flaw in the assignment, I have gradually come to realize, is that I identify the past exclusively with history and history with the kind of work that I do: academic history with its careful practices and its insistence on questioning, reexamination, and debate. I am devoted to these practices; I teach them, and I am more than ready to defend them, but this is no reason to rule out other constructions. Just because other Americans, including my own family, are innocent of what I call history does not mean they are innocent of other constructions and uses of the past.

My mother, Sara, like all of us, has constructed versions of the past. She has made memories where I seek history. It would be mean-spirited, trivial, and despicable willfully to destroy the memories of one you love. That my mother's memories are not a literal rendering of the past, not a transparent window on her experiences, is the beginning of this book not its end.

I am interested in what my mother's memories are, not what they are not. They are creations; they are a making sense; they are a conscious rewriting in the light of the person she has become and continues to become. My history needs to understand such memories, and other constructions of the past as well. History cannot afford to dismiss its rivals as simply fabricated or false, or history will weaken its own ability to understand the strange worlds we live in.

My dual fascination with history and my mother's stories, rather than any interest in my own roots or, God forbid, my identity, leads me to put history in conversation with memory. This is an anti-memoir in that it does not leave memory unquestioned, but it is not an attack on memory. It is a conversation.

It is admittedly a dangerous conversation. In forcing my mother's stories and the memories they represent to confront both other memories and a history that I can recover from places outside living memory, I may be not so much enriching the stories as diluting them and washing the meaning out of them. But having heard the stories for years now, I have more faith in them and the memories that create them than to think them so vulnerable. They are resilient, as my mother is resilient. History is more painful than memory. It is harder to repress, harder to keep confined to select audiences. It is one of the reasons we prefer memory. But my mother and my other relatives have shown me that history has its own weaknesses that memory can uncover and probe.

I have come to think of this book, of my conversations and research with my mother, as standing between history and memory. History and memory form the arcs between which the energy, the words, of this book move. It is the flash in the space between the arcs that generates the light, such as it is, by which we see. I see my mother inventing and reinventing herself to escape the inventions of others. I see my father walking toward her, forming his stories to explain what love led him to do.

And I see also the possibility of the imaginings that grow from the endless fertility of the past. I think of my grandfathers, Samuel White, voluble, friendly, and flexible, and Jack Walsh, silent, reserved, and rigid. I have vivid memories of one and only these stories and this history of the other. The two men never met, but I can imagine them passing in Canada, which inadvertently became such a land of trouble for both of them.

They couldn't have actually met, of course. Even if Samuel White had taken that vacation to Niagara Falls in 1924 instead of earlier, he would have been miles from Jack Walsh sneaking into the country at Detroit. Still, I can imagine them passing, unknown to each other. Jack Walsh's trajectory from that day was upward, slowly, unevenly, but eventually upward. It was a classic American success, except that its whole object was to leave America. And for years following that day at Niagara Falls, Samuel White's trajectory was down, nearly tragically down. I imagine them, an immigrant Irish farmer on his way to becoming a mechanic, a Jewish immigrant who had become a lawyer, and I can't tell what each would have made of the other. I do know that Jack Walsh's great hope was to go back to where he had come from and that going back to where he had come from—the Russia of his youth—became Samuel White's great fear. One achieved his goal; the other evaded what he feared. In the end, they never met. I imagine them meeting.

I imagine a past in which some truth lies. This past is a place that yields a dense, almost impenetrable, imaginative growth. Historians can only hope to tap this fertility and trim and discipline what grows so luxuriantly. Beyond history's garden gates, the thick jungle of the past remains, and memory's trails lead off into it.

My mother's stories, and my mother's silences, have made the world more dense and interesting than even I ever imagined.